2012 Shipwright

2012 Shipwright

The International Annual of Maritime History & Ship Modelmaking

Editors John Bowen
Martin Robson

Incorporating

Model Shipwright

CONWAY

New titles from Conway:

 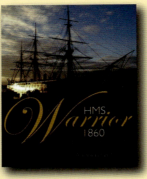  

© Conway, 2011
First published in Great Britain in 2011 by Conway,
An imprint of Anova Books Ltd
10 Southcombe Street
London W14 0RA
www.anovabooks.com
www.conwaypublishing.com

Images pp6–13 © John Lee/Conway, pp14 and 17 © Simon Stephens/National Maritime Museum. All other photographs reproduced by permission of the contributors unless credited otherwise.

A CIP catalogue record for this book is available from the British Library.

ISBN 9781844861491

Printed and bound in Malaysia

Distributed in the U.S. and Canada by:
Sterling Publishing Co., Inc.
387 Park Avenue South
New York
NY 10016-8810

Shipwright accepts advertising. For more information please contact:
modelshipwright@anovabooks.com.

Frontispiece: 'The Battle of Trafalgar, 21 October 1805, beginning of the action', by Thomas Buttersworth (NMM BHC 0553)

Contents

Editorial

Welcome to *Shipwright* 2012, the third edition of the large format, full colour annual. We have received some immensely positive feedback about the previous two annuals and we hope that will continue with the publication of this edition. One of the numerous benefits of the move from the quarterly journal to the annual large format was the extra space allotted, which allows us to accommodate lengthy articles without needing to split them up over a number of issues, as was the case with the old quarterly format. While this, admittedly, means a wait for the next exciting volume, the advantage is really brought home in this year's annual. Although it contains fewer articles than previous editions, those it does contain are what might be termed 'hefty'!

Of course, one of the other benefits from the move is the ability to include full colour imagery. Nowhere is this more evident than in the half dozen pages of the *Shipwright* Gallery, which includes a number of gorgeous models drawn from the National Maritime Museum Ship Model Collection. These range from a model of a Chinese Junk to the flat-bottomed landing craft used in amphibious operations during the late eighteenth and early nineteenth centuries, and from a 30ft motor yacht to the rather bizarrely named *Methane Heather Sally*, a Liquefied Natural Gas carrier. This last model in the Gallery reminds us that hands-on commercial ship model making still has a role to play in an increasingly technological globalised world, which often relies on three-dimensional modelling.

It is a point made by Simon Stephens, Curator of the Ship Model and the Full Size Boat Collection, in the insightful and wide-ranging interview that opens the annual. We are delighted that Simon took time out to walk Conway's Publisher, John Lee, through the excellent new ship model collections research area, model storage and access display facility at No. 1 Smithery, Chatham Historic Dockyard. As Simon points out, some of the original block models are 'coming home to roost', the happy outcome of a lengthy but extremely worthwhile process which will increase the accessibility of the Museum's collection to model makers. The move has also acted as the focal point for further research into the models themselves, pre-empted by Simon's own activities, which have included the use of a surgical endoscope and a medical CT scanner to explore the internal spaces of models that are usually hidden or obscured from view. As Simon explains, this technique has already thrown up fascinating details not included on ships' plans. Clearly a visit to the collections research area and displays will be at the very top of every model maker's wish list.

We have two articles about models which draw their inspiration from the heyday of the sailing warship. Through the inclusion of over 90 individually made scale crew members, Trevor Copp's 1:64 model of the sloop HMS *Swallow* provides a visual reminder of how busy a sailing ship would have looked. With activity taking place on deck, aloft and with officers engaged in (hopefully!) polite conversation, to the untrained eye the scene looks like utter chaos, but further investigation reveals the numerous tasks required just to keep a sailing ship underway. We have also included Trevor's short but valuable practical guide to constructing Georgian warship buckets, partly inspired by the image of HMS *Victory*'s fire buckets that appeared on the cover of *Shipwright* 2011, no less.

A more formal model, but no less inspirational, is the 38-gun frigate HMS *Minerva*, whose history and construction is

Below: A ship model from the NMM is placed in a CT scanner.

detailed at great length by Malcolm Darch. This exquisite model positively glows in the colour images here, highlighting the contrast of materials and finishes – copper, wood and striking red and blue hues. They are testament to the enormous commitment made by Malcolm (6,741 gruelling hours in total) to completing *Minerva*.

Such ships were built to fight, as Peter Goodwin reminds us with a detailed and engaging article on aspects of firing a broadside. Many of us will have wondered what it would have been like to experience battle at sea in the age of sail. Peter's empirical experiences firing *Victory*'s guns bring to mind Lt. William Roteley's recollections of the battle of Trafalgar: the fire from above, fire from below, and the fire from the middle gun deck Roteley was upon, louder than thunder, the deck heaving, sides straining. 'I fancied myself in the infernal regions', he wrote, 'where every man appeared a devil'. It also reminds us, that in an age of health and safety red tape, how important it is for people like Peter to have the opportunity and the freedom to continue to push the boundaries of empirical historical investigation.

Regular contributor John Laing's model of a pilot cutter is of the same era. The cutter was a boat type capable of fulfilling a variety of roles and John's inspiration for this model was a family connection, in this case the mysterious case of an ancestor who had his pilot cutter seized and destroyed by the Revenue Service. Thus began an exhaustive research period to source sufficient information to allow, in the absence of complete details, the building of an interpretative model. Whatever John's ancestor was up to, I am sure he would have been proud to see, and would have recognised, the completed *Palmerin* model.

Taking us into the twentieth century is Neil Howard's detailed account of an unusual design, the steam trawler *Akranes*. She was designed with her wheelhouse abaft the funnel and contained other quirky features which make for an interesting build at 1:32 scale, even more so given the problems Neil encountered with sourcing accurate information.

This year's Modeller's Draught is the *Griffioen*, a Dutch 'trawler yacht', whose particulars are described by J. Pottinger, along with images sourced from the shipyard that built the vessel and the usual excellent plans necessary for the construction of another unusual design in model form.

Also impressive is Robert A. Wilson's 1:384 model of the RMS *Carmania*. Regular *Shipwright* readers will be familiar with Robert's amazingly detailed small scale models, and this build continues his high standards while offering the kind of practical advice that he conveys so well to the reader. We are incredibly lucky this year as we are able to offer the kind of two-for-one deal usually only found in supermarkets with the inclusion of a second model from Robert, this time the *Preussen* of 1902, the only five-masted full-rigged commercial cargo carrying ship ever built. Robert goes into some depth

in this article detailing a range of techniques deployed to obtain the high standard we have all come to expect.

Moving from the delicate to something altogether more formidable is Dave Wooley's epic (in every sense of the word) build of the Soviet Aviation Cruiser *Kiev*. After charting the design history of this extraordinary class of warship, which combined the capabilities of a cruiser (including the rumoured on-board complement of tactical nuclear missiles) with organic maritime aviation assets, Dave guides the reader through the lengthy process of researching and then building the model itself. Moreover, this was to be a working model, and despite sailing only once, when trimmed and underway she certainly looks impressive. Dave generously donated the model to the Fleet Air Arm Museum at Yeovilton where it can be seen on display.

Ian Hunt undertakes his builds on a similar scale; his beautiful and painstakingly-detailed four-masted barque *Sindia* took 14 years to complete. A build which was, from the outset, designed to take to the water, the accompanying images of her with sails billowing on Wentworth Falls Lake do not leave any doubt as to the majesty of the specific subject here and the timeless grace of the tall ship in general.

The training vessel *Tenacious*, a Jubilee Sailing Trust ship, was the first wooden square rigged sailing ship to be built in a British shipyard for over a hundred years when she was launched in 2000. David Mills had already constructed a model of her sister ship *Lord Nelson*, so used the same scale of 1:64 to allow a size comparison of these vessels, which clearly give so much joy to many, in model form. The piece nicely draws the curtain on the main article section of the annual.

Alongside the usual range of book reviews organised and sourced by our intrepid Reviews Editor Steve Dent, we also have a report from Europe's largest model show, Intermodellbau Dortmund, by Dave Wooley. The diversity and sheer number of models and traders are captured in Dave's excellent images to accompany his take on the show and I think he sums it up better than anyone else can by remarking that in 2011 he did not leave the boat hall for two days of his visit!

In similar vein we are delighted to include a report by David Howell on the activities of the Royal Society of Marine Artists. His reflections on the motivations of maritime painters and the diverse styles of RSMA members make for fascinating reading. The winner of the 2011 Conway Maritime Sail Prize at the RSMA exhibition was a painting entitled 'Jack Aubrey's Minorca' by the master maritime painter himself: Geoff Hunt. We hope readers will agree that this evocative, detailed and characteristically well-researched painting is a worthy winner of the prize.

So the message from the *Shipwright* 2012 Editorial team is that, in an age of austerity, less really is more. Happy modelling!

John Bowen and Martin Robson

Interview with Simon Stephens

CURATOR OF THE SHIP MODEL AND THE FULL SIZE BOAT COLLECTIONS, NATIONAL MARITIME MUSEUM

Simon met with Conway's Publisher John Lee in June 2011 to discuss exciting developments at the new Collections Research Area facility in No. 1 Smithery, Chatham Historic Dockyard, Kent.

JL: The gallery and the new collections research area are full of magnificent ship models. It's fantastic to see a dedicated space for ship models and shipping history, and which aids interpretation by being so sympathetic to the subject itself.

Above: Simon Stephens with objects from the collections.

SS: I think the great thing is that the models are at the heart of it. Increasingly when visiting museums you tend to find that the ship models are sited in a themed gallery, and their function is to explain a specific subject or event. At the moment it is rare to walk into a gallery that is solely about ship models or model-making. We're hoping to right that here.

JL: Certainly UK-based ship modellers and readers of *Shipwright* really should be encouraged to visit. How did the No. 1 Smithery project down at Chatham come about, and what was your involvement in it?

SS: Well, a number of years ago, the Museum was looking at alternative sites to serve as storage for objects in the collections. Among the various options mooted was the No. 1 Smithery within the historic dockyard at Chatham, which, if I remember correctly, was the last derelict building on this site to be conserved. The senior directors therefore put forward the idea to combine the restoration of this building with the creation of a gallery space and model store to rehouse items from the old Museum store.

JL: A good example of joined up thinking!

SS: It was very good indeed. The HLF agreed, and provided funding. There is obviously an educational aspect to the Smithery as well as the curatorial research, and as such four museums were originally involved: the Chatham Historic Dockyard Trust, the Science Museum (who later pulled out of the project), the Imperial War Museum and the National Maritime Museum.

JL: I see. What was your role in the project?

SS: I sat on the exhibition committee, chaired by Richard Holdsworth (CHDT), which comprised the designers, the project managers, and the curators of the various collections at IWM, the Science Museum and Greenwich. We gener-

Above: Builders' half-block models in the new collections storage facility at Chatham Historic Dockyard.

ated ideas about how we would use the models and came up with themes for the gallery (managed by CHDT), including the current displays on Thames traffic and amphibious warfare that highlight recurrent aspects of the model collection. I was involved in getting the collection photographed before the move, and with logistical elements of the transition here – although in large part this was achieved by my colleagues in our collections department.

I also played a part in the conservation of the models, identifying priorities for support. So I had a range of roles within the whole project over a number of years, as of course this was a long-term operation.

JL: But here we are in the middle of 2011 and finally everything seems to be in place. I dare say we'll be hearing quite a bit more about it in the coming months. And of course we're here right in the heart of the dockyard with full-scale ships around…

SS: Exactly. That's the great joy – that you can actually look at a scale model of a rigged sloop, for instance, and you've then got the luxury of going outside the door, literally five hundred yards away, and seeing *Gannet* in dry dock. So you

can look at the running rigging, a brace, a main shroud or a back stay. If a detail is not quite there on the model you can still check it by visiting an actual ship – the same applies to the destroyer [*Cavalier*] and the submarine [*Ocelot*] at Chatham. It's all here. You can go from 5mm to full size in the space of a quick walk, which is fantastic.

JL: Superb. Some of the original block models are actually returning here too.

SS: Yes – they're coming home to roost. In particular, this applies to the block models that were made and sent to the Navy Board along with ship plans, in response to early 18th century orders; for example requesting designs for a two-decker, 70 gun ship. The dockyards would create a full hull model made of several horizontal planks of wood – what we would call 'bread and butter' construction today – which would be carved, primarily to show the hull shape, and then finished, painted with gun ports and some decoration. The model would be sent together with the plan to the Navy Board for discussion and that's the sort of model they could turn around here in a number of weeks. It was robust enough to accompany the plan, and necessary because some of the members of the Navy Board couldn't understand or interpret the complex, scientific, two dimensional ships' plans, so they needed a model in front of them to actually get an idea about the design. The models were sent to the Navy Board by the master shipwrights of one of the six royal dockyards – such as Chatham.

JL: The modern storage facilities for such models are absolutely first rate.

SS: Yes. There is a whole range, including roller racking with adjustable metal shelving to accommodate every dimension, in terms of the depth, size and length of models. Other roller racking here features high spec drawers to store smaller, more fragile objects in a much better way, while other units have vertical meshes on which to hang half models and half blocks. All these are dust-free and temperature-controlled, and sealed from the air as well – overall, a fantastic facility. I suppose the only thing lacking compared to the old store at Kidbrooke is that 'wow factor', when you walked into a room full of glass cases, but you still get that to an extent. People are still going to be impressed and coming into the collection

Below: 'A collage of models' in the Collections Research Area.

research area there are just models everywhere – it's a sort of mass visual overload of models. It's fantastic; 'our collage', as I like to say – a collage of models.

JL: And now the models are far more accessible to the public.

SS: Precisely. I think that was the whole crux of the matter. We've had so much criticism in the past – all museums grapple with how much is kept in store and questions of accessibility, and often it has been difficult, for various reasons, to get access to see the objects. This is one of, if not the, premier collections of ship models in the world , and people have the right of access to the collection.

JL: Can you explain the process for arranging to view the models?

SS: That refers to the stored collection, as we call it, which is now much more accessible. The website is searchable and also gives directions and instructions on using the Collections Research Area. Similarly, you can ring the Museum or send an email and we will respond, explaining what we've got and the images of the model that are available. If you want to come and look at a model we will book a time slot with our

staff here at the store. There are two members of staff manning the store, currently on a Thursday, Friday and a Saturday as well – that is important, because many enquiries come from model-makers and researchers who only have free time at the weekends. So we've made this facility available on a Saturday, which we hope will be a success.

Then basically you come to the dockyard and are given access to this research area. You can study, measure and photograph to your heart's content, with a member of staff in attendance. All research photography is permitted. There is a release form stating that your images are not for commercial gain, but that is a condition the Museum has always maintained. As long it's for serious research, you have access to these models. There is no charge for access to the store either. It's a national collection, so it should be that way.

JL: What do you think has been the main achievement?

SS: Well, I suppose the real success story, certainly from my point of view, is that this collection has received so much attention in the last ten years and by that I mean in terms of documentation, photography and conservation. Formerly many of the models weren't supported in any way, but now new bases and supports have been made for them, new interpretation has followed as a result, and now improved storage and accessibility too. That to me has been the real plus. It is vastly improved compared to the old storage system.

The other success has been the resulting spin-off projects themselves. For instance, the photography project – that will now allow us to put high-resolution images of models online. The collection is therefore accessible worldwide through the Internet and it is possible to search for specific models, to order images of them, and to examine various angles on-screen at very high resolution. We're cataloguing the models as well so, again, they can be searched by a whole raft of people who are interested in the collections, not just model-makers but researchers, authors, divers, programme makers, filmmakers. You can perform keyword searches and even if you Google a ship hopefully the model will pop up as well. Advances in technology have made it possible to do that – digital photography and of course the ability to search for material online.

JL: What is the true highlight of the Smithery for you?

SS: The highlight is the dedicated gallery that showcases some of our really interesting and historically important models. They've been displayed in such a way that they're nicely lit, with some interpretation, plus you can get close to and really enjoy the models. They are the focal point – the focus of the displays and also the story as well. Although we have got paintings by artists such as Norman Wilkinson, for

example – these artworks, along with other additional material, are used to support the models, which I think is going to work really well.

JL: In the context of the broader dockyard, it seems to be a similar situation. The Smithery is just one attraction that co-exists with the Victorian Ropery, the Wooden Walls exhibition, the three historic warships, and No. 3 Slip.

SS: Yes, the various parts all support each other, which is fantastic. I suppose the ship models really show why all those things are here. At the end of the day, it's the ships that explain the dockyard's existence. They were built and serviced and maintained in these dockyards and now you've got the ships in small scale – the whole range of the collection from foreign and ethnographic small craft right the way through to modern warships, modern merchant ships and small craft within that, some of which were used and maintained in this dockyard and others that circumnavigated the world.

JL: One of the centrepieces of the gallery is a magnificent model of *Victory*.

SS: It's a large-scale model of Balchen's *Victory* of 1737, which is a fantastic model. Historically it was often on display at Greenwich, but because of its size and configuration, it hasn't been on display in recent years. Again, there is a Chatham connection there. The loss of the ship is a fantastic story in itself and there's also the story behind why the model was made as well. It has always been understood that the model was made for the Board of Inquiry, which in fact it wasn't. It was made for display at the Navy Board office in London – we've got correspondence backing that up, including letters from the Navy Board asking, 'Is our model ready yet?' We have the replies saying, 'No, we need help to rig it' and similar things. This correspondence dates from the early 1740s, before the disaster in 1744.

JL: Are the models and broader aspects of maritime naval history presented in a different way than in the past?

SS: I think they are. That's quite an interesting question. You'll see that the gallery is not only a general display on the models themselves from a historical perspective and from a model-making perspective. We have also picked out key themes, like Thames traffic, which focuses on models of vessels that you would see on the Thames and the Medway, for instance. There's a display on amphibious warfare, as within the collection we've got some great models that deal with the history of amphibious warfare, from the small troop landing boats through to the tank landing craft of the Second World War. In the future we will rotate these thematic displays be-

Above and right: The main gallery at No. 1 Smithery, Chatham. Note the model of Admiral Balchen's *Victory* on the left-hand side.

cause as you can imagine, in a collection of this size, there are a whole raft of topics you can choose from: lifesaving, tugs, small craft, leisure boats, yachting – which is another big aspect of the Thames and Medway. All these have potential for focused thematic displays and exhibitions in the future.

We also plan to have themed open days, featuring a one-day conference or seminar, perhaps on lifesaving, so we'll display all our lifesaving models in one area and experts in the study of lifeboats and lifesaving will be on hand. Then the audience can view the models close up in the collections research area.

JL: Can we talk about the 1774 George III dockyard model?

SS: Absolutely. Lord Sandwich, who was First Lord of the Admiralty, was trying to encourage George III's interest in the Navy, particularly to influence Parliament to put more money into the Navy in general. George III was on a visit to Portsmouth dockyard and he was so intrigued by it that Sandwich thought it would be a good idea to have a set of models made of the six Royal dockyards: Sheerness, Portsmouth, Chatham, Deptford, Woolwich and Devonport in Plymouth. So he commissioned these models to be made

by a number of carpenters and joiners within the dockyards. They were then presented to the King together with a number of models and paintings of ship models as well – just to invigorate his interest in them.

JL: Do such dioramas present a different sort of challenge?

SS: They do present a different challenge in terms of interpretation. It's a different way of looking at a model and you either use visual or two-dimensional imagery to interpret that model. In terms of display, because generally dioramas are made on the horizontal rather than on the vertical plane, you've got to make the model accessible from all angles. Also, bearing in mind that dioramas are typically made at very small scale because you're covering a large area, you tend to find that the detail on them is minute, so you want to get up close to them as well. There are problems in terms of being able to let the public get close to the models, which is why we use technology, such as digital photography and extreme close up footage, to interpret the models and really get into them.

JL: Indeed. That leads on to the major project of photographing the collection in advance of moving it here.

SS: In some ways the photography project was started in tan-

dem with the Smithery, the store. We were in the early stages of trying to get the ship model collection online. In order to do that we needed versatile and user-friendly high res images of the models, so we started the process of photographing the models at our old store at Kidbrooke. It took four to six week chunks of the photographic studio's time and obviously a member of the conservation team and the storage removal team were also on board to facilitate that.

JL: What sorts of issues became apparent during the photographic process?

SS: The photographer was there with a very high spec digital camera, a laptop and a computer, so we would take the shot, then look at it on screen. In terms of photography we took standard shots – a broadside and if required, both sides of the vessel, a three-quarter bow view, a quarter stern view, and if the ship had a specific technical innovation or an interesting feature we would shoot that too. In that case we would do a very close-up detail of, say, the figurehead or if she was a single screw ship with a rather interesting rudder or technical feature, we would shoot that as well. We directed the photographers in terms of what was required and what we thought would appeal to the general public. Also, since we were able to zoom in extremely close, we were seeing features on the models that you wouldn't even see with the

naked eye. The painted decoration on some of the 17th and 18th century models is absolutely amazing; with high quality carving, particularly on some of the Navy Board models. You couldn't quite make out the detail but when seen on a very high res digital screen it became apparent.

So as a result of all that work, later on down the line new work will be produced on the iconography that's going on in some of the beautiful 17th and 18th century models, made possible by the quality imagery now available. You can interpret far more and there are research projects stacking up by the hundred.

JL: And you have also employed technology in the form of scanning and endoscopes, I understand?

SS: Yes. It all started with a rigid boroscope – a sort of steam-powered version of a flexible endoscope, which was primarily developed for medical reasons, as you may well know. One day we went inside a model just to see what it looked like and we were absolutely gobsmacked with the detail that was inside these models, none of which could normally be seen. It was encased, like a time capsule. So we took it a stage further by acquiring the use of a flexible endoscope, which was then hooked up to a video screen. We performed 'fly-throughs' on gun decks of primarily the 17th and 18th century sailing warship models using the endoscope. This information couldn't be seen anywhere else in three-dimensional form.

I subsequently gave a series of live lectures, endoscoping models at the museum in a lecture theatre. One of the members of the audience was a radiographer by profession and he came up to me at the end, and he was absolutely enthralled. He asked whether we had ever put one through a CT scanner. So we tried it. That was eight years ago now and the results were absolutely mindblowing. In the past we had x-rayed models and you get a certain amount of information about how the model is made, but the CT scan enables you to slice a model into hundredths of a millimetre across and along the model. Because the information is stored digitally you can reconstruct it in its three-dimensional form using a computer program and you can recreate 'fly-throughs', as we call them. It was possible to obtain details of the model internally – how it was made, the materials used, how it was fixed together with glues, fastenings and details, like the bulkheads of the cabins, details of the pumps, how they went down into the bilges, stuff that you just couldn't see on the model itself.

We found painted decorations in some of the cabins in the stern galleries of warships, which were absolutely amazing. And the real *pièce de résistance* was that in some models we were coming across signed notes from the model-makers themselves, which was incredible. So we continued with the project and when we published the results of our initial forays using CT scans in various publications, we found that our colleagues in America, colleagues of mine and friends of mine who curate models, had been doing the same on the

Below: Simon Stephens endoscoping a 90-gun three decker. The three interior views show details of the *Royal George* model (1756), namely the cooking galley, the stairwell screens and the main cabin – note the fire hearth and inlaid parquet flooring..

other side of the Atlantic and were coming up with the same results. It was absolutely groundbreaking stuff.

JL: What was the most exciting discovery you made?

SS: One of the best details was found in the stern of a three decker, 96-gun of about 1703, in the grand cabin. The endoscope revealed, on the panelling of the side of the hull (as opposed to the cross bulkheads going aforeships) beautiful painted sea serpents and heraldic figures – things that you couldn't really see with the naked eye. They were the size of a small first-class postage stamp. It was a real discovery.

When we go inside the models with a flexible endoscope you see details such as the cabin floor decoration, the panel bulkheads of the cabins and how the galley stove was set in the forecastle where meals were cooked. This information was actually used for the full-size reconstruction of Cook's *Endeavour* in Australia. Inside our models there were examples of flagstones surrounded by a wooden moulding on which the actual galley was mounted, to protect the ship from heat and fire. So it's little things like that, which helps people who are either conserving a full-size historic ship, or reconstructing or building a replica of a famous ship like Cook's *Endeavour*. It's only the models that really show that, so it's an absolute godsend. You just wouldn't get that on ship's plans.

JL: Now, a few questions about your broader role. Perhaps you could cover some of the key tasks in an average week as the curator of ship models.

SS: I suppose a fair amount of my time is spent dealing with enquiries about the collection, from members of the public, colleagues within the museum or from other museums. Those enquiries are very wide-ranging. I often get enquiries in several forms; phone calls, emails, comments coming in via the website, people turning up to the museum at the front desk. One thing I've learned working with this collection at the museum is that you never know who's going to turn up on your doorstep and it's always an opportunity to find out more about a specific model. An individual may have served on a ship during the last war and those are the sort of people you grab with open arms because that gives you a chance to talk to them about their time on board the ship and how accurate the model is.

So the enquiry side is a very interesting area of my job and also you're constantly learning from people who have looked into a specific ship or model in depth. As a curator you can't afford to devote your time to one model in that way, so you're learning too. I've always been upfront about that; I'm happy to pass on my expertise and for people to pass their knowledge back because that then builds up my expertise further, if you see what I mean. It's a circle.

The curatorial side is the housekeeping side, everything has to be managed in such a way that we can retrieve it, that we know where it is located, and also we need to know about the research side of it, where the model is from. We've got a database that has to be maintained: dimensions, condition, provenance, where it's been used, where it's going to be used. There's a whole raft of areas that we have to keep up to date. That includes images – what imagery we have of a model, what proportion is online and accessible. I also have input into exhibitions both within the museum's exhibition programme and exhibitions round the UK and abroad. We receive requests to borrow objects and are often asked to supply information for the exhibition catalogue or label – I'm also asked to verify facts in this regard.

Another aspect of my job has been as a courier of these objects. It is an amazing privilege to accompany these objects across the UK and around the world. When we loan objects abroad or to other UK museums, a condition of the loan is that a member of our staff, whether conservation or curatorial, has to accompany the object at every step of the way, whether it's by lorry, our own van, by air or by sea. We check that it's packed properly and see it loaded at this end. It's then signed off to the shippers, and we meet it the other end, in order to deal with customs via an agent. We then take it to the museum where the exhibit is being displayed, and check its condition on arrival – that all has to be logged and photographed. We help the exhibition curator with the mounting of the object in a museum itself, so it's quite a fascinating role, and a big responsibility. Some of the collections I've curated abroad have run into several million pounds' worth in value. It's enjoyable; it's nice to travel and see the world, but it comes with baggage. If there are problems with customs or if something gets damaged in transit, that all has to be logged and recorded and that's the role of a courier.

I also meet the public face to face, I give talks and lectures, and I write books and articles about the models and the collection. I also deal with VIPs for our managers and directors to encourage an association or a relationship with a corporate sponsor, for a space or an exhibition – such as the Sammy Ofer Wing or this facility here at Chatham. The curators answer questions on behalf of the managers and directors. We aim to encourage wider interest in the collection.

Finally I deal with the educational side. I have input into the educational programme – advising on suitable models to use, how models are relevant to the various stages of the curriculum. It's a very varied and interesting role.

JL: And do you also have a role in terms of acquisitions?

SS: Well, that's the other side of things. I'm constantly on the lookout for very high quality, accurate models that would add something to the collection, that tell us something new.

Above and right: Details from the topographical model of Chatham Dockyard, built c.1774, showing workshops, stores, dry docks and building slips (NMM L2712-011, L2712-007).

We have got gaps in the collection that we feel there's a need to fill, but we have a very precise and active collecting policy and a statement on our website states our areas of interest. If we're offered models that we can't accept it is necessary to fall back to the acquisition policy and refer individuals to other more suitable museums. We are offered models from private individuals via donation or as a loan if we want to borrow a specific model for an exhibition. We don't generally accept long-term loans because of the administrative issues. Bequests are welcome, though.

I also keep a watching eye on the auctions, and if we think there's a really good argument for acquiring a model that comes up, we will make every effort to acquire it for the national collection.

JL: Have there been any recent acquisitions?

SS: Oh yes. We keep a watching brief on both the commercial market and the design and technology of shipping in general – current design developments, technological milestones, etc. One of our more recent acquisitions is a full hull model of an LNG, a liquefied national gas carrier, called the *Methane Heather Sally*, which was very kindly donated to us by the BG Group. They import natural gas into the country through Milford Haven and this is a lovely state-of-the-art builder's model, which was given to the company by the Korean shipbuilders. On the one side you've got the full hull model as the ship appears and on the other side, the hull has been cut away to show how the tanks are constructed and where they are in the ship.

So there's a great interpretative use of the model, in terms of learning how natural gas is transported in its liquefied state, which was one of the reasons that the model was com-

missioned – the shipbuilders were keen to explain the concept through the model to potential clients.

JL: How does one get into the field of curating ship models?

SS: That's a tricky one because there aren't many curators of models around really. When I joined the Museum, which was in 1979, it was structured in departments that covered thematic topics – Department of Ships, Department of Navigation and Astronomy, Weapons and Antiquities, etc. Broadly those roles are still there but the curators are now more independent rather than situated within a collection department, as it were, and they're responsible for specific collections. So my role is Curator of the Ship Model and the Full Size Boat Collection, which also includes ships' equipment as well.

There isn't a course that tells you how to be a curator of ship models. There's a post-graduate museum studies course, to teach general skills in museology, but if you're really interested in paintings or ship models then aim for a job that involves those subjects.

JL: How many people are directly involved in the collection?

SS: From a day-to-day point of view, I am the main point of contact for enquiries along with my colleague John Graves, and then we've got the various support staff, including conservation, storage and movement, photography, publications and collections management. It's not a huge number – fifteen or twenty people. In the latter cases those staff aren't just dealing with ship models, they look after most objects in the Museum, so in terms of the models specifically there's just myself and John Graves.

JL: What do you see as the purpose and relevance of ship modelling in the 21st century, and how do modern digital

recreations of ship models compare with or indeed complement the real objects?

SS: An interesting question – even given the advances in CAD technology and the rise of computer simulations and games, which is 3D reconstruction in its basic form, we still see that models are being commissioned and made for various uses. Architects commission models, and even shipbuilders still use models – the small yacht designers are still commissioning models to show to clients who want to see something in 3D form. Often they don't understand a complex three-dimensional CAD drawing on a screen or in a drawn plan. They like to see the physical model.

The model provides a point of discussion where things can be thrashed out, so they're very relevant today. The great thing is that children are encouraged to use and interpret models as part of their education in design and technology.

The shipbuilding industry is still using models. Rather like the car industry, they make models of component parts of ships to get the fabrication or the production right, so models are still out there. I would hope that they continue to be made and used and the museum still collects models in that vein. We don't just collect historical 'jewel in the crown' models, like the 17th and 18th century ships, we also collect modern models. We've got examples of toe tank models, plating models, constructed from modern materials like glass fibre. I'm very keen to keep that side of the collection up and running as well.

Ultimately the public love to see an actual object, rather than something on a screen. From a remote access point of view the on-screen display is fantastic, but people still want to come and look at the actual object and just get up close and personal to it. The great thing about models is that regardless of age or sex, seeing a model in front of you is an opportunity to actually interpret the object yourself. You don't need too much explanation. The big problem that most people have is the idea of scale, but once you explain that concept, they'll go on and explore the ship, identifying the cabin, the bridge from where the captain steers the ship and so on. You can't do that from a drawing or a painting, but that's the great thing about the models.

JL: Plus, of course, the models themselves have their own history.

SS: Exactly – each has a story about why they were made and who used them, which is fascinating, as is the fact that they've survived. We've got scale models that were made in 1650. There are older models in various churches, but the idea of a scale model really dates from the mid-17th century. It's amazing that they've survived, but then again, people have always treasured them. In his diaries dating from August 1662, Samuel Pepys is promised a model by Anthony Deane, Assistant Master Shipwright at Woolwich, which he says 'will please me exceedingly, for I do want one of my owne.' It's a great quote.

The *Shipwright* Gallery (see pages 110-115) features new photographs of models from the NMM Collection. To find out more about the new gallery space and the Collections Research Area at No. 1 Smithery, Chatham, visit the following websites: www.thedockyard.co.uk and www.nmm.ac.uk/no-1-smithery/collections-research-area. For ship model-related enquiries, Simon Stephens can be contacted via email at the following address: ststep@nmm.ac.uk.

Palmerin (1813)

A PILOT CUTTER

by John Laing

While researching our family's history in England, some of my cousins were delighted to find that one of our ancestors, John Steward of Ryde, Isle of Wight, had been a Channel pilot and that his pilot cutter *Palmerin* had been seized by a revenue cutter and later destroyed by order of the court. All this had happened in 1837 and, as most of the early UK customs records were destroyed during the Second World War, we are still unsure of the exact charge brought against Steward. However, the somewhat mysterious combination of the location and the known facts: namely, the Isle of Wight,

'seized by a revenue cutter' and 'boat destroyed by order of the court' was enough for the family's combined imaginations, and romantic images of smugglers landing casks of brandy on moonless nights were the order of the day.

As this was the only maritime connection that had been found for this branch of the family, I was asked if I could build a model of our ancestor's boat, and so the search for the *Palmerin* began.

Below: Lines and framing plan.

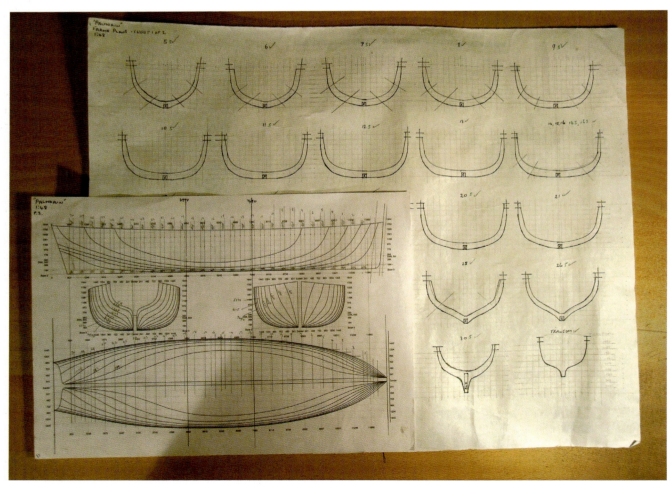

RESEARCH AND PLANS

The research phase was spread over several years as I had other models in hand at the time, and I was not encouraged by the scarcity of information that I was able to find. However a small pool of facts gradually began to emerge.

The first information to come to light was a copy of the *Palmerin*'s certificate of registration from the Isle of Wight. The registration had been transferred to Cowes when John Steward purchased the boat in 1836. This certificate gave some basic information about the *Palmerin* and stated that she had been built in 1820 at Seaton, in Devon, but gave no clue to the location of the original registration. The certificate described her as being single decked, clench built, smack rigged, 41ft 2½in (12.56m) x 11ft 2½in (3.4m) x 53in (1.34m) and with a running bowsprit.

From this information I wrongly assumed that the boat had been owned in Seaton or Beer (a fishing village just along the beach from Seaton) and continued my searching there. All the information I could find indicated that the only type of boat built in Seaton was the Beer lugger; a small open lugger designed for use off Beer's steep beach – a type of boat still to be found there today. These luggers would need to be very seaworthy for their work of fishing from an open beach – which sounded right for a Channel pilot's boat – and they were clinker built, a detail which was recorded in *Palmerin*'s registration; but the Beer boats were open luggers, typically about 20ft (6.1m) in length, while the *Palmerin* was a much larger decked smack. Even with the very limited information I had, she just did not seem to fit the description of a Beer lugger.

When I tried to find out what other types of boats might have been built at Seaton, an 'acknowledged authority' on small craft of the south coast of England had assured me that the only type of boat built at Seaton was the Beer lugger, so there the matter rested for some time. The experts told me that *Palmerin* must have been a Beer lugger – I thought she was too big – stalemate.

Sometime later when I was searching for information about another type of south coast small craft, I came across an obscure reference to a Lyme Bay boat. According to this reference, these were a type of small cargo carrying schooner built with the same hull shape as the Beer lugger, as they needed to work off the beach around Lyme Regis, but larger. Was the *Palmerin* a Lyme Bay boat?

I wrote to every museum I could find along the south coast of England seeking further information, and in due course a letter came back from the Lyme Regis Museum enclosing a copy of the *Palmerin*'s original registration. She had indeed been built in Seaton, but in 1813, and her original rig was noted as 'schooner'. She had been re-rigged as a smack in 1824. It appeared then, that *Palmerin* had been a Lyme Bay boat, but did I have enough to build a model?

If this had been just another model, I would have abandoned the project as not having enough information, but

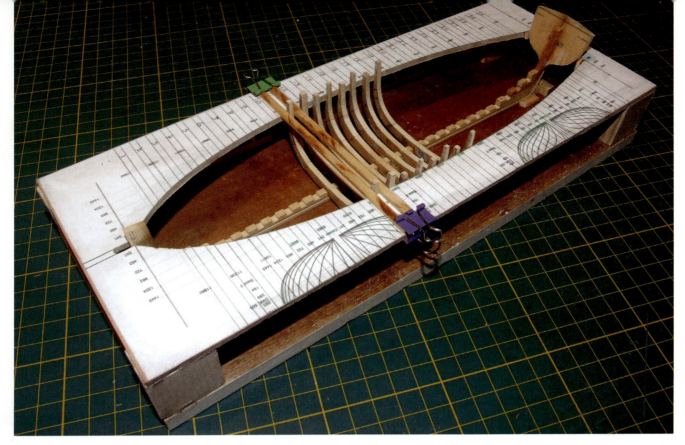

Above: Setting up frames.

given the family connections with *Palmerin*, I decided that it was worth building a model based on the best available information so that people could at least see what our ancestor's boat may have looked like. On this basis, I decided to go ahead with a set of plans.

My plans are usually pretty basic. In this case I decided that all I really needed was a set of lines plans so that I could draw up the individual frames. I went ahead accordingly and drew the lines based on the shape of the Beer lugger, but expanded to the exact dimensions of the *Palmerin*. Once

these were properly faired, I took off the shapes of the frames I wanted for the model, which were to be single 'frame and space', and drew them all full size, ready for copying on to the frame blanks.

I did not bother with a plan of the deck details or masting and rigging at this stage, as the deck fittings and rigging would all be conjectural based on contemporary practice, and I thought I would draw up any further plans required as the need arose (as it turned out, I did not draw any further plans at all).

The model was built to a scale of 1:48, rather than at my usual scale of 1:96. At a scale of 1:96 the hull would be only

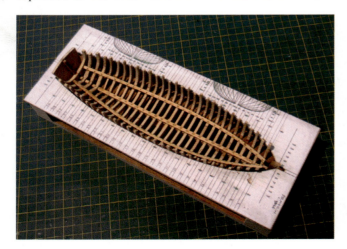

Above: The framing completed.

Above: The frames faired ready for planking.

Above: Planking in progress.

5.15in (130.8mm) long – which I felt was a little too small for the average person to view with ease.

THE HULL

The framing of the hull was constructed in the same way as that for my model of the barque *Nautilus*, which was described in detail in my article on the building of that model in *Shipwright 2010*, except that in this case I used an external jig and also notched out the keel and deadwood to take the lower ends of the frames. I had enough of the milled $1/8$in pine left over from the *Nautilus* to complete all the framing for the *Palmerin*.

The external jig was quite simple to make. A flat piece of well-seasoned wood of slightly larger dimensions than the completed hull was chosen for the base. A centreline was marked on this base and wooden blocks were glued at each corner to support the upper section of the jig. The blocks were of sufficient height so that the upper section would be fixed just below the tops of the model's frames. This upper section was made from a thin piece of MDF board on to which was glued a copy of the plan with the frame stations already marked. The hull shape was cut out using the plan as a guide, and a slot for the stem was cut from the fore end.

The jig was then put aside unfinished until the backbone of the model, consisting of the keel, stem and stern posts, deadwoods and solid transom, was completed. Once this was done, the backbone was centred over the centreline on the base of the jig and small blocks were glued to the base on each side of the keel to hold it central on the base. The upper

Above: Completed planking before cleaning up.

Above: The hull ready for deck framing.

section of the jig was then roughly positioned and glued with PVA glue to the corner blocks; the PVA giving me plenty of time to line it up approximately correctly in the fore and aft line, and with the model backbone exactly vertical when positioned in the keel blocks and the stem and transom slots. Once the glue was dry the backbone was lined up exactly in the fore and aft line by squaring up from the keel slots for the frames to the frame markings on the upper section of the jig, and chocks were then glued to the base in front of the stem and behind the stern post. This meant that the model could be removed at any time and repositioned exactly when it was returned to the jig.

As the framing of the model progressed, the frames were aligned vertically by slotting them into their respective keel slots and then lining them up with the frame markings on the jig. This system worked very well on this small model, and I may try it on a larger model at a future date.

Once the basic framing was complete, I added the keelson, stringers low on each side of hull and the deck shelf. All of these fore and aft members were glued and dowelled to the frames to give them additional rigidity, after which the frames were given a final fairing up to prepare for the next stage: planking.

I found the planking to be a very interesting part of the build, as I had never done 'serious' clinker style planking

before, my experience of this style of planking being limited to very small lifeboats and dinghies for larger models.

I had read that each plank on a clinker built hull has its own unique curve and that the curve would alter radically once the turn of the bilge was reached. That was precisely my experience. The curvature of the planks varied over the hull from 0–9mm, with the plank curvature reversing completely at the turn of the bilge from a 9mm downward curve to a 9mm upward curve.

As all planks would run the full length of the hull, the plank edges were marked on the frames amidships, at bow and stern, and also at two intermediate points along the hull before starting the planking. This was to ensure that all the planks would run evenly along the hull and to give a visual guide to the accuracy of the width of each plank. When calculating the plank widths and the number of planks for a clinker built hull, it is important to remember the additional width of the plank overlap on all except the sheer strake.

With all the preliminaries done, it was time to tackle the planking. The planking was made from my favourite model making timber – privet – milled down to a thickness of 0.5mm on my Heath-Robinson like homemade thickness sander. At this thickness the privet is amazingly flexible and bends easily to most hull shapes. It also has the very useful characteristic of maintaining its shape once bent, so it only needs to be steamed to cope with the most extreme shapes. In the case of the *Palmerin*, it was only the garboard strake that needed to be steamed, where the plank has to cope with an almost 90-degree twist at each end in addition to the curve of the hull.

First, the planks for the garboard strake were cut to size and shape. The shape of these planks was very straightforward, requiring only some minor adjustments to fit them snugly into the keel rabbet, and then curving to shape on their outer edges. All the planks except the sheer strake need to be bevelled along their outer edges to the depth of the plank overlap so that the next plank will fit snugly and not stand proud of the previous plank along its inner edge. The end of the planks require a little more bevelling so that the planks blend nicely into each other at bow and stern.

Once cut to shape and bevelled, the planks were 'steamed' by standing them in an old electric kettle and boiling them. This works very effectively for thin planks, which soften in only a few minutes. Take care to use an old kettle though, and not the one you normally use for making your morning tea, as some wood species are toxic. Once steamed, the garboard planks were twisted to shape by hand and left to dry thoroughly before gluing to the frames.

All the remaining planks needed to be carefully measured and cut to shape to conform to the curve of the plank below, and to maintain the correct shape along their upper edges. To achieve the proper shape for the planks I used card tem-

plates for the lower edges and, after this edge was cut to shape, measured the correct width for the plank with a pair of dividers using the plank width markings on the frames as a guide. This method worked very well for the entire hull except for one minor problem.

After I had fitted the first three pairs of planks I noticed that they didn't seem to be running correctly in spite of my use of templates and careful measurements. After a lot of head scratching I found that the problem was the card templates I had been using. I had chosen a very thin card so that it would bend easily around the curves of the hull as the templates were being tested and fitted, but the problem was that the card was bending too well. The card I was using was so thin that it was flexing as it bent around the hull, giving me incorrect shapes for the planks already fixed. The only solution was to rip off the planks already fixed (except for the garboards) and start again using a much stiffer card for the templates.

On the second attempt the templates worked perfectly with the stiffer card and the planking advanced at a very satisfying pace. As each pair of planks was fitted it was treenailed along its edges to the plank below. Even with the width marks on the frames and the automatic width correction that was introduced at each plank by measuring the planks from the completed section of the model, I found it a

Above: Deck framing completed.

Above: Deck planking in progress.

constant struggle to keep the plank widths down to the required size. I'm not sure why this happened, but almost every plank had to be re-sized to get the correct width before final fitting.

Once the sheer strake was reached, the plank for the toe rail was fitted flush above it (the frames had been left high enough to accommodate this) and the rubbing rail was fitted in line with the top of the sheer strake and all was then treenailed.

The next job was to clean up the hull planking and apply a couple of coats of finish so that the hull would be protected during the remainder of the build. A fine barrette file was used to clean off any excess glue along the plank edges. This type of file is an excellent tool for this sort of modelling situation, as its one cutting face ensures that the rest of the work is protected. With all excess glue removed, the entire hull was then carefully sanded, the rubbing strakes stained black, and the hull coated with several coats of matt polyurethane varnish.

DECK AND FITTINGS

With the hull planking completed, I turned my attention to the deck and its fittings. The first job was to decide finally on exactly what kind of deck openings the *Palmerin* might have had. As she had originally been built as a small trading schooner, she must have had a reasonably large hatch for working cargo, and the hatch must have been positioned between the two original masts. I reasoned that such a major structural feature would not have been altered when she was converted to a smack rig, so I decided on a realistically large hatch amidships. She would also have to have had some sort of access to the spaces forward of the cargo hold and to the cabin, which would have been aft. A simple hatchway would, I thought, be right for the forward access, and some sort of companionway aft to the cabin.

The mast position and rake also had to be decided at this stage so that the mast step could be positioned in the bottom of the hull and the mast partners incorporated into the deck framing. I studied all the drawings and photographs of very

Above: Deck planking completed and major fittings in place.

old smacks that I could find (not many, as it turned out), and finally decided on a mast position almost exactly one third of the hull length back from the stem and with virtually no rake.

With the position of the major deck opening settled, the deck framing could now be undertaken. Firstly, the mast step was glued and dowelled to the keelson and the deck was then framed in pine, using the same material that had been used for the hull framing. I decided to use a solid block drilled slightly oversize for the mast partners – the slightly oversize hole to allow for final adjustment of the mast to ensure it would be absolutely plumb when fitted.

Once the deck had been framed, a broad margin plank was fitted around the outboard edge of the deck. The margin plank was made in three sections down each side – two long sections with a short section at the bow. This configuration made for easier fitting around the more severe deck edge curve at the bow. Each section was fitted around the toe rail

stanchions by trial and error as follows: the rough shape of the plank was first obtained by tracing the shape from the top of the toe rail as this was not far above the deck level; the final shape was then checked by offering the plank up to make sure it was a good fit along the rail stanchions; once the rail was a good fit the position of the stanchions was then marked on the plank and the rebates for the stanchions cut out a little at a time with constant checking for their position and depth. This method resulted in a margin plank that fitted closely all around the hull.

The deck planking was then carried out by laying the first plank down the centreline and working outboard on each side. Where the planks needed to be joggled into the margin plank, their length was marked against the margin plank, the 'snipe' cut out, then the margin plank marked from the now prepared plank and cut out to fit. This may sound a difficult procedure to carry out neatly, but it is actually quite simple provided a very sharp knife blade is used. The edges of each plank were marked with a black permanent marker prior to

Above: Deck fittings completed.

fitting to simulate the deck caulking. After treenailing to the beams, the deck planking was then carefully sanded and given several coats of polyurethane varnish before going on to the capping rail. The shape of the capping rail was found by laying the strips of privet along the top of the toe rail and drawing around the shape. The rail was then cut out in several sections and, after staining black, was glued and treenailed to the top of the toe rail and given its protective coats of varnish.

The next part to be tackled was the main hatch. This, as well as some of the other deck fittings, was made from Chilean myrtle as a contrast in wood colour. The reason for choosing this timber was simply that it was available from a local speciality timber yard. It's perhaps a little soft for some applications (such as carving), but is nevertheless a very nice timber to work with and has a lovely reddish brown colour.

The hatch was made up of a simple box structure with a ledge built into the inside to support the hatch boards and also to be a sliding fit into the hatch opening in the deck. The hatch boards were made individually so that they would look authentic on the model. The handholds in the boards were marked out and drilled to a realistic looking depth with the tip of a large drill. The drill was held in a pin vice and turned very slowly to avoid the edges of the hole chipping out and

Above: Masting in progress.

also to be able to control accurately the very shallow depth required. Small grooves were cut on each side of the hand-holds and a piece of brass wire glued across each hold flush with the tops of the hatch boards. The cleats for the hatch wedges were bent up from thin copper sheet and glued and pinned to the hatch sides, with the pins left standing proud of the cleats to simulate bolts. The metal work was painted matt black after the hatch was varnished so that any over painting would not soak into the wood and would be easy to clean off. The hatch has been left as a push fit so that it can be removed to show the internal framing of the hull.

The fore hatch was veneered with Chilean myrtle over a plug to fit into the deck opening and with a fitted cover. The after companionway was sided with the myrtle, but with a pine top. The curved top of the companionway gives, I think, a little visual interest and, as I had seen this type of companionway in old drawings, it's also an authentic design for the period. The hinges and door lock for on the after end were made from scrap brass and, like the hatch fittings, painted after varnishing had been completed.

The only other major fittings on deck were the windlass and bitts. I decided on a simple 'log' windlass as appropriate for this sort of boat and it was made from myrtle and pine. The barrel of the windlass is octagonal, cut by hand in two separate pieces, with squared holes at each end for the bars. These square holes were made by first drilling them out to the appropriate size and then carefully filing out with the end of a square escapement file. The pawl-rim was made from a plastic gear wheel from the scrap box with the teeth cut down to a more suitable height. The drums, pawl-rim and standards were then assembled and glued on a length of thick copper wire, which was allowed to protrude from the sides, and small collared brass washers (again from the scrap box) were fitted over these ends as the outside bearings.

The bits, which are offset to starboard to accommodate the offset bowsprit, were made up from scraps of pine and myrtle with brass wire belaying pins and cleats. The windlass pawl is fitted to the after side of the port bitt and it too was made up from scrap copper. I remembered to drill a hole through the bitts to take the bowsprit fid just before it was permanently glued in place.

The other smaller fittings followed. The rudder was made from narrow myrtle planks glued and dowelled together with

Below: Rigging in hand.

Above: The completed model.

the cheek pieces added separately and through-dowelled. The tiller was from privet, shaped to an agreeable curve so that its inboard end sat at the right height. The pintles and gudgeons were, again, from small pieces of copper from the scrap box. After trial fitting the rudder I decided it looked a bit bare, so decided to dress it up with a little marlinspike seamanship as may have been done by a proud boat owner, and finished it off with a little fancy seizing work and a three-stranded Turk's head knot.

The remainder of the smaller fittings, starting from the stern, were the main sheet horse, made from bent brass wire; a pair of wooden mooring bitts, made from pine and through-drilled to take the brass wire arms; several small wooden cleats on the deck which were carved from privet as they needed to take some strain from the rigging; eyebolts in the deck made from soldered copper wire to attach the running backstay tackles; the bitts at the mast, also from pine

with brass wire belaying pins; the spurling pipe for the anchor cable, which was a length of brass pipe bent at right angles with the aid of a piece of soft wire inside it to stop it from crushing as it bent; the spectacle iron, which was bent up from scrap copper shim and the anchor cable stem roller, carved from privet with a concave copper bead as the roller. I usually cut my anchors from brass, but as the *Palmerin*'s anchor was to be painted I decided to try a different technique and make it from wood. I cut the shank and arms from a single piece of privet and then glued and dowelled privet palms to the arms. The ring was made from copper wire. I decided on a wooden stock as the period when the *Palmerin* was sailing was during the time when wooden-stocked anchors were giving way to metal stocks. I reasoned that a thrifty boat owner may well have chosen to keep his 'old faithful' wooden-stocked anchor rather than buy a new one. The stock was made from myrtle with paper bands glued on. The chain cable was a length of purchased small chain; common links being chosen rather than stud link, as this was (and still is) quite common on smaller craft. The only problem I found with my wooden anchor was that it took some time to make it hang naturally in its lashings due to its relative lack of weight.

The channels were shaped from small pieces of myrtle with grooves cut into them to accept the chain plates and they were then glued and dowelled to the toe rail. The lower deadeye strops were bent up from copper wire after small eyes were worked into each end of the strop. The chainplates were made from thin sheet copper cut to the appropriate length and drilled for the 'bolts' (lengths of copper wire) and the end of each one worked into a small loop by bending around a drill bit. A pin was then passed through the eyes in the stops and the loop in the end of each plate and the whole assembly fixed with a touch of soft solder at the joint. It's quite safe to use soft solder right up against wood like this, provided the job is done quickly, as the heat generated in a quick soft solder joint isn't sufficient to scorch the wood. The assembled chainplates were then positioned over the channels, shaped to fit snugly around the planking, and glued and pinned to the side of the hull.

Below: Starboard quarter view of completed model.

MAST AND SPARS

The mast and spars were shaped by hand from pine. First, the spars were cut to length and shaped square to the correct size and taper, then cut eight-sided and finally rounded using files and sandpaper. The heel of the bowsprit was left square inboard of the spectacle iron, and the heel of the mast was cut square to fit the mast step. Once they had been shaped, each of the spars was completed ready for rigging.

The bowsprit first had to have a hole drilled through the heel for the fid. Two wooden cleats were carved from privet and fixed to the upper side of the heel just forward of the bitts to secure some of the head rigging. A sheave was fitted vertically in the outer end of the bowsprit for the outhauler. Originally I was going to make this a dummy sheave, but the bowsprit was large enough to cut a slot and fit a sheave made from brass rod. The slot was cut by drilling through the bowsprit along the length of the slot and then finishing off the edges with a fine file. The sheave was held in place by a piece of copper wire fitted through the bowsprit and filed off flush. The band at the end of the bowsprit has a single eye on its lower side for the bobstay. This band was made from thin copper sheet, as were others on the model. A hole was first drilled in the end of the length of copper and then bent up to form the eye. The band was then rolled around a metal rod of appropriate diameter and the joint soldered. The band and eye were originally made wider than needed as I find a slightly oversize band easier to make. It was finished to width by rubbing on fine emery paper after soldering. The only other bowsprit fitting was the traveller, which was bent up from copper wire and soldered. As the bowsprit was a tight fit through the spectacle iron, both the band and the traveller were put aside until the bowsprit was ready for final fitting.

The boom and gaff were very similar in construction to each other. The jaws to clench the spars to the mast were made from pine, cut roughly to shape and then glued and through-dowelled into rebates on either side of the heels of the spars. The jaws were then shaped to blend into the spars and to fit loosely around the mast. The parrels were made from very fine copper wire with very small matt black beads used for the rollers. The gaff was fitted with two eyes for the peak halliard blocks and a strop looped through holes in the heel at the jaws to take the throat halliard block. The boom only required the addition of a band where the sheet block was fitted and a pair of small thumb cleats for the topping lifts to rest against.

The mast collar was made from privet as it was quite delicate, even at this scale, and the privet was easier to work with than softer species. The collar was cut accurately to fit the mast then finished to its final outer shape after fitting and gluing in the brackets, as this made a much more stable structure to sand. Next to go on were the mast hoops. These were made from thin pine shavings, glued and then wrapped around a former of the right size to form a wooden tube. This tube was then sliced into narrow sections to form the hoops, which were cleaned up to the correct thickness by rubbing on fine sandpaper. It was necessary to make the hoops at this stage while they could still be fitted over the masthead. A pair of pine bolsters was fitted for the shrouds to rest on, and the throat halliard crane, made from sheet copper with an integral pin to attach it securely to the mast, was fitted just above these.

Eyes needed to be fitted for the various blocks attached near the top of the mast. A pair of wooden cleats was also fitted near the foot of the mast to secure the boom topping lifts. The mast coat was simulated from myrtle cut to shape to fit the base of the mast.

RIGGING

Before starting work on the rigging I made sufficient blocks to complete the model. The blocks were made from English boxwood salvaged from carpenter's discarded folding rulers in the same way as that for my model of the barque *Nautilus*, which I described in my article on the building of that model in *Shipwright 2010*.

Below: Showing deck detail.

The first spar to be rigged was the bowsprit, and this might be a good point to add a cautionary tale concerning planning and thinking ahead. I was about to glue the band to the end of the bowsprit when I remembered that it would not fit through the spectacle iron with the band attached. Therefore I fed the bowsprit through the spectacle iron, pushed the fid home to hold it securely in place and was about to glue the band on when I remembered that the traveller had to be positioned first as it would not fit over the band. When rigging even the simplest model, it is essential to keep on

Below: Bow view of model.

thinking several stages ahead.

The only standing rigging on the bowsprit is the bobstay. This comprises a length of chain shackled to an eye in the stem and to a single purchase, the other end of which is shackled to the eye in the bowsprit band. The running end of this tackle is taken straight inboard and secured to a metal cleat on the knee of the bitt.

The next to be fitted was the mast. The blocks at the head of the mast were rigged before it was stepped, as it was easier to do this while the mast could be held in the hand. The jib halliard block was rigged on a long strop as was the practice on many traditional craft. The throat halliard was also spliced to the upper halliard block strop prior to the block being fitted. This was due to the fact that when the boom was rigged, this block would be difficult to access between the topping lifts. As the throat halliard is quite long it was coiled and the coil seized in several places so that it would stay clear and untangled until it was needed.

The mast coat was then slipped over the heel of the mast and the mast located in its step and wedged at deck level before gluing on the coat. The glue I use for this sort of work is a two-part epoxy which gives me about five minutes to double check that everything is properly aligned and plumb before the glue sets.

The gaff and boom had to be fitted to the mast at this stage as it would be almost impossible to secure the ends of the parrels to the jaws after the shrouds were rigged. Once they were secured to the mast, they were allowed to lie across the hatch until it was time for them to be rigged.

The pennants for the running backstays were put over the mast and bedded down on the bolsters, and then the shrouds were rigged; the starboard pair first and then the port pair. The lanyards were set up tight and tied off, but not finally secured at this stage, as other rigging can affect the final tension.

The forestay was the next to be rigged. The upper end sits over the throat halliard crane and the lower end is set up with a deadeye on the stay, with the lanyard being threaded through three holes in the top of the stem and then seized back on to itself. Like the shrouds, the forestay was not finally secured at this stage.

The last pieces of standing rigging were the running backstays, which were set up as Spanish burtons, with the lower part of the stays leading from an eye on the deck, up through the block on the stay pennant, and back down to the upper block of the stay tackle. Once again, the backstays were rigged, but not finally secured.

The running rigging was quite straightforward, as would be expected on this type of craft. The main sheet is a twofold purchase with the lower block being shackled to the sheet horse. The two topping lifts have eyes spliced in their ends where they rest against the thumb cleats on the boom, from

Above: The stern.

where they lead up through the blocks on the bolsters and then down to be secured on to the cleats at the bottom of the mast. It was then simply a matter of adjusting the sheet and topping lift tensions until the boom was resting at a pleasing angle before securing them.

The gaff was rigged with peak and throat halliards, both of which were secured to the after bitts at the mast. Before finally securing the halliards, lashings were put on between the boom and gaff so that everything could be set up with realistic tensions on all lines.

Then, the fore staysail and jib halliards were rigged, together with the fore staysail downhaul; the jib halliard was shackled directly to the bowsprit traveller. Both halliards were rigged double and the running ends were secured to the forward bitts at the mast. The staysail downhaul was secured to one of the belaying pins in the bow. At the same time the outhaul and inhaul were spliced to the traveller and led back along the bowsprit to be secured on the cleats at the heel of the bowsprit.

With all the running rigging secured, the various parts of the standing rigging were given final minor adjustments before being permanently secured.

The last jobs were to add a touch of dilute white glue to all the knots and splices to ensure they would remain secure, trim all the ends of the rigging and make dummy rope coils for the various locations where they were needed around the model.

This model of the *Palmerin* is currently still on display on its building stand at the Australian National Maritime Museum in Sydney, but will be moved to its permanent home at a later date and displayed in a permanent display case.

Introducing a New Series on the Frigates of The Royal Navy

The first subject will be
HMS EURYALUS (36) 1803

Text and model by Allan Yedlinsky
Plans by Wayne Kempson

This will be a plank on frame model using David Antscherl's upright method. Euryalus was part of Nelson's fleet and served at Trafalgar. This book is part one of a two-part series. This volume covers building a model through the lower deck. The second part, to be published in 2012, will complete the model.

Part one contains 14 sheets of plans in 1:48 using multiple colors for easy interpretation and use. All of the frames' drawings, showing front and back of each one, will be found on a CD in the book. They can be printed out from your computer on 8½" x 11" or A4 paper.

The text and photos will take you through the building process. Passages from the ship's log and an actual builder's contract are included.

- 9"x12" hardcover with jacket
- 164 pages of text, photos and drawings, 14 sheets of plans
- CD of frames

$80.00
+ shipping and handling

All of our titles are in stock. Please go to our web site, **www.seawatchbooks.com** to pick out your favorites. Plus there is now a free download on how to build *HMS Sussex* as a solid hull model.

NEW INFORMATION ON SHIPPING COSTS:
We are now using US Post Office international flat rate boxes for shipment of 3-4 books.
Pay shipping for the first two books only.

SEAWATCHBOOKS LLC
19 Sea Watch Place
Florence, OR 97439
Tel: 541 997 4439
Fax: 541 997 1282
email: seawatchbooks@gmail.com
www.seawatchbooks.com

PAYMENT:
Visa, MasterCard, Discover, and checks in US $ (made out to SeaWatch Books LLC) accepted. Also place orders by phone or on our secure web site.

RMS *Carmania* (1905)

CUNARD LINER

by Robert A. Wilson FRSA

Without a doubt the Cunard liner *Carmania* of 1905 is one the most complicated passenger liners that I have ever attempted. This 19,524 gross ton ship had an overall length of 672.5ft and a breadth of 72ft. The scale I chose was 1:384 (1in = 32ft). This gave the hull of the model an overall length of 21 inches.

The hull of the *Carmania* is really very simple as there is no raised poop or forecastle to deal with and the large 'midship structure is further simplified by having bulwarks along the bridge and promenade decks. The sixteen lifeboats were stowed on the boat deck and served by basic radial davits. The resulting model was very impressive. Despite its apparent simplicity, it was quite a complicated build in other ways because of the vast number of items that had to be duplicated such as side stanchions, portholes and lifeboats.

From the top down, there is the boat deck, which is obvious because the boats are stowed on it. Directly beneath that was the promenade deck, designated as 'A' deck. Beneath the promenade deck, and rather oddly named was the bridge deck, designated as 'B' deck.

The initial task of shaping the hull was relatively simple, the stem being vertical, although camera distortion in the first photograph makes it appear to have a slight rake. The counter stern was made following my usual method of sandwiching a piece of wood the depth of the counter from knuckle to top between two pieces of 0.005in brass shim. The shim is thin enough to be cut accurately with nail scissors. I use contact adhesive to glue these two pieces of brass to the top and bottom of the wood. These act as templates to carve the counter, simply sloping the top down to the knuckle with a scalpel. So many counter sterns in small ship models are ruined because they lose the sharpness at the knuckle

1. RMS *Carmania*. Port view of completed model.

2. Top of counter.

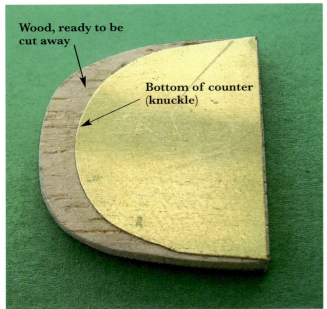

Wood, ready to be cut away

Bottom of counter (knuckle)

3. Bottom of counter.

during the carving. This method is foolproof and, provided the two pieces of brass are correctly cut to shape, it is impossible to go wrong. A recess was cut into the stern to take the counter and it was faired into the hull with automobile filler paste.

The brass shim was left in, and was so thin that it did not hinder the process of cutting a vertical slot in the stern to take a brass insert, complete with rudder. The three stages of the construction of the counter are shown in Photographs 2, 3 and 4.

The whole length of the top of the hull was covered with an overlay of $^1/_{32}$in marine plywood. The centre section beneath the bridge deck was plain wood, but the two ends were scored to represent the wooden deck planking. The decks may be scored by hand, or using the scoring device that I described in detail in *Shipwright 2010*.

The first raised level of the accommodation (the bridge deck) was then added with its scored decking on top. This did not go right out to the sides of the hull, but was set in slightly by the thickness of the white plasticard side plating that was fitted later.

At this stage, I drilled the portholes. There were three rows in the black section of the hull and I made two simple jigs from flat pieces of steel bar of about 10mm by 2mm. These were bent over at right angles by the simple process of placing them vertically in a large vice and beating the protruding half over with a hammer to form a right angle. Two jigs are required because one will be run over the top of the raised central part of the accommodation. In Photograph 5, the jig in position, is over the raised deck, with the top row of portholes (1) in the top of the black section of the

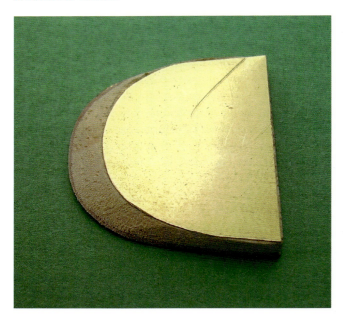

4. Completed counter.

hull. The white plating that is to go above the top row (with another row of portholes) will be added later.

The portholes were drilled through the holes, 1, 2 and 3. These jigs ensured that the three rows faithfully followed the sheer of the hull all along the ship's length.

Photograph 6, shows how the horizontal spacing is achieved. I stuck a piece of paper masking tape lightly along the plan (that is printed to the size of the model), and marked off the spacings, in this instance for the top row. I then stuck it lightly to the hull. The portholes were drilled in through the relevant hole in the jig. In this instance, I have just

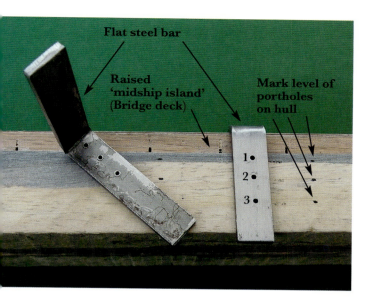

5. The two porthole jigs.

Labels in image 1: Flat steel bar; Raised 'midship island' (Bridge deck); Mark level of portholes on hull; 1● 2● 3●

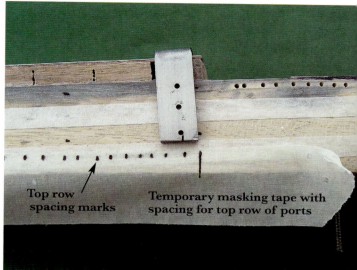

6. Method of obtaining correct spacing of portholes.

Labels in image 2: Top row spacing marks; Temporary masking tape with spacing for top row of ports

finished using the shallower jig for the top row of ports under the foredeck. Using the second jig over the raised deck, I continued drilling the top row through hole '1', using the marks on the tape to get the correct spacing. I drilled each row in turn, working from top to bottom and completing both sides of the hull before moving down. The red underwater colour was sprayed on using a red oxide matt primer aerosol from an automobile supplies store. The planked deck should be well masked with paper tape during the spraying. The area that is to be painted black does not really matter as the black paint covers any red on the sides very well. The black was hand-painted using water based artists' paint. The border between red and black was covered by the white stripe. This was made from a thin strip of paper masking tape that had been sprayed with white matt primer whilst stuck on a long piece of scrap acrylic.

The black clogged the portholes to some extent, but it didn't matter, because they could still be seen and were cleaned out by running the drill through them after the paint was dry.

Carmania had a large number of side stanchions along the side decks and, following my usual practice, I etched them from 0.002in brass shim. The etching process was covered in detail in my article '*Stella Polaris* and *Rose*', which appeared in *Shipwright 2011*. Since then, I have simplified the process slightly. After numerous experiments to find a pen that uses acid-resistant ink, I discovered that the best for the job appears to be the ZIG Opaque Writer. Although these pens are manufactured in Japan, they may be found quite easily on the internet and seem to be available World-wide. I used a black one, but I assume that other colours would work just as well. There was no need to back up the lines ruled on the brass shim with tape stuck over the top. I did, however, leave

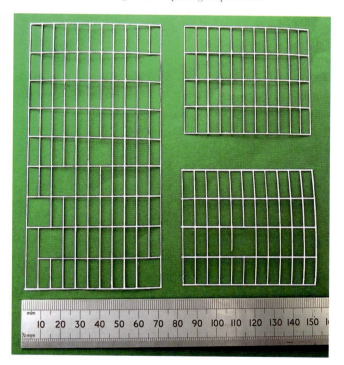

7. Completed etchings.

the prepared brass overnight to allow the ink to dry thoroughly. The back of the shim was, of course, painted to stop the etching fluid eating its way through from the back.

I also dispensed with the bowl of warm water in a separate dish under the bowl containing the etching fluid. This meant that it took six hours to etch instead of two, but the results were very good. The stanchions were ruled on the brass with sufficient vertical depth to cover both open side decks. This ensured that they were all in line. I ruled far more than were necessary in case some did not etch properly. After

8. Ventilator shaft with cowl ready to solder on top.

10. Ventilators ready for painting – one shown before the base is fitted.

9. Cutting the square brass ventilator bases using the lathe.

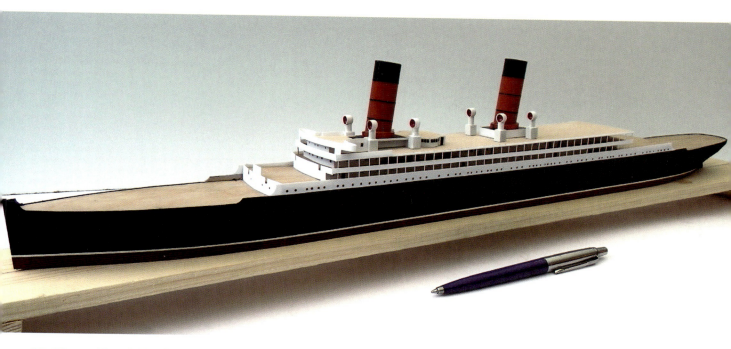

11. Side stanchions, bulwarks and large ventilators fitted.

the etching was complete, the paint from the back was removed by leaving it in a shallow dish of white spirit. This did not remove the black ink on the front and I found that only methylated spirits would do that!

As can be seen on Photograph 7, a small number of stanchions got etched away, but more than enough were left for the model. They were sprayed with matt white primer whilst still joined up. Then they were cut off leaving the top horizontal strip intact, but the bottom ends open and just of sufficient length to reach the deck below.

The white belt of side plating with its single row of portholes was made next. This was made from thin white plasticard sheet. I found it easier to drill the holes in the plasticard before cutting it down to the correct size. The drilling was done along the edge of a steel ruler using a small 12- volt hand-held electric drill. The fact that they were drilled in a straight line without bothering about the sheer did not matter. The plasticard was flexible enough to bend to the slight sheer when it was glued along the hull above the black part, covering the lower ends of the side stanchions. The solid bulwarks along the promenade deck were then cut from thin plasticard sheet and glued on with contact adhesive. The

12. RMS *Carmania.* Starboard view of completed model.

13. RMS *Carmania* completed and in display case.

top horizontal rail of the stanchions that was glued along the boat deck was covered with a thin strip of white plasticard. The result was an extremely neat array of stanchions along the sides of the ship, as shown in Photograph 11.

Another slight problem was a number of large cowl ventilators on the boat deck that had square bases. I made them using my normal method and then adding the bases afterwards. The cowls were made by placing a brass rod of the correct diameter in the lathe and rounding off the end. This formed the back of the cowl. It was then parted off by holding a jeweller's saw against it. The cowls were hollowed out by placing them in the lathe chuck, rounded end first and putting either a round dental burr or a drill in the tailstock and advancing it into the flat face of the cowl to hollow it out. The shafts were also made from brass rod with the end reduced to glue into holes in the deck, as shown in Photograph 8. The cowls were soldered onto the ventilator shafts using soft solder.

The length of the shaft should be the full length from deck to cowl. The square section was made from a piece of square brass tube cut to the correct length. I find it very difficult to cut pieces of square brass tube accurately, so I do it in the lathe and that guarantees a perfect square cut every time.

A cutting disk was inserted in the lathe as shown in Photograph 9. The square brass tube was inserted in the tool holder and it was turned round so that it was horizontal. I advanced the tool holder until the end of the brass tube slightly overlapped the cutting wheel, and then advanced the

cross-slide gently so that the cutting disk cut off the end squarely. I then moved the cross slide back until the brass tube was clear of the disk and then advanced the tool holder by the required amount, and cut off the brass square to the required length. I did not bother with the vernier markings on the wheel for this, but just counted the number of full or half revolutions of the wheel to obtain the required length. The brass squares were then slid over the end of the ventilators and fixed with a spot of superglue. Ventilators ready for painting, and one waiting for the square base to be fitted are shown in Photograph 10.

The tiny gaps in the top of the square bases may be filled in with a spot of white glue before painting. The painting was done using a white matt primer spray.

The lifeboats were vacuum-formed from white plasticard sheet using a simple home-made miniature vacuum box into which a normal household vacuum cleaner was plugged.

The remainder of the deck fittings, masting and rigging, etc., were made using similar techniques already described in *Shipwright* annuals 2010 and 2011.

With a hull length of 21in, this was rather outside my comfort range and in many ways, I found it hard-going on account of its physical length, although the scale was my usual 1:384 (1in = 32ft). This was because of the length of my work table, which is really more suitable for much shorter models. Photograph 12 shows the completed model before fitting into the display case, whilst Photograph 13 shows it in the display case.

HMS *Minerva* (1780)

38-GUN FRIGATE

by Malcolm Darch

HMS *Minerva* represented a bold step forward in frigate design when she took to the water on a windy and cloudy afternoon at 2.30pm from building slip No. 4, in the Royal Dockyard at Woolwich. The ship's log, written by her Commander Charles Fielding Esq., tells us that she was launched on the 4th of June, 1780. This was a Sunday, but time and tide wait for no man, and the vessel was needed to protect England's shores. She had been built under the watchful eyes of Master Shipwright George White and was completed by John Jenner.

Until the launch of this new frigate, designed by junior surveyor Sir Edward Hunt, a 38-gun frigate did not exist in the fleet. *Minerva* was also the first frigate to be designed to carry heavier firepower in the form of shortened 18lb cannon, as opposed to the previous 12lb guns. The 18lb cannon were cast to a length of 8ft instead of the usual 9ft. She was a very expensive ship to build, costing £25,000, and as a new design *Minerva* was constructed in a Royal Dockyard to iron out any potential problems more efficiently.

After launch she was immediately warped to the sheer hulk and had her masts and bowsprit fitted prior to being put into dry dock to be copper sheathed the following day, which took a week. All the while the vessel was alive with riggers and ballast trimmers, loading provisions – including fresh meat and anything else required to keep 280 crew and many others fed, watered and supplied when at sea. Twelve days later she was afloat and completing final outfitting.

Minerva was the second Royal Navy ship to bear that name. Her predecessor was a 32-gun frigate captured in the West Indies by the French vessel *Concord* in August 1778.

The first British frigates appeared in 1757. They were designed as single-decked warships to act as convoy escorts, but primarily to hunt out the enemy and report back to the main fleets as the eyes of the navy. Their speed and light construction made them highly capable of fulfilling this role – they were much faster than ships of the line, but unable to withstand a full broadside from the multiple-decked First and Second Rate ships. Instead they were intended to outmatch anything from the largest privateer down, so the frigate's lot was cruising to find and engage the enemy; with the promise of prize money for successful crews.

Minerva was to be the first of four frigates in her class launched as 38s; a fifth vessel, *Melampas* (Bristol), was fitted out as a 36, as it was found that the design was short of space to work the extra cannon. Her sisters were *Arethusa* (Bristol), *Phaeton* (Liverpool), and *Thetis* (Rotherhithe). The four took to the water over a period of two years and three months. As

Left: My favourite angle for taking a portrait of a frigate.

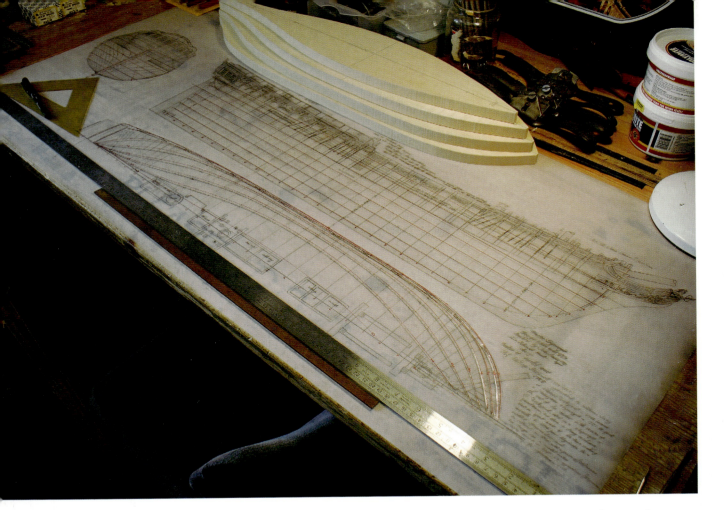

Above: The Admiralty draught for *Minerva*, traced and with
added researched detail on drawing film. This formed the basis
for the start of the model's construction.

it turned out, *Minerva* stood alone with regard to the design of
the new class, because *Arethusa*, the second built, was constructed with a reduced sheerline, flattening out some of the
beautiful swept quarterdeck rail line. Evidently the navy's
habitual tendency to build ships nearly straight in the sheer
was prevalent even then. *Minerva* was also unique in having
her hawse pipes between the cheeks and not above like her
later sisters.

The last two of the class were modified underwater
forward and aft, introducing extra buoyancy to prevent the
vessels pitching in a heavy sea. It was found that the giant
step of introducing a greater number of (and heavier)
cannon, and subsequently moving the gun ports closer
together, had put more weight in the vessels' ends, creating
this pitching tendency. Another milestone in naval ship construction at the time of building *Minerva* was the Admiralty
order to sheathe the fleet in copper, starting with the frigates.

With regard to the armament, the carronade came into
service at the same time, although *Minerva* apparently carried
just four 18 pounders on the quarterdeck.

As with all vessels that were new experiments, there were
many changes to her armament during her lifetime, which
was to be twenty-three years.

The vessel – identified as a 38-gun frigate by her fourteen
gunports on each side at launch – carried 28 x 18 pounders
on her upper deck (main gun deck), plus 10 x 9 pounders on
her quarterdeck and forecastle decks. In addition she carried
two long nines bow and stern, as chasers. Carronades were
not included in the gun count, but were very useful weapons
– especially for frigates, because they packed a punch but did
not weigh as much as a proper cannon. This meant that 18lb
balls could be fired from the quarterdeck without making the
ship top heavy. Some frigates were later converted to an all-
carronade armament, but the drawback with this was its lack
of accuracy, which made close quarters fighting essential.

Minerva measured 141ft on the lower deck and 38ft 10in in
the beam with a tonnage of 940t. Her sisters were all heavier.

The fitting of four carronades to *Minerva* introduced the
solid barricade to the frigate's quarterdeck, whilst still retaining the timber headed fo'c's'le. The forward end of this
barricade was elegantly finished with a scroll, while the later
frigates simply had a rather harsh-looking vertical cut off.

Taking an overall look at the frigates in the navy, *Minerva*
must rate as one of the prettiest, highly decorated vessels

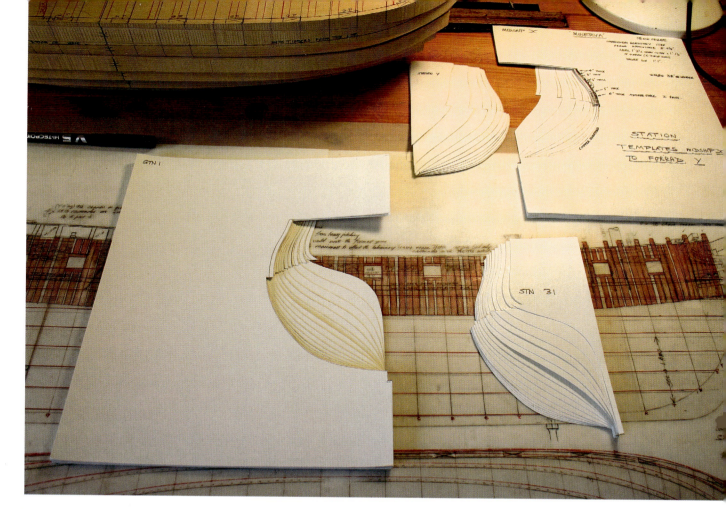

Above: Card templates for each hull station cut to shape, to ensure accuracy when shaping former and frames.

launched. It was in 1790 that the Admiralty dictated that frieze painting must be phased out, and the extensive carved decoration kept to a minimum, as a cost cutting exercise.

As a result, when the next batch of 38-gun frigates began to be launched in 1794, with the start of the Napoleonic war the year before, the *Artois* class such as HMS *Diana*, incorporating all that had been learnt from the *Minerva* class, were quite austere with regard to decoration. They featured plain painted backgrounds where there had been frieze painting along with much less carving.

Minerva therefore really represents one of the last of the ultimate frieze-painted and carving-decorated frigates, and as such makes a wonderful subject for a model.

Minerva had three years at sea including the relief of Gibraltar in 1781 before the war stopped in 1783. She had on occasion sailed with the Grand Fleet in company with HMS *Victory*. She then swung at her moorings in ordinary in Portsmouth until 1789, when she was re-coppered, and prepared for a four-year voyage out to India and the Far East.

She was to become the flagship of Rear Admiral Cornwallis at this period, involved in the blockade of Pondicherry, before coming home to fight on the blockade with the Channel Squadron under Sir John Borlase Warren, with other heavy frigates including her sisters *Arethusa* and near

sister *Melampus*. Edward Pellew (later Lord Exmouth) commanded *Arethusa* to great effect.

On one occasion, it was *Minerva*'s intelligence upon returning from India, with Cornwallis aboard, that led to the famous action off Guernsey on the 23 April 1794 (St George's Day) when three out of four French ships were taken, the 36-gun frigate *L'Engageante*, the 44-gun *Pomone* and the 20-gun corvette *La Babet*.

As a consequence of this action, upon return to Portsmouth, where *Minerva* was swinging at mooring number 43, Pellew sent a butt of beer from *Arethusa* to the crew of *Minerva* in gratitude.

Whilst in Ceylon (Sri Lanka) *Minerva* was careened to clean and check her copper bottom at Trincomalee. It ended in near disaster, because local coconut fibre (shortstrand) ropes were used to haul the near 1,000-ton vessel on to her beam ends (having stripped the interior of stores, cannon etc.). Unfortunately the ropes parted, bringing the ship upright with a rush, causing her to partially flood and straining the timber structure. This was the cause of fresh water leaks through the decks that plagued the ship thereafter.

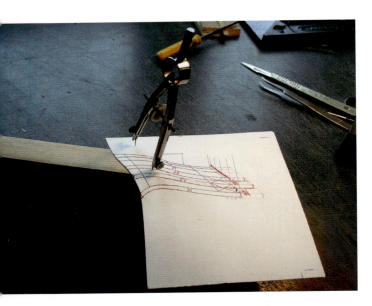

Left: Marking out the sections of frame onto the edge of the boxwood, to incorporate all the alterations of the hull shape within that section.

Minerva was docked at Portsmouth and given a large refit. She went back to sea with Sir Richard Strachan's Squadron patrolling the Channel and further afield at times. Apart from a grounding and a collision, which both needed serious repairs, she continued as HMS *Minerva* until 1798, when much of her armament was removed and she was converted to a troopship. She was renamed *Pallas* – the previous *Pallas*, a 32-gun frigate, had recently been lost at Plymouth. The name was still apposite – Pallas Athena was simply the Greek name for the Goddess that the Romans called Minerva. In turn, this meant *Minerva*'s name was now vacant, and so the keel of the next Minerva, number three, was duly laid down.

As a troopship she visited Ireland, and Ostend in May 1798 when a force of troops were landed to damage the canal and lock systems, to prevent French invasion barges getting to England.

Eventually she arrived at Sheerness in April 1802, in a sorry state, and was docked in December at Chatham for survey. Her copper bottom and some planking was removed, and it was found she had gone very badly rotten with fresh water ingress, as a result of her accident in Trincomalee, and was too far gone to rebuild. As a result she was 'taken to pieces' and existed no more after 1803.

Her three sisters, on the other hand, fared a lot better and lasted into the 1820s. Still, *Minerva* was involved in some

Above: The hull was built in three sections to enable each topside half model to be laid flat on the bench for delicate work.

important events in British naval history, and captured several enemy vessels in a solid career. As such she was worthy of being immortalised as a good example of a beautiful British-built frigate of the Georgian Period.

THE MODEL RESEARCH

I have been making ship models constantly for thirty-five years, building to commission for connoisseur collectors worldwide. *Minerva* is commission number 54. My initial brief was for a frigate of C.S. Forester's 'Hornblower' period in the Napoleonic Wars.

Having done some basic research, it seemed sensible, given that Hornblower first went to sea in 1794, to choose a frigate of that era. Consequently the *Artois* class was first choice, with David White's book *The Anatomy of the 38-Gun Frigate Diana*, which had taken him over three decades to research, as a basis to work from.

Negotiation with my American client went well, until I mentioned that the *Artois* class was developed from the *Minerva* class. This name piqued some interest and resulted in *Minerva* being chosen as the subject instead. In model-making terms, the fact that *Minerva* was highly decorated with carving and frieze painting represented many hours more work and more problems to resolve than would have been the case with HMS *Diana* and her sisters.

Above: Card templates were made to establish the true shape, lengths and heights of the quarter gallery and stern gallery windows.

With hindsight, the client's choice (made because he has a home at Minerva) was the right one. Although it seemed daunting at the time, to have the opportunity to build a frigate at all was a grand commission, and having gone to all that trouble, it was a good thing that we went the extra mile, and built a model showing the best the artisans could produce, rather than a plainer example.

I was born in Bristol and grew up visiting the Bristol Museums, where I admired the naval frigate models built by James Martin Hilhouse of Bristol, who was a shipbuilder for the navy from 1776 to 1815.

There are several models now in the Industrial Museum in Bristol, one plank-on-frame model of *Minerva*'s near sister ship *Arethusa*, and two models of *Melampus* (36), the fifth in the class. Of the two models of *Melampus*, one is an exquisite example at 1:64 scale ($^3/_{16}$in = 1ft), though carrying little carving and no frieze painting. This model in particular captured my imagination from an early age.

After I had completed ten years' service in the timber yacht building industry on the Solent at Hamble and at Salcombe, I returned to study this model I had so admired, to see if I could understand and interpret her better. She still looked amazing and I was in awe of the work involved in building it. So when asked to build a frigate I knew that the scale needed to be 1:64.

In the early 1970s, my first visit to the National Maritime Museum at Greenwich introduced me to many of the Navy Board Models which were then on display. I was qualified as a timber shipwright by that time, so I had a good look at them all, and studied them in close detail. Of the whole collection, I found that there were a couple that really stood out in my mind, and I analysed why this was.

I realised it was because, first and foremost, the smaller 1:64 scale, as opposed to the usual 1:48, produced the same exquisite result as the model of *Melampus* in Bristol. The standard 1:48 scale models were an ideal means of conveying aspects of a ship's design – which, after all, was their purpose, sent as they were with the draughts supplied by the shipbuilder – but they were too large to be exquisite.

Hence the scale chosen for the *Minerva* model was 1:64, giving an overall length of just under 4 feet fully rigged.

The other reason that two models in particular stood out in the National Maritime Museum collection was their colour. They had been made from boxwood, and it seemed to me that the shape of the vessels and their beautiful design was enhanced by this beautiful timber; especially when the carving was not gilded, the lightness of the colour enabling much greater contrast between light and shade on all the mouldings and details.

Why did the original craftsmen use boxwood for many of the Navy Board Models? I had often asked myself this question, and I now know the answer.

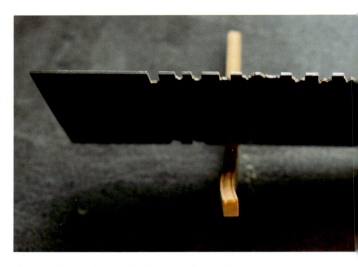

Above: The tooled steel cabinet scraper, which was altered and then utilised as the moulding scraper. The different sections of the moulding required have been ground into its edge.

The obvious reasons are its attractive colouring, excellent carving qualities and easy availability. With the complex shape of the models being built, however, the first and foremost consideration was the need for a timber that would steam-bend well, and boxwood, believe it or not, is the best timber I have ever steamed.

In addition its carving characteristics are absolutely perfect; it holds a sharp edge and this was the reason it was used so extensively in the printing industry for blocks and for wood-cut illustrations, which were carved into the end grain.

So my choice of scale and materials was clear: build in 1:64 and in boxwood. I managed to buy some timber in Bristol that had been in stock for twenty-two years.

DRAWINGS (DRAUGHTS)

As is well known, the National Maritime Museum hold the vast majority of all the old Admiralty draughts, and so I ordered a batch not only of *Minerva*, but also of *Arethusa* and her sisters to cross-check between the vessels in the class.

I also ordered a contract of 1780 for a sister of *Minerva* (*Phaeton*), which itemised each part of the ship's structure.

I was amazed at how organised the Admiralty were, with their tabulated pre-printed paperwork, whereby a standard contract could be used for any rate of warship, the appropriate blank sections simply being filled in with a quill; the basis being that everything was sized by proportion relating to the number of guns.

The marvellous book *The Shipbuilders Repository 1788* was published, unsurprisingly, in 1788, in an edition of just 200 copies, and is today one of the rarest books on shipbuilding. Fortunately Jean Boudriot Publications printed a further 750 copies as a facsimile edition in 1992 (ISBN 0-948864-13-3),

Above: Some of the results obtained using the moulding scraper.

with the addition of ships draughts to represent each rate of ship. I am happy to say I own copy number twelve.

The original book was anonymously written – just as well, for the author would have been hung, drawn, and quartered had he been discovered. His work virtually amounted to treason against the navy. The book contains the tables of measurements for every rate of ship, for each structural member within the hull, and was obviously the master plan from which contracts were created, as all the sizes and tables match. It is an amazing book and proved most useful.

The next breakthrough came with the information that the original Navy Board model of *Minerva* still survives, and is part of the famous Henry Huddleston Rogers collection of models, sold to the United States in the 1920s, and now displayed in the Museum of the US Naval Academy at Annapolis. It was misidentified in the early catalogues and listed as a 36-gun frigate (with fourteen gun ports per side on the main gun deck).

When the draughts for *Minerva* were drawn up, the introduction of the carronade, which was to appear halfway through her build, was not foreseen, and so a rough tree rail is shown on the quarterdeck. The model has a solid barricade as would have been built into the ship on the stocks.

The decision to lower the sheer line in the next build in the class, *Arethusa*, whilst she was on the stocks, demonstrates how executive decisions were made during construction, causing a modification to the original draughts. This must have come about as a result of observing *Minerva*'s final appearance when fitted with barricades on the quarterdeck.

One interesting point of note was that *Minerva* had the four carronades fitted on the quarterdeck, but because of difficulties found with flame and blunderbuss style blast effects from the short barrelled weapon, they required a longer gun port, so as not to do damage to the ship. The original sized ports shown, which match the cannon ports, had a facility for the lower part of the port to hinge open, creating a bigger port when in use.

The model at Annapolis is varnished and frieze painted, carrying full boxwood carving – a marvellous record. I had nearly 200 photographs of this model taken under my direction and sent to me on disc by the very helpful staff.

A second Navy Board model at the National Maritime Museum has been identified as *Minerva*, although in my opinion it may be an early attempt to show how the new 38-

Above: The use of medical clamps and wooden clothes' pegs to plank up the solid boxwood wall of ship's timbers.

Above: The tip and butt joints used in the heavy wale planking.

gun class might look. However, it is very similar to the Annapolis model and has an owl carved into her stern decoration. Minerva was the goddess of wisdom, of which the owl is representative.

When interpreted correctly, the carving on the Annapolis model conclusively identifies the ship as *Minerva*. This of course requires a knowledge of Roman or Greek mythology, another skill I had to acquire. The Annapolis *Minerva* carries a serpent at the foot of the figurehead, which ties in with the mythology, and also symbolizes wisdom.

Minerva was also goddess of craftsmanship, especially shipbuilding, and of the fine arts and music. She was also an overseer of peace and war. The latter attributes are depicted next to the carved serpent as a phoenix rising from the flames, with a cocoa flower in its beak representing peace, and all the banners and weaponry of war as a backdrop located in the trail boards. Similarly, the frieze paintings, which feature thunder and lightning, illustrate *Minerva*'s connections with these qualities.

The stern taff rail carving in the middle top carries a cameo of *Minerva* held in a wreath by two cupids. Two further cupids hold shields with a carved anchor, covering the joint in the wood-carved panels. Next, outboard at the top, are a British lion on the port side and a horse on the starboard side – Minerva had the ability to tame wild horses. Decorative panels at the rear of the quarter galleries (instead of a false window) show two ribbon-handled baskets of olives. The olive tree featured prominently in Minerva's/Pallas's mythical lives. On each quarter is a full-length figure. On the port side this figure is a warrior, very similar to the one recovered from the seabed a few years ago off the Isles of Scilly from the wrecked *Colossus*, which had carried all of Hamilton's china collection from the Mediterranean, much of which was destroyed. The starboard quarter carries a female figure of the same era.

The model at Greenwich differs noticeably from the draught of *Minerva* in the position and spacing of gun ports. It also has a stepped deck where the quarterdeck joins the gang boards, whereas the model in Annapolis is flush-decked. The figurehead also has what appears to be a replacement head.

A drawing exists in the Museum which has only been catalogued in recent years, because it was admitted into the Museum's collections with an assortment of different drawings from a source other than the Admiralty. Several experts have decided that it is possibly a drawing, and not a draught, produced for the French model maker to build the early model in the Museum, as it matches it exactly. The name *Minerva* is not present on this drawing, whereas the actual draughts carry *Minerva*, and where applicable her sister ships' names, with written annotations relating to modifications. As

Above: *Minerva* on the workbench: the model is still in three pieces even at this quite late stage. Having established that the method works for the starboard side, the port side takes shape.

with all evidence of this period, nothing is ever conclusive, but the indication in this case seems to be very nearly so.

Extensive searches to date have failed to produce any images of *Minerva* of 1780 in either drawings or paintings, although all of her sisters are represented.

Much research and consultation was done with the draughts department at the National Maritime Museum, and with Robert Gardiner, specialist in frigate history. Marine artist Mark Myers has always been a great help to me.

I have to say that this model is my first attempt at a frigate; my only other eighteenth-century vessel built to commission was a 1799 privateer/whaler conversion built for a client in Chile. There are many very talented model makers and maritime historians who specialise in just this period, so I knew I had to be thorough with my research, and cross-reference everything. I was pleased to consult all the written works available, and everyone who I felt was able to offer construc-

tive advice, prior to the construction of this commission.

THE METHODOLOGY FOR CONSTRUCTION OF THE MODEL

Building a model for one's own pleasure and building to commission are two completely different things. The most important differences are firstly building to a fixed price and secondly attempting to build within a certain time frame.

With a model as complicated as this, it is very difficult to calculate the time needed and hence the cost. But is has to be done: I have yet to meet someone who would commission with an open ended contract at an hourly rate.

In my case, I felt three years of intense work in excess of 6,000 hours would cover the project. The client suggested two years; I said it was not possible. We settled on two years and eight months with a possible review. This proved necessary, and the final result has been three years plus a bit. This has required working six days a week for the majority of that time. Previously, the largest model I have built in terms of hours spent had been a plated and rigged four-masted

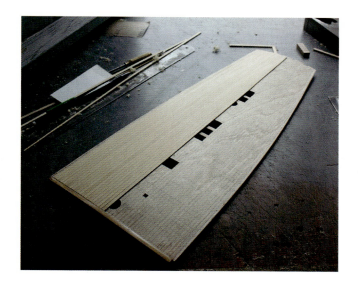

barque, *Pamir*, which took me 3,840 hours and seemed a lifetime over a 20-month period.

To spend over 6,000 hours on one project over a sustained period is a severe strain, but the one thing that kept me going was looking at the original Navy Board model photographs and saying to myself, 'Well, if they were able to do it in 1780 with only candlelight and daylight, I must be able to do it'.

Since starting the model it has been revealed, however, that the Georgian model makers had a specialist team to carry out the carving and frieze painting, copper sheathing, etc. Hence the models were assembled in double-quick time, but they did cost a great deal of money. As a result the Admiralty were always making cuts, cancelling framed models in 1750, and so on.

Ships' logs are held at the National Archives. They are very useful for confirming details of boats and other items carried on board, especially in *Minerva*'s case, where I found references such as '...launched the red cutter'. It was possible to ascertain that the cutters were painted in different colours – red and green – to differentiate them.

It was an amazing stoke of luck that seaman William Richardson, who wrote a book (still in print) of his life story, *A Mariner of England*, was press-ganged aboard *Minerva* having just been shipwrecked in a merchant vessel in India. He gives a detailed account of the voyage back to England, which in conjunction with both Master's and Captain's logs give a wonderful insight into shipboard life. A Master's log was located via the internet in Brisbane, Australia.

When *Minerva* was careened at Trincomalee, all equipment was removed from the ship and itemised in the log, which was most useful – except of course, the model represents the vessel before that date, so care had to be taken as to which items were aboard at an earlier time.

MAKING A START

This required a great deal of thought as to just how I was going to tackle the project with the time restriction in mind.

Firstly, I consulted my *Model Shipwright* library, referring back to every issue that covered building frigates and the different techniques past model makers had employed.

Having studied these in my spare time whilst finishing my previous commission, I established that the easiest way to go about it was to build an underwater body (which would be copper sheathed) in a laminated bread-and-butter method, using jelutong, constructing the topsides as two half models, with the ability to lock into position on the under body. This would give me the facility of working on the intricate decora-

Above: Boxwood gratings with 1mm laser-cut apertures.

tion of the topsides, the frieze painting and small details, with each half lying flat on the bench. The stern would incorporate a separate laminated section, which could also be laid on the bench for painting and carving.

That was the theory. Putting it into practice was more difficult and brought its own problems.

All the frieze painting on the original model of *Minerva* had been done on paper, which was then glued and fitted around all the gun ports and topside detail. But although it had been done very well, it is still possible to see it is paper.

I wanted to do the job properly and paint directly on to the model, to prevent blistering in future years – a problem

Below: The large gratings in the waist, prior to adding the cannonball racks around their perimeters.

that has affected the original Navy Board model.

I created a central vertical spine of jelutong ½in thick, which keyed into the under body fore and aft, and created a backing for the half models to fit against. All the joints would be covered when assembled by the laid decks.

For strength and speed, the topsides were framed down to the bottom of the main wales. This was achieved with great difficulty, by producing solid sections of boxwood framing of the correct moulded dimensions, joining between the gun ports with grain and joint running vertically.

This of course requires some skill, as the frame covering that distance fore and aft changes shape in three dimensions, and it was my shipwrighting experience that allowed me to pull this off, risking my fingers when cutting out each section on my miniature bladed band saw. Normally on a model of this scale, the frames would be separate or doubled. I was building a complete solid wall of framing with no spaces. The bottom ends rebated flush into the under body former, screwed and glued with epoxy for strength, and also glued to each other on the edges.

With extreme care, this produces a highly accurate wall of framing. When given the final fairing with glass paper, it is a wonderfully strong base upon which to mark out all the topside detail in pencil, giving an exact finished plan in three dimensions before even starting on the planking, but still retaining the ability to work on the two halves of the topsides flat on the bench. The framing is not for the faint hearted and no doubt health and safety would have something to say about my using the band saw in this way. I do still have eight fingers and two thumbs!

With all model making, but especially so with eighteenth-century naval vessels, the order of build is critical and that was one of my biggest challenges, especially as I was building it in an unorthodox manner. It brought advantages but other

Above: The ship's boats; at left the launch, the pinnace in the middle, and at right one of the two cutters.

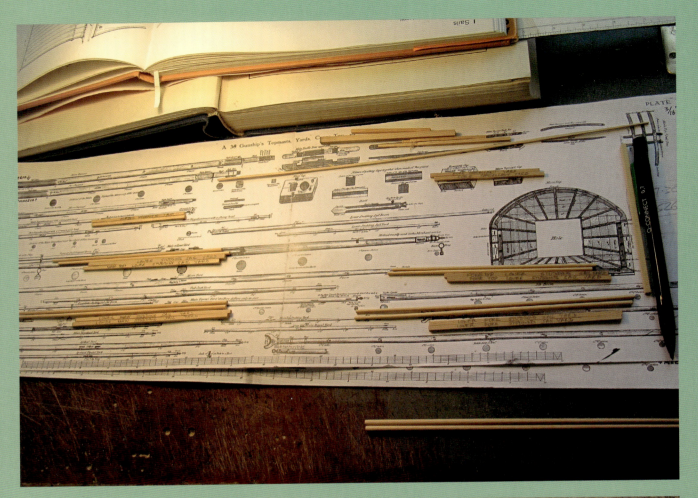

Above: Making a start on the spars, using a multitude of references to ensure accuracy.

Right: Carving in boxwood with a No. 11 scalpel blade. A basket of olives with ribboned handles, part of the starboard quarter decoration.

Left: The trailboard decoration for the port side. The carving depicts a serpent with a phoenix holding a cocoa flower (symbolizing peace) in its beak, rising from the flames and weaponry of war.

Below: The copper sheathing showing all fastenings and laps is just $^{1}/_{1000}$in thick.

Above: The stern decoration and carving starts to take shape.

problems cropped up as a result, each in turn having to be resolved before proceeding, thinking about ten moves ahead at each stage.

I had read many harrowing accounts in *Model Shipwright* of keen model makers spending upwards of two to three years working splendidly, and then finding they couldn't complete the model because they had built it in the wrong sequence, meaning it had to be scrapped and started again. This was a nightmare which I could not let happen, as I was building to commission and being paid for each month. To go backwards could not enter the equation. Really it is a matter of common sense, but even the best model makers, unless they are building this type of vessel regularly, have to be on their toes in looking ahead. In my case, I seem to have managed without too many false starts (maybe a few sleepless nights!).

The planking continued inside and outside of the framing; obviously the framing at the stern had to be individual to be able to look through the great cabin windows, along the upper deck (main gun deck) which is shown cleared for action, giving a clear field of view up to the fo'c's'le, with the cannon rigged and the under deck detail visible.

I managed to buy a set of stainless steel long reach medical clamps, which were ideal for planking the hull with the addition of some plastic shoes over the metal serrations on the ends of the clamps, to prevent damage to the wood, and to space the arms out from the tumblehome. Decks were laid whilst the model was still in two halves, with the central planks being added once assembled, when the whole was very carefully cleaned up.

As the deck planks were all tapered towards the ship's ends, it might be thought possible to make a jig to taper them equally all at once. Unfortunately in practice this does not work and each plank had to be tapered individually.

At this scale, deck caulking with black paper is not really very practical; but because I used boxwood for the decks, for the first time I was able to produce the deck seam on the edge of the planking, with permanent black felt tip, without the

Above: The great cabin and its chequered floor in blue, prior to the quarterdeck being added. Note the groove for the tongues at the side of the deck to slide in.

ink ingressing into the wood. The result was marvellous and quickly done; the excess on the top surfaces easily cleaned off when the decks were cabinet scraped.

The quarterdecks and forecastle decks were made separately and slid into position in rebates built into the inner planking. In order to achieve this a laminated underlay was made from the thinnest aircraft model makers' birch 3 ply, glued into layers with the planking on top. There is enough room to slide the quarterdeck aft once the model is assembled, because the sides of the ship are getting narrower on approaching her ends, allowing the gaining fit of the deck to be fitted and removed at will until quite late in the construction and assembly of the finished model. This had advantages and disadvantages. In my case the advantages

won the day. Disadvantages are that when the period demands that the hanging knees fit tight to the deck head alongside the beams, they cannot be shown because it would not be possible to slide the deck in, as they would obstruct deck detail whilst being fitted. On the other hand though, all lodging knees may be fitted with ease on the underside of the deck between the beams, which are cut to fit flush with the inside timberwork when the deck is in position. The fact that the long quarterdeck has openings for skylight and gangways allows for two-way bend (compound curves) when used in conjunction with the grooves each side, into which the plywood under deck tongues locate the edges of the deck in the correct position whilst the cambered beams maintain the curvature at the correct amount. The advantages of building the model in this way are immense – keeping it clean under the decks until the last minute is a great help.

The original model of *Minerva* at Annapolis is not framed but a carved bread-and-butter hull planked inside and out.

The commission required a rigged model, and so I had to introduce boxwood framing in the topsides, to make them strong enough to withstand the pull of the rigging on the chain plates, and to avoid any possibility of very thin fore-and-aft grained jelutong splitting with the tension amongst the frieze painting.

One of the jobs I was dreading was producing all the boxwood mouldings, which are found all over the ship. Each is of a different and unique design.

Eventually I found a small mention in a *Model Shipwright* article which stated that any moulding may be produced using a scraper! This required a great deal of experiment and thought, but again I worked on the basis that if they could produce such intricate carving in the eighteenth century there must be a simple modern solution.

The answer is indeed a scraper. I modified a cabinet scraper by grinding all the female contours required for the model into its edges, to the exact scale proportions.

The next stage was to prepare the boxwood blanks to the exact external dimensions needed to produce the moulding.

I cramped the boxwood to a flat, smooth working surface – I would recommend a formica top or similar – and used the cabinet scraper at a forward leaning angle, as if scraping a piece of timber. The ground edges of the moulding were sharp enough to cut the required shapes. When the moulding depth was nearly achieved I gradually altered the angle of the scraper to the vertical, thereby ensuring that the cut was not too deep. The fact that the edge of the scraper came into contact with the surface of the bench created a constant depth and accuracy, avoiding any undulations in the finished design of the moulding . It also polished the finished job.

As I was working to 1:64 scale, I found the best way to form the designs in the steel tool scraper was to use a circular dental grinding disc, ground prior to use against another one where necessary. This enabled me to create the tongues of very fine metal, often paper thin, which cut these beautiful deep insets in the mouldings with ease.

Despite my thirty-five years of professional model-making, this technique of creating mouldings (once the hard work of grinding the scraper was done) was an entirely new skill. It proved to be quick and simple but very satisfying; a superb method to create something of extreme beauty very easily. It opens up so many possibilities for future models.

Having dealt with parallel moudlings, I moved on to the next job. How did they manage the tapered mouldings in the eighteenth century? I had all sorts of theories but none of them worked until I forced myself to think simply.

The answer was to create a female half-moulding in the scraper using the method described above, but this time I left a clearance aperture for the piece of timber being worked, so only one half of the moulding was created at a time. Care had to be taken because of the need to keep the pressure on the side of the timber being cut, and so as not to create undulations, since this time the scraper was not guided by the

width of the timber. When the first side was finished I turned the tapered piece of timber around and did the other side, the taper being absorbed by the central section of the design of the moulding. Of course it was still necessary to create the scrolls by hand but none the less a scraper did help.

The Annapolis model does not show the jointed wale planking. It would seem that, depending on date, anchor stock jointing was used on the inner strings while tip and butt jointing was used on the main wales, with the joints staggered between upper and lower strakes.

At the bow and stern the shape of the hull was such that I steamed the wales to achieve a good fit, thereby avoiding any structural stress to the model. The wales were not finally fastened until quite late in the build, being held in position by tight-fitting pins to keep the timber well in place.

My policy in regard to the order of build is never to attach something permanently to a model until required to do so in

Below: The view from my workshop window provides a touch of reality and has often given me inspiration when the going gets tough.

order to move to the next stage. This sometimes gives me the option to build in an unorthodox order, which occasionally gets out of hand – because I should have made something permanent before attempting to build the next components, which may be more difficult to fit as a result.

At about this stage I started to paint, varnish, and then stain varnish in a light oak colour. If a stain varnish is applied directly to unsealed boxwood it will stain unevenly, as boxwood is often a little porous in certain places. It is therefore necessary to seal the wood first with ordinary clear varnish. The ability to remove planks, wales and mouldings to paint and varnish has the obvious advantage that no cutting-in with the paintbrush is required, though where different colours appeared on the same structural piece I masked with brown parcel tape. Always buy a good brand, because some of them leave a sticky brown residue when the tape is removed, which is most annoying.

The frieze painting was a real challenge. Having never tackled this before, I consulted various experts in the art world to ask their advice. They all explained how it was done, but shuddered at the idea of doing it on such a small scale. However, the ability to lay each topside half flat on the bench made the job easier and took much of the stress away.

With the photographs of the Annapolis model in front of me I was able to make a master drawing on a long strip of plastic drawing film, the length of the model. Two had to be made because the design was different on each side.

The first stage was to lay the film over the half model, and spile it like fitting a plank. It was cut exactly to the required dimensions to cover both upper and lower friezes for the length of the model. It was then taped in position and all the gun ports and mouldings traced on to it, thus giving the true shape and size of the surfaces to be decorated. It was then removed from the model, and using the photographs, the designs were copied on to the film flat on the bench, to the correct scale of course, because it had to fit into the spaces available between the gun ports.

The film was once again attached to the model, above its proper place but positioned correctly fore and aft. The whole process was repeated freehand, applying the design to the

Below: The break of the quarterdeck looking aft, prior to rigging.

model, using the tracing above as a guide. I found that using a brush for applying the gold leaf 'effect' was a non-starter at this scale. I am sure there are many modellers who have the ability to do this, but I decided to try another method.

My solution was to use a gold fibre-tipped pen, drawing the design very carefully without smudging it. This was difficult to accomplish. I knew that it was important not to make

a mistake with the gold, because it would be almost impossible to remove from the background colour of beautiful Prussian blue (plus the two coats of light oak stain varnish). It would leave a horrific-looking stain – I knew this because I had done some test pieces.

It was necessary to concentrate to avoid making a mistake. The finished result with the gold applied looked a little amateurish, but I didn't worry about this, because once it had dried it was brought to life with other two colours, the

Below: The complexity of the bow has its own beauty.

very dull red and black. These were applied very carefully using a No. 5 brush. Once in the swing of it confidence builds and it becomes a very satisfying job to do, with beautiful results, using the photographs of the original model as a guide throughout. Once the model had all the extra detail added, even any bits over which there was some slight uncertainty were hardly noticeable.

I did not attempt to seal the gold by over varnishing as I was concerned that the varnish would melt the gold and spread it – a potential disaster.

If done correctly, the quarter galleries on vessels of this period are an exquisite part of the model. If not, they let the model down terribly. The biggest problem is achieving the true dimensions of the structure, because no matter what

angle it is viewed from nothing in a normal two-dimensional drawing is a true length, since the surfaces are leaning and curving away from the vertical or horizontal. There are ways of unravelling these curves by geometry, but even though I have qualifications in technical drawing it was all too much for me.

So, working on the old adage that 'if it looks right, it is right', I played for many hours with thin card and tape (in tiny pieces), on which the final design including all decorations had been temporarily drawn in pencil.

When I was happy that I had captured the correct curves and rakes, I drew out the true shape of the design on the same very thin birch aircraft modellers' 3-ply that I had used for the deck underlay.

This gave rigidity to the structure, as a basis for wrapping around the carved shingle-roofed block of boxwood that formed the top of the quarter galleries. The very fine fretted design running around the top of the roof was achieved using photo-etched brass.

As this model was to be imported by my client into the USA, certain restrictions applied with regard to materials used on a model of this type. Many of the original Navy Board models used bone or ivory for parts of the white decoration in the stern and quarter galleries. As the import of ivory is strictly controlled my client and I decided to avoid both bone and ivory – we didn't want the model being tampered with by Customs Officials to establish whether a specific material was bone and not ivory.

The decision was made to use an alternative – the same also applied with the use of ebony. Instead I used white Plasticard, varnished once fitted to resemble the lustre of ivory. I sent a sample with the model for Customs to establish just what the material was. The semblance of ebony was achieved by employing black paint of the correct sheen.

Styrene (Plasticard) is in fact quite a useful material for modelling. When carved with care a lot of detail can be achieved – moreover, fluting the pillared window supports was made easier because of the softness of the material.

The area around the stern gallery windows was built up from two layers of thin birch plywood, to achieve the laminated curve required, whilst permitting removal from the model for fine detailing on the bench. The curved lower areas of the structure were cut from a solid piece of boxwood, and thinned down until daylight could be seen through it, prior to varnishing and painting. The mouldings were also cut to shape to accommodate the curved stern, and then moulded using the scraper. The mouldings, of course, are all on the cant here, because of the angle of the stern windows. These methods meant that the whole structure was removable for finishing on the bench. The white window

Below: This shot simulates the view a Georgian seaman would have had of his ship when approaching prior to boarding.

frames and glazing bars were made from the Styrene. The glazing bars were made in sections of very small dimension to give the correct Georgian style. Careful use of liquid poly was needed when glueing these glazing bars – a great deal of patience is required here, and a steady hand.

At this stage the model was still in three pieces, but the time was drawing near for final assembly. As this was my first attempt at this type of construction, I had worked more on the first side as a prototype, so that any bad moves were not repeated on the other. Having therefore done most of the details on the starboard side, this left me with the disheartening task of starting again on the port side. This was, I suppose, the lesser of two evils – at least I didn't have to redo both sides!

The day eventually arrived when the whole model was assembled to enable the main deck to be finished and cabinet-scraped clean. There is no going back at this stage, so I was careful not to forget any bits.

With time ticking away, I was very pleased to find a quality set of gun carriages and brass cannon available in kit form, suitable for this model. I had to rework the muzzles of the barrels of the 18lb cannon in the lathe, but otherwise once assembled and painted they didn't look too bad. The assembly of all 42 cannon and 4 carronades took three weeks.

Rigging them all took another three weeks, so if I had made them all from scratch the time really would have run away with me. The brass photo-etched gun locks look very well – I did add extra detail to the cannon to bring them up to the standard of the rest of the model.

If available and of sufficient quality, other items of detail were also purchased and assembled, but only because of my deadline. The galley stove was a good example. The model kit industry has made huge strides during my time as a professional model-maker. It is always worth keeping abreast of the industry to see how manufacturers have utilised modern technology to the advantage of the model-maker. When I actually received a catalogue of fittings available, the variety of items on the market was quite an eye opener.

In the past, even if a specific fitting could be purchased it tended to be a disappointment. Today there has been a revolution and, provided the correct scale is available, certain items are amazing in their quality. One of the biggest surprises were laser cut grating bars and laths at 1mm square aperture size. I have made my own gratings for years, using various methods. However, there is no way any human is able to match the quality and precision of laser-cut boxwood parts. Obviously the model-maker uses them as a raw component, making the grating frame to accommodate them once assembled and introducing the correct camber when finished, but the parts are excellent. I defy anyone who is able to do better, and was delighted to use them for this model.

The next big challenge was the ship's boats. A heavy

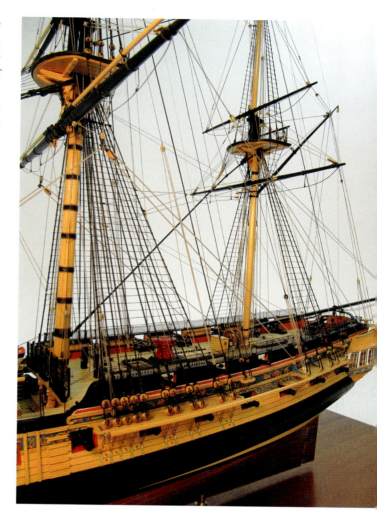

Above: The hammock nettings. When full of rolled-up hammocks they would have had waterproof tarpaulins hung over them, creating a higher defensive barricade.

frigate of *Minerva*'s size during this period carried two cutters, a launch and a pinnace. A little later in her career she carried a jolly boat as well, when davits had been introduced.

The construction of clinker-built ship's boats is something I have done happily for many years, down to quite small scales. Making carvel-built ship's boats is a little more difficult. Invariably these days the model-maker overcomes the problems of rigidity (given that there is no clinker overlap in the planking to provide strength) by producing a shell for the hull, either to be planked over or used as is. I looked into this and found that ship's boats were available in kit form for a frigate of this period. I bought them to see whether I could adapt them. On arrival I was a little disappointed. Although the basic shape was there they needed a great deal of work to fair them up outside, prior to thinning them down to scale thickness inside, so that daylight was nearly visible through their hulls. This took time and great care but the results were very acceptable. I put aside the materials that came with the kits for fitting out, and scratch built the insides from boxwood instead. I did use the photo-etched oars, grapnels and boathooks, introducing photo-etched miniature gratings for the sterns. A great deal of time was spent with timbering out. Having first glued in the gunwales, one end of the timbers was glued tight against one gunwale, sprung in at the other end, and cut off to exact length against the other gunwhale. This meant that the timbers hugged the inside contours of the hull. The hulls were all pre-painted internally to eliminate the daylight showing through prior to timbering. Then many more hours were spent making all the knees, details which make a real difference in the finished model.

As I had never built an eighteenth-century naval launch before it was quite an eye opener. I found the introduction of a removable stern davit quite enlightening. this was used in conjunction with a windlass midships to break out the frigate's anchor flukes using the anchor buoy rope. I was

Below: An overall shot of the finished model on its Cuban mahogany plinth from above the port quarter.

pleased with the result – indeed, people who have seen the finished model invariably say, 'I love the boats, they are so exquisite. How much would just a boat cost?!'

I am keen to point out that most of the fittings on the model were made, so please do not get the impression that I assembled a model from manufactured parts!

The next job was making the masts and spars. As with all items on a model of this period, care has to be taken not to introduce detail that hadn't arrived yet. Steel's drawings are of a later period; however certain aspects of them could be used. *Minerva*, for example, was built before masts were iron-hooped, but she did have rope wooldings on fore and main masts. The masts and spars were made from boxwood and when finished were stained in the same way as the hull to tone them down a bit. They were made so that external appearance was correct, with the appropriate front fish, etc.

The demands of this commission meant that it was necessary for me to invest heavily in the reference books available on eighteenth-century naval vessels, particularly frigates. It was quite amazing to find how different every aspect of the design, the shipbuilding and the rigging was in comparison to nineteenth- and twentieth-century vessels. It was a completely new world, and one which I had previously only had a superficial knowledge of.

All parts of the vessel incorporated intricate design, especially the bow and stern details. The head rails and all their fine details sweeping towards the figurehead constituted a massive achievement in the development of naval architecture over hundreds of years. The design was eminently practical, yet turned into a thing of extreme beauty by clever use of timber.

The decoration in the form of the woodcarving was the 'icing on the cake' of this period. All my carving was done in English boxwood using a dental laboratory handpiece with diamond burrs to remove the bulk of the excess timber. The carving was always finished with a No. 11 Swan Morton scalpel blade to achieve the requisite crispness. Boxwood does hold its edge beautifully.

The carving of the trailboard detail demonstrates just how strong boxwood is; the serpent and phoenix with a cocoa flower in its beak all conjoined with the rising carved flames at the base. Making the mirrored pair was an interesting challenge. As with the original model, the stern carving was done in three panels. Two extra cupids with anchor carved shields covered the joints between the panels, added afterwards.

Sheathing the hull with copper is a feature that I have quite happily done for many years on my models, slowly developing new methods and adding to the detail achieved with each step forward. For this commission the client had requested that I showed all the copper nail heads on the sheathing.

Having copper-sheathed vessels during my career as a shipwright, and knowing that the system was the same back in the eighteenth century, I was aware that when nailing into the sheathing to attach it to the hull, the underlay of felt and paper etc. causes the nail head to be below flush when fully driven home. This can be seen on the *Trincomalee* at West Hartlepool.

In the early days of making models I had copper shim sheared for me to the correct width for the scale of the model I was building. This was very expensive. I used to glue each plate on individually – very time consuming and tricky not to get glue on the outside surface, which caused it to oxidise unevenly. Then, many years ago now, when taking annual leave on the Isles of Scilly, during a visit to a local stained glass craftswoman I noticed she was using copper tape in rolls, to attach to the edge of her glass on each component prior to soldering the two together.

On closer inspection I noted that the tape was available in different widths, and that it had a peel off paper backing which exposed an amazing adhesive able to stand the heat of the soldering iron. Basically the copper strip that attached and folded over the face edge of each piece of glass was replacing the leaded extrusions used in the past to hold the whole together.

This tape is made in America, but is available from any stained glass supplier in the UK. I tested it on a piece of jelutong timber for adhesion and left it in the sun in my workshop window for six years. When I pulled the tape off after that time, it pulled the grain off the timber with it, so I knew then I had a product that would stand the test of time.

For this model to satisfy the client's wishes, I devised a method using toothed wheels (watch sprockets, in fact) to mark the appropriate number and pattern of nail heads on the sheathing, before it was applied to the model. The paper backing of the copper meant that when set up on my worktop with a jig, I was able to reproduce all the nail heads with two differently spaced sprockets, the paper absorbing the teeth of the wheels and leaving an even depth of impression. This took four intense days of work, with many rejects. Eventually, having also marked out the plate laps (visible from aft only) by impressing into it with a metal edged tool , I was ready to start laying the copper strips as opposed to the individual plates.

It took 11 hours' work to do both sides of the model. I did it all in one day, having rubbed my (acidic) hands once down each strip to introduce an even amount of oxidation to the raw copper. Spreading the work over several days would have meant that the oxidation would have been different for each day's work, creating bands of different colour. There were no belts in this frigate's sheathing, so it was a straightforward process – due, no doubt, to *Minerva*'s quite fine lines, which gave her a speed of 9 to 11 knots 'without pressing', according to her captain's official reports. It is also possible to edge bend this $\frac{1}{1000}$in thick copper. The most effective technique is to peel the paper gradually when applying the copper. With practice this evolves so that the hand is capable of peeling the paper progressively when laying the copper.

Back inside the frigate, I was adding detail in the great cabin aft. The model is represented with the vessel cleared for action, with all bulkheads removed, and stowed in the hold. I did the chequered floor covering, having marked it all out carefully beforehand. The original model showed a medium blue check. The rudder head was boxed in, the housing having a radius running aft as a seat to the stern windows. Care was taken with this, to allow visual access along the length of the gun deck when the model was finished, through the stern windows.

One of the problems of building high monetary value models is the inability to take the model out of the workshop into the sunshine to photograph (which always introduces realism with the shadows caused) because of the insurance factor. To try and get around this a few photographs were taken in the workshop window with the sun streaming in.

The small detail was also added at this stage: hammock cranes and netting, capstans made from boxwood using the lathe, the knees on top of the channels, all with moulded edges. These details seemed to be endless – was I ever going to finish this model? – and that was before the rigging was started. The upper lengths of the chainplates were modelled as bare brass, as in the original model, with varnished boxwood deadeyes. To some extent I was limited in my

Below: The starboard bow, showing the intricate tracery of the moulded and tapered headrails. *Minerva* was the only vessel in the class to have her hawse pipes between the cheeks.

Above: The elegance and majesty of the finished stern is a delight.

choice as to how to decorate the model because of the requirement to copy the original model. The client and myself did decide, in our opinion, to improve on the colour scheme in small areas.

The quarterdeck details included a mix of 18lb and 9lb cannonballs. The 18lb balls were the carronade ammunition. When I eventually felt that I had done the deck and hull detail justice, it was time to start the rigging.

Obviously I had thought about this at the beginning of the project, and discussed the spinning of the rigging with friend and modelmaker/author, Will Mowll, who has devised an efficient method of producing left- and right-hand lay rope to my requirements, including cable-laid rope when necessary. His is the alternative ropewalk in Kent to Chatham, which of course does the full size commodity. I had decided, as the vessel was a new approach in 1780, to cable-lay the shrouds, with of course the fore swifter served all the way up. I did get a little carried away, and did the main swifter as well!

Cable-laid shrouds were a little unusual at this time, but became the norm a few years later. The only previous experience I had with eighteenth-century rigging was with a 1799 Merchant/Privateer rigged as a Whaler. There were similarities, but the frigate of course was a great deal more

complicated, naval practice being a little different to the merchant service.

James Lees' book, *The Masting and Rigging of English Ships of War, 1625-1860* was very helpful in sorting out most problems. However, as with all reference books discussing this period, the sources do not all agree with each other. I was delighted to find out at the outset of the model that Lennarth Petersson's book, *Rigging Period Ship Models*, was based upon *Minerva*'s later 36-gun sister *Melampus*, using the models in the Bristol Industrial Museum. His illustrations, broken down into each stage of the rigging, are absolutely brilliant. But although *Melampus* was launched in 1785, both models in the Museum are for some reason rigged for the post-1810 period.

I found, therefore, that I had to do a juggling act, referring to Mr Lees' accounts for dates of introduction to changes in rigging procedure, and not using later introductions which appear both in the book by Mr Petersson and on the *Melampus* models. I was using additional references, including the *Anatomy of the Ship the 24 Gun Frigate Pandora*, by McKay and Coleman, which was right on date for *Minerva*. I also used, selectively, David White's *Anatomy of the Ship the Frigate Diana*, launched 14 years later than *Minerva*. These rigging introductions were so precise date-wise, when answering Admiralty changes to procedure, that I felt where possible I had to stick with the written word, very much realising that the whole thing was a 'minefield' to the unwary. I have attempted to show the finished model to as many experts in the field as possible, but have finally accepted that I could do no more than make the model as accurate as possible within the time frame.

Asking even the experts in the field to criticise a model of this complexity is a lot to ask, because no one, to my knowledge, is able to keep all the variations of rig in their heads, or at their fingertips for comment. It all requires thorough research to cover many periods of change, as I found out. So at time of writing I hold a clear conscience.

A few words on the photography of the model might be helpful. I never use flash when taking my photographs; this was especially the case with *Minerva*. A great deal of care was taken, when painting the model, to scale down the density of the colour. It is well known that, when depicting strong colours such as red on a model, if 'post office red' is chosen for an item, when fitted to the model it will be far too bright, more akin to a 'day-glow red'. So realism is created by toning down the brightness or density of the colour.

In the same way the amount of light used when photographing a model should not be too bright, in order to create atmosphere. The type of light used is also important, warm or cool light. Daylight bulbs are a cool light, whereas an anglepoise bulb may be a warm light. Over-use of either will ruin a model photograph.

HMS *Minerva*'s new home will be the small town of Minerva, in the United States, which is quite fitting really

because she was built to counter the new big American frigates being launched, and indeed she did manage to capture a few American vessels.

The total number of hours taken to build the model from initial construction to final completion was 6,741.

Above: A peep through the stern gallery windows shows the main gun deck cleared for action. Light illuminates the port gunports, showing their red edgings. Also visible are the lower capstan, the chain pumps and deck pumps, the accommodation ladder and the companion ladder. (Photograph by Alan Harper)

Below: Photographing the ship – lighting is so important.

Firing a Broadside

THE PRACTICE AND POWER OF FIRING BROADSIDES IN BRITISH MEN OF WAR

by Peter Goodwin MPhil. I. Eng. MIMarEST

THE BROADSIDE AND THE LINE OF BATTLE

The concept of broadside fire from ships formed into a line of battle into an opposing line of enemy ships was created during the Dutch Wars in the mid-17th century. Prior to this naval warfare followed a more fluid form of engagement, with ships manoeuvring independently when attacking an opposing fleet. This tactic was used by Hawkins and Drake against the Spanish Armada in 1588. This freestyle method of engagement was quashed during the 17th century when naval warfare was put under the restrictive control of 'Generals at Sea' appointed into the Navy by Cromwell. In effect the Commonwealth Navy was largely organised in a military fashion; commanders of ships and squadrons being directed to operate like regiments on the battlefield.

The line of battle, much employed by Blake and Torrington, maximised the control and effect of gunfire into enemy ships. Broadside firing in line ahead also dictated the design of ships, leaving their heads and sterns weak in construction and consequently vulnerable if attacked from afore or abaft. The only ships built with provision to avoid this were the galley frigates and 20-gun ships such as the *Blandford*, which, built to specifications of the 1719 Establishment, could manoeuvre under sweeps.[1] The only other vessels generally furnished with sweeps were sloops, armed cutters and gun boats.[2] Although later frigates were provided with sweep ports (for war only); *Trincomalee* (1817) being one example, it was uncommon in two-decked ships – the 50-gun *Bristol* is a rare exception.[3]

Above: English and Dutch fleets engaged at the Battle of the Gabbard, 2 June 1653, during the First Anglo-Dutch War. (NMM BHC0276)

The tactic of broadside firing was to prevail as standard naval practice until the War of American Independence in the 18th century, when Admiral Rodney broke away from the rigid Admiralty instructions at the Battle of the Saints against the French fleet under De Grasse on 12 April 1782.[4] Prior to this any officer who did not fight in the authorised line of battle 'did so at his own peril' and faced the wrath of the Admiralty. Nelson is repeatedly given considerable credit for using an unauthorised tactic of attack at the Battle of Trafalgar, when he directed his ships to pass through the enemy line. Although his line of attack proved successful at this battle, this overrated misconception wrongly fortifies 'the Nelson myth', whereas the plaudits for this revolutionary form of naval warfare should rightfully be attributed to other tacticians like Rodney and Boscowan.

The key elements of British naval supremacy were good seamanship, gunnery and training.[5] Ironically the form of fighting employed at Trafalgar, where ships individually or jointly attacked and subdued single ships piecemeal under consolidated broadsides, very much returned to the type of tactics used against the Armada at the end of the sixteenth century. The breakaway from the rigidity of the line of battle also provided ship designers greater scope to build ships with less vulnerable heads and sterns. The introduction of the round bow and stern can in large part be ascribed to the influence of Robert Seppings, who became Surveyor of the Navy in 1830. The round bow and stern also provided the ability to mount guns in these parts of a ship, giving 360° defence.[6]

HMS VICTORY FIRES A BROADSIDE

On 18 September 2009 Her Majesty's Ship *Victory*, the world's only surviving 18th-century 100-gun ship, fired a simulated single broadside to commemorate the official launch of Britain's National Museum of the Royal Navy from her starboard broadside battery of guns. The simulated broadside was created to good effect by the company Master Gunner Ltd under the direction of Charles Payton, with his expert team comprising Martin Bibbings and Brian Miller. Martin Bibbings provided all the gunnery expertise for the successful 20th Century Fox film *Master and Commander*, directed by Peter Weir and starring Russell Crowe.

To understand the destructive capability of a real broadside fired from the *Victory* the significant point we must realise is that the *Victory* carried more firepower in weight of shot than Field Marshal Wellington had at the Battle of Waterloo in 1816. Although classified as a 100-gun ship when serving as the flagship of Vice Admiral Nelson at the momentous Battle of Trafalgar on 21 October 1805, *Victory*'s ordnance actually totalled 104 guns, mounted on her three full gun decks and upon her quarter deck and forecastle, and comprised the following armament.[7]

Victory's Ordnance

Deck	No. of Guns	Gun Type
Lower gun deck	30	Long 32-pdr carriage guns
Middle gun deck	28	Long 24-pdr carriage guns
Upper gun deck	30	Long 12-pdr carriage guns
Quarter deck	12	Short 12-pdr carriage guns
Forecastle	2	Medium 12-pdr carriage guns
Forecastle	2	68-pdr carronades on slide carriages

TOTAL 104

Note: According to the Gunner's records the *Victory* was also carrying an 18-pdr carronade, which was probably reserved for mounting in the ship's launch should a boat attack be called upon.[8]

FIREPOWER

The weight of iron discharged from single shotted guns fired from one broadside of the *Victory* is 1,148lb (522kg) or 0.65 imperial tons.[9] If firing both larboard and starboard broadsides simultaneously the combined broadside weight of *Victory*'s firepower is doubled to 2,296lb (1.25 tons).[10] This weight is 35% greater than the massed firepower of 1,704lb (0.76 tons) discharged from the 161 guns that Field Marshal Wellington had at his disposal to support his allied army in the field at the Battle of Waterloo against the French in 1815. *Victory*'s first opening broadside at Trafalgar, fired through the stern of the French flagship *La Bucentaure*, was triple shotted; the weight of broadside in this instance was 3,444lb (1,566 kg) i.e. 1.9 tons.[11] The total broadside weight of iron round shot expended if all guns from each of the thirty-three British ships (frigates and smaller vessels included as well as the line of battle ships) present at Trafalgar fired one round only amounted to 51,944lb (23.21 tons).[12]

MUZZLE VELOCITY

The larger 32-pdr Blomefield pattern guns were very powerful. Using a full charge of about 11lb (5kg) of gunpowder, i.e. $1/3$ the weight of the shot, the muzzle velocity (MV) of these guns firing a single 32lb (14.4kg) shot would be between 1500 and 1600 feet per second (487 metres per second). These figures equate to between 1023 and 1091 miles per hour (1646 and 1755 kilometres per hour). Consequently projectiles fired from smooth bored muzzle loading guns were supersonic, the shot taking 3.3 seconds to travel 1 mile.

Note: One of the most remarkable incidents recorded about gunfire was the death of Thomas Whipple, who was serving in the *Victory* as Captain Hardy's clerk at Trafalgar. Whipple actually died unmarked. His death was caused by

the vortex created by a round shot passing his head; the resulting vacuum sucked all of the air from his lungs. In effect he was instantly suffocated as he stood on the quarterdeck.

RECOIL

According to Isaac Newton's law of physics, 'for every action there is an equal and opposite reaction'. This statement, in relation to the gun or other contrivance that discharges a projectile under force, be it either round shot, rocket or even the simple arrow, is called recoil. The recoil of a naval gun is constrained by heavy breeching ropes secured to both the breech of the gun and to a pair of ring bolts firmly secured in the ship's side.

The length of a breeching rope is calculated as three times the length of the barrel of the gun measured from the muzzle to the breech ring. Not only does the breeching rope ensure that the gun is secured to the ship's side, its actual length is determined such that the gun can only recoil a sufficient distance to bring the muzzle about 18in from the gun port, thereby providing sufficient room to swab and reload the gun. If the breeching rope was any longer then greater physical effort and time would be wasted in hauling the gun forward, back to its firing position with its muzzle outside the gun port. My colleague Major Adrian Caruana, Royal Artillery, who carried out an experimental firing with an unrestrained 32-pdr carriage gun using a full charge of powder and a projectile, recorded that the gun and its carriage totalling a weight of 69 cwt 2qtrs 11lb (31.2 tons) recoiled a distance of 50ft 2in (15.3m), i.e. about 3ft (91cm) greater than the breadth of the lower gun deck of a 74-gun ship. Calculations made by another colleague, Major Denny Elvin, also Royal Artillery, determined that the gun and carriage were reversing (recoiling) at a speed of 6 feet per second before overall weight brought the gun to a standstill.

The forces exerted upon the two ringbolts at the ship's side to which the two ends of a breeching rope are secured are therefore quite considerable. Calculations infer that the total weight exerted by a single 32-pdr is estimated as 8 imperial tons per ring bolt; 7 tons for a 24-pdr and 6 tons for a 12-pdr. Using these figures as a guideline, when the *Victory* fired a single-shotted broadside the total estimated forces exerted upon the hull frames on one side of the ship would be somewhere in the region of 1300 tons. Because of this colossal strain imposed upon the fabric of the hull the practice of firing a broadside in a ripple form from head to stern was introduced. This method allowed the hull to absorb a diminished shock as opposed to the concerted force exerted if all guns fired at precisely the same time. For virtually identical reasons a similar concept was introduced into armies when they were marching across bridges, where they would break step to prevent the resonance of concerted foot movement weakening the structure of the bridge.

GUNPOWDER AND ITS PROPERTIES

The propellant force that produced such muzzle velocities was standard gunpowder, which is made from three constituent materials. In brief the saltpetre provides extra oxygen and potassium nitrate, which reacts with sulphur and carbon to form nitrogen and carbon dioxide gases and potassium sulphide; the expanding gases, nitrogen and carbon dioxide,

provide the propelling action.[13] Rated a highly explosive compound, gunpowder is only 35% weaker in destructive power than modern trinitrotoluene (TNT). When gunpowder is ignited it expands to 300% of its own volume, providing a highly effective propellant.[14]

The Constituents of Gunpowder

Chemical	Quantity	Purpose
Potassium nitrate (saltpetre)	75%	Provided oxygen to increase the combustion rate.
Charcoal. (carbon)	15%	Provided fuel and heat in the form of carbon dioxide to assist the combustion process.
Sulphur	10%	Acted as a catalyst (chemical reaction) with the charcoal in the combustion process

Above: The shot damage display set up on *Victory's* orlop deck.

The total broadside weight of gunpowder expended by the thirty-three British ships present at Trafalgar if firing one round only amounted to 16,032lb (17.7 tons).[15]

DESTRUCTIVE POWER

At a point blank range of 370 yards (338.33m) a 32lb shot travelling at these velocities could pass through 3ft (0.9m) of oak or 6ft (1.83m) of fir or pine. A superb example of this can be seen on the battle-damaged section of the *Victory*'s original pine foremast, now displayed in the ship, which was shot clean through at Trafalgar.[16] The MV of the smaller calibre 12- and 24-pdr guns was only marginally slower than that of the 32-pdrs, albeit that the fire power was proportionally reduced. In comparison to the long guns, the carronades had a considerably low MV, but firing a proportionally heavier shot at low velocity these guns had the advantage of creating greater damage at short range. Rather than punching its way through timber the shot virtually 'churned its way through', making repairs to the hull far more difficult.

SHOT DAMAGE DISPLAY

A realistic shot damage display has been created for the public in the *Victory* on the starboard side of the orlop. This demonstrates the effects caused by a 32lb solid iron round shot fired through the ship's side just below the waterline. The production of this display required the expert assistance of Nick Hall, Keeper of the Royal Armouries Fort Nelson, Portsdown Hill, Portsmouth and his team to set up the necessary experiments.

One early morning in June 2009 we fired two single 32lb solid iron round shot from an original cast iron 32-pdr gun through oak planks 9in (22.9cm) thick and 12in (30.48cm) broad. These timbers represented the internal planking forming the strakes of the lower gun deck clamp (beam shelf) supporting the lower gun deck beams in the *Victory*. The firing was undertaken at a range of 25 yards (22.9 metres) i.e. 'pistol shot range', the distance at which most sea battles were fought. The gunpowder charge used for this experiment was only 4lb (1.8kg), whereas the normal charge for a 32lb shot was about 11lb (5kg). This reduction in the charge was calculated to account for the fact that the shot would have lost part of its kinetic energy having theoretically passed through the ship's hull at the determined point. The total thickness of timber forming *Victory*'s hull at the chosen point is 2ft 7½in (80cm). This comprised the main wale 10in (25.4cm) thick, the ship's frames 12½in (31.75cm) thick and finally the internal deck clamp 9in (22.86cm) thick. The display clearly shows entry and exit holes and the deadly splinters that inflicted terrible wounds upon the men.

Besides providing the effect required, this experiment created exciting new information about the impact of shot. One shot hit a knot in the timber, and although it continued to pass through the timber the wood surrounding the knot sprang back and reformed due to the inherent strength of its growth around the knot. This type of damage indicated that it would have been more difficult to seal when attempting to effect repairs than that needed to stop up a clean punched hole.

Although we know from historical records that flying wood splinters inflicted horrendous physical wounds upon the men, which certainly kept the surgeon and his mates busy below decks, the most surprising thing we discovered from this experimental firing was that wood splinters, driven by the kinetic energy generated by the impact of the shot, penetrated firmly into nearby timber. This result indicated that the same effect would have been produced inside ships during battle. Colloquially known as 'spalling', the same kind of effect is produced by fragmented metal inside military tanks when they are hit by shells, the shards mutilating the crew within. The section of the framing used to hold the experimental 'target' affected by spalling has been displayed in the *Victory* as an example of this feature for interpretation. To expand on this matter Brian Miller, a retired military explosives expert and advisor for Master Gunner Ltd, has since informed me that when experimenting with explosives he had experienced instances where straw had been driven into timber by the same kinetic forces. The opening scenes of *Master and Commander* provide a superb visual effect of a ship receiving broadside fire and the damage inflicted.

As *Victory*'s Keeper & Curator at that time, I supervised the assembly of the entire display in situ by volunteers of the NMRN (National Museum of the Royal Navy). The display has since proved a popular feature with the public.

PSYCHOLOGICAL EFFECTS

Despite the awesome damage, horrendous carnage, casualties and injuries inflicted by a well-timed broadside it was often the psychological effect that had the greatest impact. Creating sudden mass impacts to mentally break human conditioning and the will to fight has long been used in warfare, from the fast chariots used as archery or javelin platforms by the Egyptian king Thutmosis III (1504–1450BC) during his campaigns in Syria and the Euphrates Valley[17] to the loosing off of millions of arrows at the start of the Battle of Hastings in 1066.

Other classic examples of creating terror are the prolonged barrage bombardments of the trenches before infantrymen went 'over the top' during the First World War; the London Blitz and bombing over Germany in the 1940s; and more recently the use of napalm during the war in Vietnam. Such overtures to conflict have a devastating effect

Above: HMS *Victory* fires a broadside, Portsmouth, 2009. (Courtesy of the National Museum of the Royal Navy)

on the human mind and nervous system, a condition commonly called 'shell shock', something with which the comedian and eccentric Spike Milligan suffered greatly when fighting at Monte Cassino in 1944.[18] My own father, who also fought at Monte Cassino, was blown up when the Bren gun carrier he was driving hit a mine. As the only survivor of his crew the trauma of this explosion did unfortunately affect his temperament.[19] Military and naval records from the eighteenth century do not provide statistics of those who suffered from such mental phenomena.

THE NOISE OF GUNFIRE

It is said that the noise of gunfire at the Battle of Trafalgar taking place some 12 to 15 miles out at sea could be heard 60 miles inland in Spain. The explosive noise of a broadside was tremendously terrifying; enough to break the morale of a ship's crew under fire. Although it is popularly conceived that our gunners suffered temporary or sustained deafness after a sea fight, gunfire noise is only created at the muzzle end of a gun. This point was recognised when partaking in the firing

of guns in HMS *Warrior*. I found that the external noise was far greater than that heard inboard upon the gun deck. This salient fact clearly informs us that the effect of noise upon the ship being attacked would have a profound psychological effect upon its crew.

If they were returning fire then this may have been negated by a great sense of release – despite the fact that each individual could be a casualty within seconds. The act of firing an opening broadside and the noise it created provided a mental release and quiet jubilation to the guns' crews delivering the broadside, particularly after the often prolonged anticipation · of fighting as opposing fleets manoeuvred in preparation for battle. A well-timed broadside could defeat an enemy ship in a very short time, boarding and hand-to-hand combat being the final process of taking possession of a ship. Not only did getting in very close alongside an enemy ship and hitting them hard have the desired effect upon an enemy, it reduced the inevitable waste of shot and powder used in ineffective long range gunnery. Because manning and operating naval guns is both physically and mentally exhausting, getting into close action quickly also kept the guns' crews alert for as long as possible.

Such tactics were employed by Captain (later Admiral) Edward Hawke during Rear-Admiral William Rowley's engagement against the French off Toulon on 11 February 1744. During this action Hawke closed his 70-gun *Berwick* within half pistol shot range of the 60-gun *Poder* and fired his opening broadside, killing 27 men and dismounting several of the *Poder*'s lower deck guns. Within 20 minutes the *Berwick*'s broadsides dismasted her opponent and inflicted over 200 casualties, compelling the *Poder* to strike her colours. Losses in the *Berwick* comprised just 6 men.[20] This concept of getting in very close and causing high casualties was to be used by Admiral Edward Boscawen at the battle of Lagos in 1759 and successive admirals including Nelson.[21]

RATE OF FIRE

As well as the necessity to get into close action, it was essential to deliver a fast rate of fire in order to inflict as much damage in as short a time as possible. This would swiftly subdue an enemy ship. Similarly it was also necessary to establish a faster rate of fire than that of the enemy, which would effectively reduce casualties within one's own ship.

At Trafalgar most British ships were firing off three broadsides to every single broadside fired by the enemy. The success of the British Navy in most naval engagements was primarily due to the extensive training given to gun crews in order for them to fire and reload their guns rapidly. Most captains expected their gunners to complete the entire cycle of firing, i.e. swabbing, worming and loading the gun with its charge, wad and shot, in 90 seconds. Records do indicate that this sequence was quite often achieved in under a minute. The gun crews trained by Martin Bibbings for *Master and Commander* were achieving times of less than a minute. Firing rate however could only be maintained at the opening of battle as fatigue, injury or loss of life began to deplete the efficiency of a gun's crew.

The number of men in a gun crew was devised by calculating the total weight of the gun and its carriage and dividing the sum by 500, the number produced being the maximum weight for a single man to haul. Furthermore, and this must be clearly understood, the number given for a specific gun type also includes the gun's crew that would man the gun on the opposite side of the ship. For example, a gun crew manning No. 6 gun on the lower gun deck larboard (port) also served No. 6 gun lower gun deck starboard. Although this theoretically reduced the ship's manpower, the limitation was necessary as the physical and provisioning constraints of the ship made it totally impractical for berthing and feeding such numbers of men. As a result, if the ship was fighting on one side only then a gun would be fully manned; however if the ship was fighting on both broadsides the entire gun's crew was halved between the guns on each side. Alternatively the gun crew would cross the deck after firing one gun to fire its opposite number. This practice is clearly shown in *Master and Commander*. The total number of gun crew for each type of gun is shown below:

Number of Gun's Crew per Gun

Size of Gun	Total Crew	If firing both broadsides
42-pdr	16	8
32-pdr	14	7
24-pdr	12	6
12-pdr	10	5
9-pdr	8	4
6-pdr	6	3
4-pdr	4	2
3-pdr	4	2

In the case where a ship was suffering with a depleted crew, perhaps caused by disease or misadventure, reduced numbers of men were sometimes divided into groups working along one side of the deck. Commodore Anson used this method in the 60-gun *Centurion* when he attacked a Spanish treasure galleon in the Pacific. Here the crew 'used an ingenious system of fire power. Since their guns were less than half-manned down a crew of flying cannoneers ran from one gun to the other reloading and firing so that the firing into the enemy ship was continuous. Within a half mile range the *Centurion*'s guns were able to inflict heavy damage'.[22] Although the physical acts of swabbing, loading and firing were fully reduced, when employing this practice the firing rate remained consistent.

MANPOWER

Individual members of gun crews were also designated to undertake emergency tasks in battle. These were given on the ship's Quarter Bill. Taken from the Quarter Bill of the 74-gun *Goliath*, for example, these were specified as follows:[23]

Task Allocation from each Gun's Crew

Letter	Task or Station	No.
B	Boarding or repelling borders	2
S	Sail Trimming	2
P	Manning the pumps	2
F	Fire fighting	1
L	Holding Lanthorn (night action)	1

In such circumstances each gun crew would be reduced by the same number of men, according to the emergency arising. Thereby reduction of manpower was proportional, without detriment to overall efficiency, albeit that firing rate was equally diminished proportionally. The men would return to their guns on completion of their allotted duties. Naturally firing rate would greatly diminish in a hard-pressed fight due to casualties; therefore under these extreme circumstances firing rate would be controlled by individual gun captains, firing when able and ready. A system similar to that adapted by Anson would have been used if boarders, sail trimmers and fire fighters etc. were called away from the guns in the midst of engagement.

The problem of suddenly depleted gun crews would have been apparent in the 80-gun French flagship *La Bucentaure* at Trafalgar, when the *Victory* fired her triple shotted larboard broadside through the stern. Dismounting 25% of its guns and causing some 360 casualties, all manner of confusion compounded with the shock of devastation must have reigned between the decks of the French ship. The fact that the British warships following in *Victory*'s wake likewise raked *La Bucentaure* in a similar manner utterly broke what remaining crew were able to stand. Totally dismasted, *La Bucentaure* drifted off until boarded and taken.

Below & Opposite: Peter Goodwin and the Master Gunner team in action at the Dockyard 500 event at Portsmouth in 2007. (Courtesy of Martin Bibbings)

DAMAGE CONTROL AND REPAIR

The previously mentioned shot damage display set up in the *Victory* also provides examples of the damage control methods used by the carpenter and mates during battle. Damage below the waterline was critical because the volume of seawater flooding into a ship's hold greatly affected the ship's stability, speed and manoeuvrability. Unlike modern warships, there were no watertight subdivision bulkheads to reduce the free surface area and lessen the leverage effect of lolling water. After the battle of Trafalgar the *Victory* was making 12in (30.5cm) in depth of water in her hold with the pumps constantly manned. During battle Mr. Bunce, the *Victory*'s carpenter and his crew were stationed below the waterline in the orlop wing passages to undertake immediate damage control stopping up shot holes and shattered planking. The original orders directing the requirement for carpenters to be stationed below decks in battle were first authorised in the Tudor Navy of Henry VIII. The prevalence of naval artillery as the primary weapon for sea combat had important ramifications in ships like the *Mary Rose*.

Tools used by the carpenter's crew for stopping up holes comprised pin mauls, hammers, large wooden mallets, hand saws, adzes and measuring battens. The latter are similar to

the Gunter battens used today in naval damage control. The materials used to effect repairs would have included conical wooden plugs, softwood wedges, sheets of lead to cover shot holes, flat headed nails to secure lead sheets, pads of oakum[24] used with lead sheeting, wooden pads to cover shot holes or retain plugs, and timber shores to hold sprung planking or retain wooden or lead pads. Other items close at hand may also have been used to stop up holes – bedding, hammocks, clothing, etc. It is notable that the methods of damage repair used in 1800 differed little to damage control applied in the Second World War.

EXPERIENCE

Working with Master Gunner Ltd and the HMS (Historical Maritime Society) we formed into re-enactment gun crews, firing simulated broadsides using gunpowder charges only. Acting as a gun captain with my own gun crew and personally firing a gun during the act of staging this event brought to light the reality of the practice of broadside firing. I found the most significant aspect of the whole experience to be that one becomes so focused in getting your own gun's crew swabbing, worming, loading, running out, priming and firing the gun within a very short time span that you become totally oblivious to events, noise and people around you. Moreover, despite being well-rehearsed, people did get accidentally hit with rammers and gun tools as they were being passed, and gun captains could get minor flash burns from the gun vent as it fired. Although we were not actually under fire, the entire re-enactment scenario provided a great perspective on what naval gunners experienced in a hard-pushed and closely-engaged sea fight, in extreme personal danger as others died or fell around them. The entire gun drill and practice of firing a broadside is, as Martin Bibbings aptly quoted; 'like a well rehearsed ballet' [25] – to which I would personally add: 'and dance of death'.

SOURCES AND NOTES

1. Goodwin, P. *Anatomy of the 20-Gun Ship Blandford*, London, 1988, passim. See also Lyon, D. *The Sailing Navy List*, London, 1988, passim.

2. Lyon, D. *The Sailing Navy List*, London, 1988, passim. See also Goodwin, P. *Anatomy of the Naval Armed Cutter Alert*, London, 1989, passim.

3. Goodwin, P. *Nelson's Ships*, London, 2002, pp64-72. See also Lyon, D. *The Sailing Navy List*, London, 1988, passim.

4. Clowes, W. L. *The Royal Navy: A History from the Earliest Times to 1900*, Vol. 3, London, 1898, pp520-530.

5. Goodwin, P. *Nelson's Men of War*, Greenwich, 2003, p8.

6. Goodwin, P. *The Influence of Industrial Technology and Material Procurement on the Design & Development of HMS Victory*, University of St. Andrews, 1998, Chap. 4, pp59-70 and Chap, 8, pp104-110.

7. Goodwin, P. *Nelson's Victory*, London, 2004, p28.

8 NMRN. Mss.1998/4. The Rivers Papers: Journals of Master Gunner William Rivers in HMS *Victory* 1793-1811.

9. Op. Cit. *Nelson's Victory*, p31.

10. Op. Cit. *Nelson's Ships*, p234.

11. Goodwin, P. *The Ships of Trafalgar*, London, 2005, p22.

12. Op. Cit. *The Ships of Trafalgar*, London, 2005, p241.

13. Ibid.

14. Author's notes from 'Royal Explosion!', Museum of Naval Armament, Gosport.

15. On loan to HMS *Victory* from the Royal Collection by kind permission of HM Queen Elizabeth II.

16. Author's Notes from Royal Armouries, Fort Nelson, Portsmouth.

17. Sometimes called the 'Napoleon' of the 18th Dynasty, Thutmosis III used his chariots in blitzkrieg fashion, keeping them hidden below a hillock before suddenly striking. Partridge, R. *Transport in Ancient Egypt*, London, 1996, p105. See also Shaw, I (Ed.) *The Oxford History of Ancient Egypt*, Oxford, 2000, p243.

18. Parker, M. *Monte Cassino*, London, 2003, pp104-106 & 202.

19. Goodwin, Albert Victor Basil, former Lance Corporal Royal Fusiliers British 8th Army. Africa, Sicily and Italian Campaigns WWII.

20. Burrows, M. *The Life of Edward Lord Hawke*, London, 1904, p39. See also Clowes, W. L. *The Royal Navy: A History from the Earliest Times to 1900*, Vol. 3, London, 1898, p100.

21. Clowes, W. L. *The Royal Navy: A History from the Earliest Times to 1900*, Vol. 3, London, 1898, pp213-215.

22. Heaps, L. *The Log of the Centurion*, New York, 1974, p227.

23. NMM,WQB/11. See also Lavery, B. *Nelson's Navy*, London, 1987, pp196-199.

24. Oakum – loose hemp fibre made from old rope mixed with tallow and tar.

25. Bibbings, Martin, 2005.

HMS *Swallow* (1745)

278-TON SLOOP

by Trevor Copp

BACKGROUND TO THE PROJECT

Everyone has heard of James Cook, but very few have heard of Philippe de Carteret (1733–1796), a figure who deserves greater recognition in the history of maritime exploration. He commenced his second circumnavigation of the globe on 22 August 1766, having arrived back from his first circumnavigation less than three months earlier. For this voyage he was given his first command, as Master and Commander, of the 278-ton sloop HMS *Swallow*. The expedition was led by Captain Samuel Wallis in HMS *Dolphin*. The third member of the flotilla was the supply ship *Prince Frederick*. By the end of the year *Swallow* had become separated from the rest of the flotilla, and continued alone.

In the summer of 2006 I had no project under construction, and I asked Doug Ford, Director of Education at Jersey Heritage if there was any model he would like constructed for display in the Jersey Maritime Museum. He suggested that I build HMS *Swallow*, as he was engaged in researching and writing up the career of Philippe de Carteret, a Jerseyman, and a model of the vessel would suit the Museum's needs.

A copy of the original line drawings that subsequently arrived from the National Maritime Museum, Greenwich, were disappointingly lacking in detail, but then, *Swallow* was a very ordinary workhorse. The drawings were headed 'copy sent to Mr Bird 17 Apr 1745'.

So *Swallow* was built by Bird at Rotherhithe. This rang a bell. Several years earlier I had built the Jotika kit HMS *Supply*, also built by Bird at Rotherhithe. Examination of the two sets of drawings showed that both vessels were similar to within a few inches in length, although in beam they differed. A decision was made to purchase another *Supply* kit as a source of material.

On a previous model displayed at the museum (*Earl of Pembroke* aka HMS *Endeavour*) I had included about fifteen commercial figures, which gave added interest to the model, especially for the younger visitors. At that point I decided that a scratch-built model required scratch-built figures, although at that time I did not know how I was to tackle this.

Moving forward to the present day, the model was finally completed in December 2009, and went on display in January 2010. It was chosen as one of the Jersey Museum's ten objects as part of the national 'History of the World' project. The model is displayed in a case, under sail, on a sea base measuring 90cm x 60cm. Working the vessel are 94 figures, of which only 5 were commercial examples. There is a pod of nine bottle-nosed dolphins (*Tursiops truncatus*), a species with a world-wide distribution, leaping around the vessel (Photograph 1). A little licence was employed here, as it is not known if any dolphins were present at the time the diorama is set; 2 July 1767 when Midshipman Robert Pitcairn, positioned on the foremast crosstrees on the model (Photograph 2) sighted the island that bears his name. The dolphins were added to provide interest for the younger visitors, as this species is found in the waters around Jersey. The Museum's technician has done a superb job in lighting the model, and as one walks past the model the sea sparkles and has an appearance of movement.

CONSTRUCTION

The copy of the original drawings from the NMM were to 1:48 scale. The majority of the contemporary models displayed in the NMM, and the Science Museum, London are built to this scale. This would have produced a larger model than I wanted, as all the other models I had made were to 1:64 scale, and I wanted *Swallow* to fit in with the others.

Reference marks were made on the drawings, and the drawings scanned into the computer in sections. The reference marks were important, as my scanner and printer can only cope with A4 paper, so the rescaled drawings would be printed in sections and joined as accurately as possible. Using the computer the drawing sections were reduced to give the working scale of 1:64. The individual sections were then printed and joined together.

The drawings from 1745 showed a side view, hull sections and sheerlines, and a plan of the deck illustrating the position of the hatches, ship's wheel, capstan and bitts. Also depicted was a plan of the lower deck showing the positions of the various cabins, which would not be shown on my model. There was also a plan of the forecastle and the poop deck, which was labelled 'quarter deck' in this example. The drawings demonstrated a high standard of draughtsmanship, with beautiful lettering, and connected me immediately with the period. Unfortunately, there was no stern view, and it was difficult to see from the side view whether stern windows were fitted or not. The finished model does not have stern windows, even though during the build I made and fitted stern windows, as somehow they just did not look correct. I also agonised over the fitting of a stern lantern, and once again it was not finally fitted. Reading around the subject seemed to suggest that this size of vessel was often not fitted with a stern lantern. Did this contribute to *Swallow* becoming separated from the rest of the flotilla early in the voyage?

Another anomaly was that the 1745 plans show a two-masted brig, whilst all the pictures of the vessel represented on stamps and other sources showed a three-masted vessel. This was not resolved until building was well under way, and Doug found in one of his reference books 'built in 1745 as a two-masted brig, third mast added in 1755'. No drawings were available for this modification. The drawings depicted the positions of the fore and main chains, and backstays, but no further rigging details. It was clear from this that the finished model could never claim to be a scale model of **HMS** *Swallow*, but only a 'best guess' representation of the vessel.

The bulkheads were traced from the plan, scanned into the computer, reduced to 1:64 scale, and printed onto card. The outline of the individual bulkhead sections was reduced by just under 2mm, this being an allowance for the thickness of the two layers of 1mm thick hull planking, and an attempt to allow for the thickness lost in sanding the hull. Notches of 5mm width were marked on the sections to locate the keel. The card sections were numbered and cut out, and used as templates to transfer the sections to 5mm birch plywood. The keel was made by drawing directly on the 1:64 scale side

1. Model ready to leave workshop.

view, paying particular attention to the positions of the bulkheads, and transferred directly to 5mm birch ply. The outlines of the stem, sternpost and false keel were similarly taken from the side view drawing, and cut from 5mm walnut stock.

The bulkheads were dry assembled in their positions on the keel and checked. There appeared to be no major discrepancies, so they were permanently secured with PVA adhesive. When this assembly was thoroughly cured, I added extra stiffeners at deck level between the bulkheads to provide a greater gluing area for the false deck and the gun port patterns. These were drawn on the side view, and transferred to card. Because of the curvature of the hull, the gun port patterns would be longer than the flat side view. But by how much? That calculation was way beyond my abilities, so I used a card template, trial fitting and trimming until I was satisfied that I had obtained the best fit. Using the template, port and starboard gun port patterns were drawn on 0.8mm birch ply and cut out. A final check was made on the fit of the gun port patterns and the gun ports cut out. The final sizing of the gun ports was carried out with port and starboard patterns clamped together to ensure best possible symmetry.

The gun port patterns were then permanently fixed, pinning to the bulkhead extensions, and the horizontal stiffeners between the bulkheads until the PVA was fully cured.

The first planking of 1m x 4mm lime was started below the gun port patterns, down to the false keel following the standard practice of using PVA adhesive, and pinning each plank to the bulkheads until the glue had set.

Looking around for a suitable wood to cut the planks for the second planking, I found at one of the Jersey Heritage sites an old chair, made of beech, which had been put aside to provide kindling for the baker's oven. I was given a few pieces from which I cut a suitable number of 4mm x 1mm planks for the hull. I wish I had not! The planking was quite pleasing to the eye, but when it came to sanding down the hull, it was very troublesome. Never again with beech!

The second planking continued with the 1m x 4mm beech, from the top of the gun port patterns, down to the false keel, using cyanoacrylate adhesive. The garboard strake and the two planks above it were fitted early in the planking process, so that when the planking progressed down from the water line, the final planks, and little areas where things never quite work out were in a more accessible position. The position of the main wale was marked on the hull, and a row of pins inserted in the hull along the midline of the main wale. The beech planks making up the main wale were painted before fitting. The first (lower) plank was then positioned against the pins, giving it a positive location, the pins removed, and the second plank butted up against the first.

The bulkhead extensions above deck level were removed, and using the re-scaled admiralty drawings a cardboard template was made for the main deck, and the positions of the hatchways, masts and deck fittings were marked on the template, transferred to 0.8mm ply and cut out. It was at this point in the construction that it was discovered that *Swallow* was fitted with the aforementioned mizzen mast in 1755, possibly in attempt to improve her sailing qualities. In the event Philippe de Carteret had inherited the command of a leaky, poor sailing vessel, long past its best, which had a tendency to be caught in stays, the ship's boats and sweeps being used to haul the vessel through the eye of the wind. This is suggested on the model in that some of the crew are stowing the sweeps, or are they preparing them for use?

The position of the mizzen mast was deduced as 'the best guess' as no drawings were available for this refit, and with the aid of James Lees' *The Masting and Rigging of English Ships of War, 1635–1860* the dimensions of the mizzen mast and its associated spars and booms were deduced.

The false deck was fitted and glued with PVA, and the deck planked with pre-sanded strips of 1m x 4mm Tanganyika. On previous models I have represented the pitch caulking between the planks by running a black marker pen along the thin edge of the planks before fitting. I have seen models where this was done with black cartridge paper, but at 1:64 scale it appeared overstated. On *Swallow*, and on other models I have not emphasised the pitch lines, just fitted the planks as they are, and to my eye it looks about right.

Whilst the early stages of the hull were under construction work was started on the masts and spars. It is my usual practice to build other parts early in the project, such as hatches, ship's wheel, anchors and cannons, which would be needed later. The 6-pdr cannons and swivel guns were bought as kits from Jotika. The cannons and associated tackles, and some of the crew members would need to be fitted at a fairly early stage, certainly before the masts were stepped (Photograph 3).

As I had never built a model with sails before, it was time to start thinking about how these would be made. There appeared to be a choice of two materials: tissue paper or cotton. In *Modelling Sailing Men-of-War*, author Philip Reed explains how to make lifelike sails from tissue paper. Unfortunately, this did not work for me, as I was totally incapable of handling the material, mostly ending up with shredded, wet tissue paper! I finally settled on a thin white cotton fabric for the sails, which did not fragment under my clumsy handling. It was really much too bright, so I set about dyeing the material a more realistic colour. I tried coffee and tea, and finally settled on very dilute gravy browning. For me and the techniques I was using, this gave just about the right hue.

The dyed cotton was allowed to dry, then ironed and sprayed with dilute PVA to stiffen it. Individual sails were marked out on the fabric, and the seam lines drawn with a hard pencil. Reinforcing pieces, which were small pieces of the same material, were cut out and glued onto the sail with

3. Deck fittings and cannons prior to masting and rigging.

PVA adhesive. In making the individual sails great help was again obtained from James Lees' work, as well as *The Anatomy of the Ship Endeavour* by Karl Heinz Marquardt. Bolt ropes and cringles were added, and holes pierced in the tabling for the robbands. In a similar way the reefbands were pierced ready for reefing ropes, which were small lengths of 0.10mm linen thread threaded through the holes and glued in place with PVA adhesive. The bolt ropes were simply glued in position, but the cringles were also stitched for extra security as they would be under tension when the rigging was added.

It was hoped that the stiffened fabric would hold a realistic shape when in position on the model, but this was not the case when making up some 'test' sails. To give an effective curvature to the sail a length of 0.14 thou. diameter stainless steel wire was incorporated in the foot of the sail when the reinforcing strip was glued in position. This could then be bent to the desired curve in an effort to represent a wind-filled sail. The individual sails were attached to their respective yards using a 'continuous' robband, which is threaded through the holes in the tabling of the sail, and tied off at each end of the yard. If the sail was to be shown furled, it was a very simple sail with much of the reinforcing detail omitted. The sail was attached to the yard, brushed with

dilute PVA and furled. It was easier to arrange the folds in the sail when it was wet, and when dry the stiffened fabric held the folds nicely (Photograph 4). The same technique was used on the main topsail, which is shown being unfurled (Photograph 5). All the fittings including the foot ropes were fitted to the yards before the sails were attached (Photograph 6).

I find that if I make the foot ropes from linen thread, it is difficult to get them to hang correctly from the yards. They are easily deformed when the model is handled, and nothing is worse than taking photographs of your finished model, only to later discover that the foot ropes are all awry. I now make the foot ropes from twisted copper wire as described by Philip Reed in the aforementioned publication. As a source of thin copper wire, I strip the insulation from domestic electrical flex, which provides an adequate supply of thin copper wire for rope making. If two or three strands are twisted together and painted very serviceable foot ropes can be made. The wire ropes are very suitable in situations where a rope hanging in a catenary curve is required.

The strands can be twisted together by hand, but a more presentable job can be achieved using a lathe or a suitably

4. Sail fitted to yard and stiffened with diluted PVA.

5. Main topsail unfurling.

clamped drill running at low speed. Select an offcut of dowel, about 5cm in length and crossdrill near one end with a 2mm diameter drill. Alternatively, a small hook could be bent up from stiff wire. Clamp in the lathe or drill chuck, thread the copper wire strands through the drilled hole, and twist together to secure. Grip the free ends of the wires in a pair of pliers, gently pull straight, and turn on the power (slow speed) and watch the ropewalk work for you. I found it best to start with fairly short lengths of about 30cm until you can judge if the set up is working satisfactorily. The newly made wire rope will need to be painted, and Philip Reed's method is to put a blob of paint on an offcut of hardboard or similar non-absorbable material, hold the wire rope in the paint with a paintbrush, and gently draw the wire through the paint. Hey presto! It takes longer to describe than to do.

While work progressed with the sails, the Jotika cannon kits were assembled and painted. This company produces a wealth of firepower in 1:64 scale.

Much help in the design and construction of the deck fit-

6. Rigging the yards progresses.

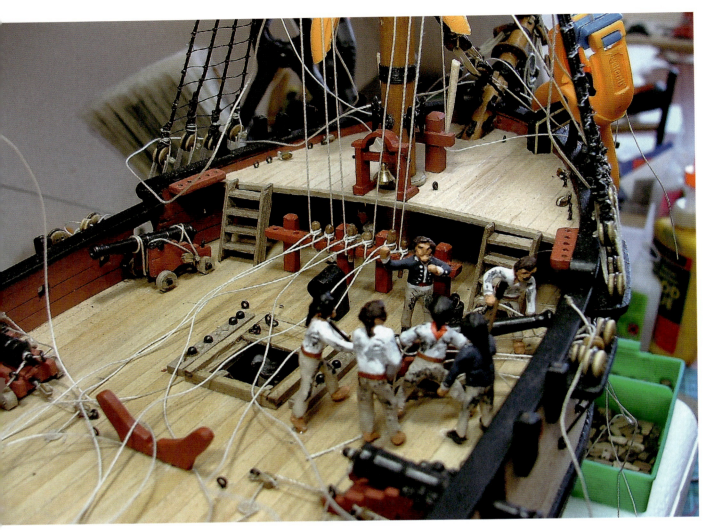

7. Belaying points and belfry. Note the cocktail stick holding line temporarily in the forebitts.

tings was found in *The Construction and Fitting of the Sailing Man of War 1650–1850* by Peter Goodwin. The posts for the bitts and belaying points were cut from 3mm x 3mm walnut stock, the cross pieces from 2mm ply, and drilled for the belaying pins. Commercial belaying pins were used, and at this stage it is as well to check that the holes drilled will accept the belaying pins. It can be a fiddly job attaching rigging lines to the belaying pins. I now thread the rigging line through the relevant hole in the crosspiece, insert the belaying pin, which immediately traps the rigging line in position. It is a much simpler procedure to adjust the tension on the rigging line if using this method. The line can be carefully pulled through the belaying point with the pin in position until the desired tension is achieved. When satisfied with this, a couple of figure-of-eight turns around the belaying pin, a half hitch and a dab of diluted PVA to secure (Photograph 7). It is then finished off by adding the false coil, also securing this with a dab of PVA or cyanoacrylate.

The barrel of the capstan was turned from 8mm dowel, and the whelps cut from thin ply. The base and head were cut from separate pieces of walnut, and holes drilled in the capstan head for the capstan bars. The holes for the capstan bars were made square using a simple device described in *Ship Modelling from Stem to Stern* by Milton Roth. File the point of a suitable nail to a tapered square section, cut off the head, grip in a pin vice, and press the tapered square point into the round hole; the visible part of the hole is then neatly squared off.

The gratings were made up from the parts supplied in the Jotika HMS *Supply* kit, as were the pumps. The shot garlands were cut from 1.5mm ply, and to hold the shot a starter hole was drilled (but not completely through the wood) and finished with a round burr in the Dremel (Photograph 8). I have made shot from Milliput putty, but shot is now available in several sizes from Jotika, so it is far easier and quicker to use a commercial alternative.

The curved top to the belfry was carved from boxwood, the bell turned from 6mm brass bar in the lathe (Photograph 7).

Once the hull was finished and painted, the finished

8. Shot garlands, capstan and pumps.

cannons and tackles were rigged. A number of the crew were positioned at this stage – helmsman, marine sentry (James Sealey) at the captain's door, and a gun crew working one of the 6-pdrs (under the watchful eye of Quarter Gunner Francois Jegger) – as it would be more difficult to do this once the rigging had been completed.

The masts were constructed in sections, lower mast, topmast, and topgallant mast, using various diameter beech dowels as supplied in the *Supply* kit. The tops and crosstrees were made from the kit, but as *Supply* is a brig, a third set was made for the three-masted *Swallow*. At the present time I finish the masts with light oak satin varnish, as this seems to give about the right hue. Wooldings were added, and as much 'hardware' as possible: cleats, eyebolts, and rigging blocks. Before the masts were stepped, rigging lines were threaded through the blocks under the tops, which are the

9. Belaying points on foredeck. Note crewman on 'seat of ease' in the heads.

10. Wooden plug and fibre-glass hulls.

11. Completed launch.

rigging lines to the lower yards, as this can be a difficult area to reach once the rigging sequence is under way. The lines were tied loosely in a bunch to keep them out of the way, and to prevent them being pulled through the blocks. The bowsprit and jibboom were assembled early in the building sequence, as its passage through the foredeck to its securing point on the bits needed to be determined before the fore-deck was planked. The bowsprit was not finally fitted until the majority of the standing rigging had been fitted, to prevent possible damage to it during the rigging process. The masts were stepped, and rigging commenced, following the well-known sequence, which as always, becomes more diffi-cult as it progresses, i.e. starting with the standing rigging, working from the centre line, upwards and outwards, leaving the standing backstays until the rigging was almost complete.

In most cases I added the finishing coils to the belaying points as each group of rigging lines was belayed (Photo-graph 9). I do it this way rather than when rigging is complete, as I have found that if I leave this to the end I nearly always miss some belaying points, and others can be extremely difficult to reach. I would also find it tedious to have to make perhaps 100 or so coils and hanks when the fin-ished model is sitting in front of me. As it is, at the end or beginning of most modelling sessions I make up several coils and do some work on several figures. This seems to work, as I nearly always have rope coils of the correct diameter to hand, and to date I have made about 200 figures, about 90 of which are on *Swallow*, and the remainder are being made for the next project – but more about the figures later. My way of making rope coils (after Keith Julier in *The Period Ship Kit Builder's Manual*) is to use an old paintbrush, the tapered handle giving a wide range of suitable coil sizes. From time to time I give it a rub over with a candle to give a non-stick surface. Take a length of linen thread of the required diam-

12. Towed pinnace and fishermen.

eter, about 15cm is sufficient, put a dab of PVA on the fore-finger, and draw the length of thread between the forefinger and thumb, thinly coating the thread with the PVA, and quickly wrap the thread around the paintbrush handle at a point to give the required size of hank or coil. The coil can be slid off the handle almost immediately, and tied off to make a hank for a belaying pin, or left as a coil to lie on the deck.

The spars of circular section throughout were made in one piece. Those with an octagonal centre section were made in three pieces, and dowelled together with brass rod. The octagonal centre section was either made from dowel rod of a slightly larger diameter than the spar, and sanded down to an octagonal section, or from square stock, the corners planed and sanded off to form an octagonal cross section. To taper the spars, I fix a spar in the lathe chuck, and sand to size using tungsten carbide sanding sticks, which produce a rapid result, finishing with finer grades of sandpaper.

Blocks, cleats and sails were attached to the spars before fitting to the masts as described earlier. Where possible, I attached each spar using two brass dowels, this helping to prevent the spar pivoting when tension is applied to the running rigging. As I worked my way through the running rigging, more figures were added, hauling on ropes, and belaying others. The majority of the figures have a 5mm extension to a leg, which is secured with cyanoacrylate in a hole drilled in the deck. This ensures that the figures are firmly fixed, and will not be pulled out of place by the tension on the rigging lines. Others were fitted on the footropes, secured by a small brass pin in the trunk, and glued into a hole in the spar. When the rigging had been completed figures climbing the shrouds were added.

SHIP'S BOATS

Usually I start building the ship's boats early on in the construction of the model. The scratch builder can tackle this project in several ways. I have made plank-on-frame models,

13. Base board with cut-outs for boats and waves added.

14. Christian Sibiern and John Harris at work on a sail.

15. HMS *Swallow* with a slight heel.

double planked on bulkheads, the bulkheads removed once the glue holding the planking has cured. This method can be very time-consuming, especially if several boats are required. Reed suggests the hot forming of an acrylic shell, which is then finished to the builder's requirements.

Jotika produce an excellent range of ships' boat kits to 1:64 scale, using a plank-on method on a preformed resin hull. Again, it is a question of how much time is available, and how much detail should be scratch built in a scratch built model, and what is a museum quality model? I suppose ultimately the scratch builder should start with a tree, but I digress.

Previously I had carved a set of wooden plugs, a launch, a cutter and a jolly boat (Photograph 10). The plugs were sanded smooth, sealed, and mounted on short lengths of dowel (about 30mm, it is not critical). The dowels were glued into holes in an offcut of ply or similar, but were a push-fit into holes drilled in the plugs, so that the plug could be removed from its stand.

The plug is given a liberal rub over with a candle, as a separating medium, and using the thinnest chopped strand glass mat, sold here as 'finishing tissue', and resin, a fibre glass hull is laid up on the plug, using two or three layers of the chopped strand mat. Working with glass fibre can be a messy business, and this operation should be carried out well away

from the model building area, preferably in the garage. Once the resin is set, the plug is removed from its base, and the hull shell gently prised away from the plug, and trimmed to size. The inside of the hull will be smooth, the outside will be rough, but this can be smoothed with sandpaper or on the belt sander. The hull is then planked with 3mm x 0.5mm stock and the false keel and stem added. The inside of the hull is then detailed, the ribs (timbers) can be represented with thin wood stock or even paper, and the riser for the thwarts is added; this must be wood. The bottom boards are made and the thwarts added. Further details can be added, such as oars, ropes, buckets, to the builder's requirements, and if scratch building these items further thought and experimentation will be required (Photograph 11).

In the *Swallow* diorama the cutter is towed astern, and in it three crew members are engaged in fishing; there are buckets, lines, fish and oars in the boat (Photograph 12). The jolly boat is stowed on the deck; the sail maker, Christian Sibiern (born in Elsinore, Denmark), and his assistant John Harris, are seated in the boat mending a sail (Photograph 14).

MODELLING THE SEA

By this time it had been decided that the model could best be displayed as a waterline model, in fact, as displayed, the model is still in its building cradle. In order to fit the display

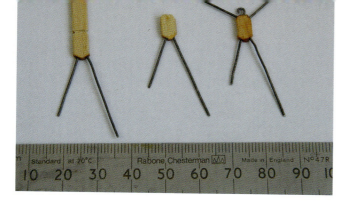

16. Construction of figure armature.

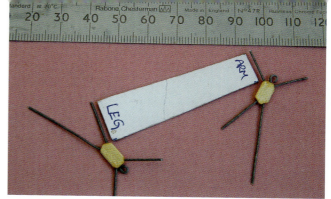

17. Trim leg and arm wires to length.

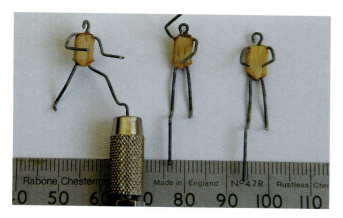

18. Armatures bent to shape.

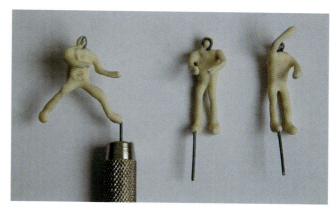

19. First coat of thinned wood filler applied.

20. Face moulds and faces.

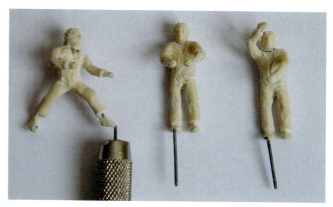

21. Final details added and figures carved.

22. Finished figures.

23. Selection of completed figures for future project.

case, the sea would be about 60cm x 90cm. This in itself was another modelling challenge as at that time I had not attempted to model the sea. Verticals were dropped down from the waterline of *Swallow*, and a card template of the hull shape at the waterline prepared. This was transferred to a piece of 6mm ply, and the hull shape cut out. This made the ply a bit too flexible for my liking, so it was reinforced on the underside with some 30mm x 30mm stock. *Swallow*'s hull was a reasonable fit in this cut out. A small cut out was also made for one of the ship's boats, as it would be towed by *Swallow* (Photograph 13).

I contacted a professional modeller, James Main, who had made a model of one of the Jersey Heritage sites, Mont Orgueil Castle. The castle is on a promontory, surrounded on three sides by the sea. From his home James kindly talked me through his method of representing the sea. I made several smaller trial 'seas' before attempting the larger sea for *Swallow*. He said:

'Brush PVA adhesive liberally on the baseboard, and prepare a "sloppy" mix of "Polyfilla" or similar plaster-based filling material. [I also mixed some PVA with this mix.] Brush the sloppy mix liberally over the base board, and then cover it with kitchen paper, tamping it down into the plaster mix. Decide on the wave or wind direction, or you might even decide on wind against tide for really choppy sea. Put your hands on to the now wet kitchen paper and push it in the desired direction to produce waves.'

The first few attempts will probably end in disaster, mine did, but persevere! It provides a nice relaxation from the intricacies of rigging. Allow this to harden, prepare more of the mix, and stipple it all over the kitchen paper with a paint brush, building up the waves as required, and creating wavelets between the main waves.

For some slightly bigger waves I used the paper rolled into a sausage shape, and impregnated with the mix to achieve this. I used this method to create the ship's bow wave and wake. Do not attempt too much at each 'sitting', as the larger waves will need blending in with the rest of the sea. Set this aside to dry thoroughly, which may take a week or more. When everything has dried, examine the sea carefully; there will probably be a few air holes that need filling, and the waves may need further shaping by adding more of the mix.

When any such additional work is dry, spray all over with a basic sea blue paint. When dry, brush on a couple of coats of gloss varnish. Decide on the direction of the light, and brush or spray darker shades of blue and green. It will need

24. On show at the Jersey Heritage Maritime Museum.

25. Activity on the main deck.

26. Philippe de Carteret, Captain (windward side); Erasmus Gower, Lieutenant; Alexander Simpson, Master; Thomas Watson, Surgeon; Edward Leigh, Purser.

a couple more coats of varnish, and more texturing with the blues and greens. Then more varnishing; decide if there are any breaking waves, and use some lighter shades at the breaking crests. Yet more varnish, and by this time the sea should be appearing to have some depth to it; darker shades in the hollows will assist this. The last task for now is to use white gloss to highlight any breaking crests on the waves and wavelets. I used very small quantities of silver sparkle, obtainable from craft shops, to produce pin points of light. Take the sea outside into the sunlight, change the angle slightly, and the sea will sparkle just like the original on a sunny day.

The next task was to fit *Swallow* as accurately as possible into its cutout. I intended to give it a heel to show two or three strakes, any more and I would need to heel the crew as well, and this was now not possible (Photograph 15). Masking tape was fixed to the hull at waterline level, after rubbing a candle on the non-sticky side of the tape as a separating medium. The vessel was placed carefully into its cutout in the sea, and any spaces between the hull and baseboard filled with a thicker mix of the plaster based filler. When hardened, Swallow was removed and the masking tape removed from the hull. The newly added filler was further contoured to represent the white, bubbly water created as a ship moves through the water. This was painted white, sparkle added sparingly, the whole sea examined, and further colour added where necessary, and finally given a final couple of coats of gloss varnish.

FIGURES

From the outset I had decided to include crew figures working HMS *Swallow*. The figures would be representative,

as an inordinate amount of time could be spent detailing each figure. I first became enamoured with the addition of figures during a visit to the National Maritime Museum at Greenwich. The superb model of HMS *Endeavour* displayed has the complete crew aligned before the model, each individual named. At 1:48 scale the adult figure is about 36mm in height, and is very detailed. Using the 1:64 scale chosen for *Swallow* the figures would be around 26mm high. I am deliberately imprecise about the height, as it is important to vary this for the overall effect.

I had used commercially made cast figures on earlier models, but this has the drawback in that only a few poses are available. I read literature on how to modify stock figures, but it became apparent that it would be quicker to make them from scratch. Wishing to make some 90 or so figures, it was imperative to devise a method that was not too time consuming, and I had in mind that I did not want to spend more than an hour on each figure. I wanted to use materials that were easily available, inexpensive, clean to use, low odour, and could be used safely indoors, using the same tools. I will explain the making of the figures in some detail. This method can then be modified as required.

The individual figure is built up on an armature. I usually make up a couple of these at the end of a modelling session. Checking my present stock, I have 25 ready to use. The measurements which follow are approximate for 1:64 scale.

Prepare or obtain lengths of hardwood 5mm x 2mm, and lightly round off the corners. I am using odd lengths of ramin as I have found that softer woods do not do the job.

27. Starboard view, lower stun sail being rigged.

Mark off a length of 9mm (Photograph 16). Sand the end in the shape of an apex, and using a triangular file, make a nick on each side just below the 9mm mark. Prepare lengths of wire; I use 0.7mm galvanised garden wire, and after making 200 or so figures it has proved admirable for the job. Lengths required are: long leg 30mm, short leg 20mm, arms 15mm, and a small eyelet for the head. I have a piece of card with the lengths marked, and snip off the lengths. The longer leg enables the figure to be held in a pin vice or similar during construction and painting. The torso requires drilling with four 0.7mm diameter holes to accept the limb wires, and I centre pop before drilling with a pin held in a pin vice. Using cyano, glue in the leg wires, and when the glue has set, saw off at the 9mm mark, glue in the arm wires, centre pop and drill for the head eyelet, and fit. I have three or four lengths of wood in use, and when the legs have been secured in the third, the first is ready to be parted off. The final task is to trim the short leg to its working length of 15mm, and the arms to 11mm, using a simple card jig (Photograph 17). If a shorter figure is needed a further millimetre or so may need to be trimmed from these measurements.

Next, decide which figure is to be made: officer, marine, seaman, midshipman, and what the figure is doing; hauling on a rope, climbing rigging, working one of the great guns and so on. Strike the pose, and look where the arms and legs are placed, and bend the limb wires of the armature to match. Bend up a couple of millimetres on the short leg for the foot, on the longer leg a double bend is required (Photograph 18). Using a scalpel, the hips of the wooden torso may need tapering slightly.

The next task is to put flesh on the bones. I have several shades of Ronseal wood filler, as well as other makes; all are good provided they are of the low odour type. Straight from the pot it is too thick for figure making, so put a quantity on to a mixing pad (thin plastic sheet, cut from a margarine tub), dip a spatula into water, and mix this into the wood filler until the desired consistency is obtained. It is difficult to describe this, but a consistency that will almost drip off the spatula is about right. Using a cocktail stick or similar apply a thin coat over the armature, including a small blob on the back of the head eyelet. The idea is to cover it quickly, not worrying too much about the details of the anatomy of the figure, as the diluted wood filler will tend to slump on the framework (Photograph 19). If the wood filler is too thick it will take longer to apply and is more difficult to manipulate. Set the figures aside to harden overnight. I use an off cut of wood with holes drilled to accept longer leg wire as a stand for the figures.

The figures will need a second coat of wood filler – mix up a portion as before and build up the figure. The torso will probably need very little, as will the arms. The legs and hips will need the most attention. Do not add any more to the back of the head, and keep the front of the head clear of any filler. Carving will commence when this layer has hardened, so it is always better to have the figure a little over-built at this stage. If batch building, add the first coat of wood filler to the armatures made previously, and make three more armatures, and so on.

At this point I roughly carve the figure, using a scalpel and rotary instruments. I aim to trim the limbs and torso to their approximate shapes; some areas may be found to need further building up. Now is the time to add the face. This can be done by building up the front of the head and carving with a small inverted cone burr to define the eye sockets and nose, but although some of the figures on Swallow were depicted in this way, I was never completely happy with the result. I had a war-gaming friend cast a couple of suitable figures, and then made several small silicone moulds of the faces. A thicker mix of the wood filler is pressed into the moulds, left overnight, and the faces removed. No separating medium is necessary. I then apply a coat of thin cyano to the faces, to prevent the detail from being rubbed off during subsequent handling. Hollow out the rear of the faces with a round bur, and they are then ready to be fitted to the figures, using the filler as an adhesive (Photograph 20). I used this method to represent figures standing with arms folded. It was taking far too long to carve the folded arms on an individual figure, so I made a couple of moulds of folded arms, and fit the arms to the figure after the rough carving stage.

Further carving is now done and the final details added; hair, perhaps rolled-up shirt sleeves and trousers (Photograph 21). Coat tails are made from paper and faired in with wood filler. Details such as belts, cross belts and hats are added after painting. Origami paper in a variety of colours is ideal for making belts, epaulettes and similar.

Before painting, detail the hair and add a few creases to the clothing using an inverted cone burr. Paint the figures using enamels or acrylics, and when satisfied with the paint job, add 'grime' to the clothing, using thinned matt black. Finish with a coat of flat matt varnish (Photographs 22 and 23). The leg extensions can be cut off completely, or trimmed to about 5mm to enable later fitting into drilled holes in the decking. Final figures were added, the model checked over for damage, paint work touched up as required and deemed completed and ready for the museum at the end of 2009.

The completed model was transferred to the Jersey Heritage Maritime Museum, set up in its case in January 2010, in time for the start of the BBC's 'History of the World' project (Photograph 24). In all, I estimated that the diorama had taken some 1,400 hours to complete. Photographs 25 to 29 show some aspects of the completed diorama.

Attempting to build a model from scratch is extremely time-consuming, and my thanks go to Doug Ford at Jersey

28. Bottle-nosed dolphins bow riding alongside HMS *Swallow*.

29. Port view from aft.

Heritage for delving into the literature to solve some of the problems concerning HMS *Swallow*. A big thank-you to the technicians at the museum for the case work and lighting.

I am pleased to have devised an effective way of constructing figures at 1:64 scale. The figures look better in context when viewed at normal distances; photographs depicting them larger than life will never be flattering. They undoubtedly add interest to a model.

Never plank a model with beech.

With hindsight, there are clearly errors in the model, and as for the stern windows – well, they can be added later.

Buckets for the Georgian Navy

A MODERN METHOD OF SCALE CONSTRUCTION

by Trevor Copp

I have always put a scattering of buckets on the decks of my completed Georgian Navy models, but not nearly enough. I usually work in 1:64 scale, and have never been completely happy with my bucket making attempts, and using commercial alternatives often had cost and availability implications. On receiving my copy of the *Shipwright 2011* annual, I spent some time looking at the cover picture depicting fire buckets on HMS *Victory* before opening the volume. As a sidetrack from the model under construction the aim would be to make buckets for my models, in some cases to retrofit them, aiming to achieve a time of approximately 10 minutes to make each bucket; this would give interludes during the longer sessions involved in planking and fitting copper plates.

During the last two weeks or so I have evolved the following method.

CONSTRUCTION

The basic material in my scale is 6mm dowel, cut into about 6in lengths; as I am making the buckets in batches of 12, I cut six lengths. Mount the dowel in the lathe, using thick paper between the wood and the chuck jaws to avoid bruising the wood. Square off the end of the dowel, centre drill, and drill (a 4mm diameter bit is about right, it is not critical) to a depth of about 3mm (Photograph 1). Set the cross slide of the lathe to give a taper of about 3 degrees, and cut the taper for the body of the bucket. Give it a quick sand, and mark off what will be the height of the bucket. In Photograph 2 I am using a piece of card for this. Saw completely around the dowel at the mark using a razor saw, but do not part off. Remove from chuck and repeat process on the other end of the dowel. Then repeat for the other, in my case, five dowels. There are now twelve embryo buckets. Give them a coat of sanding sealer or quick drying varnish to seal the grain, and then paint inside and out with the appropriate colour chosen earlier: in this case Humbrol Matt 186 looked about right. When dry, remount in the lathe and add the rim detail (Pho-

1. Drilling dowel.

tograph 3), using Humbrol Metallic 56 (Aluminium). Now the GR emblems are added. These are 4mm in height, 3mm wide, and will be explained in the Artwork section below. When dry, I touch up the edge of the decals with the matt brown. The finished buckets can now be given a coat of matt varnish (Admiralty Varnish Flat Matt AV9105). Crossdrill just below the metallic rim and add the rope handles (0.10mm natural rigging thread). I secured the handles with a drop of superglue inside the buckets (Photograph 4). Finally, saw off the completed buckets, go back to the beginning and make another twelve.

Photographs 5 and 6 show the completed items. The addition of 'weathering' would probably enhance their appearance further. Magnified images of small objects are never flattering, but when viewed at 'normal' distances the appearance is quite acceptable.

ARTWORK

The royal cipher on the buckets is easier to produce than it might appear. The only question is the colour fastness, but in this respect, only time will tell. The technique makes use of a home computer with a photo-edit programme and scanner. The second half of the process utilises special papers and solutions to produce decals or water-slide transfers.

The first stage is to draw or trace the royal cipher – examples can be found on the internet. These will be

2. Taper dowel and mark length.

coloured images, so it will be necessary to trace the letters in outline only, as they will be coloured later. It is advisable to make the letters slightly wider; if not, when they are greatly reduced in size, the letters become virtually invisible.

Scan the completed outline into the computer to produce a JPEG image. The programme may only recognise this as a black-and-white image, and it will be found that it is not possible to fill it with colours. If this is the case, paste the cipher image on to any colour image, merge, and then crop the image to leave only the cipher image, which will now be a colour image. Then fill in the letters and crown. Originally I

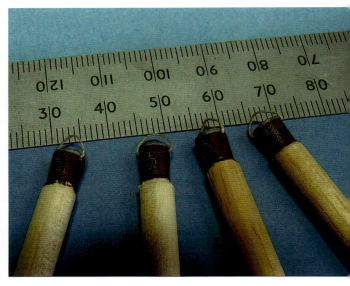

3. Add rim detail.

4. Completed buckets ready for parting off.

used yellow ochre for this, but the letters did not stand out enough, so in the latest batch I have used yellow. Next fill the lines surrounding the letters with yellow, or it may be decided to leave them as black lines. The final stage is to fill the background. If this is for the emblem on a cannon barrel it will be black, and will present no problems, but for the buckets under consideration it will be necessary to match the colour of the bucket. Once an acceptable match has been achieved, note the RGB combination of the colour for future use. Photograph 7 illustrates the fill sequence, and Photograph 8 shows the RGB values which I am currently using.

Finally save the completed artwork, as a small image, 3mm wide in the example shown in Photograph 9, but at very high resolution, 12250 pixels per inch in this case. This will give a very crisply printed decal. The final size of the decal to be printed is decided at the print stage, as is the position of the image on the paper. At the moment I am printing one decal at a time, and adjusting the position of the printed image on the paper for each pass through the printer.

PRINTING THE DECAL

This came about with the development of colour inkjet printers. At that time there was no special paper, in fact

5. 1:64 scale buckets and a 1:48 scale bucket for comparison.

6. Buckets on deck!

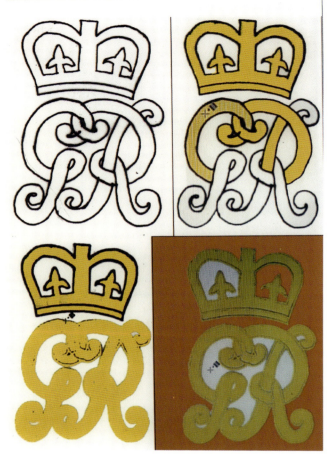

7. Royal cipher filling sequence.

glossy photo GGG paper was just coming onto the market at affordable prices, and the decal was printed on standard inkjet paper, coated with a special varnish, and then soaked in warm water, at which point it was just about possible to lift the image off the paper. It did not work all that well, at least in my hands.

The system now offered works really well. The images are printed on a special decal film paper, which is sold and packaged by the sheet. The images are then given two coats of a varnish type material called Liquid Decal Film. When dry, the image is cut out, and is then ready to use. Decal adhesion is aided by the second solution, Micro Set, which is brushed on to the area where the decal is to be applied. The decal is soaked in warm water, carefully lifted off the backing paper – they are thin and delicate – and applied. I obtained the materials from Hobby's, London.

This system has many possibilities for the marine modeller, such as the manufacture of nameplates for ships, or notices and lettering on more modern vessels. Lettering can be produced at any size, in any colour or font. Modern inks have improved vastly, and the image is protected by several coats of varnish, but only time will demonstrate the colour fastness of the system. However, with the current museum trend of changing display items on a regular basis, I am sure the method will suffice in the short to medium term.

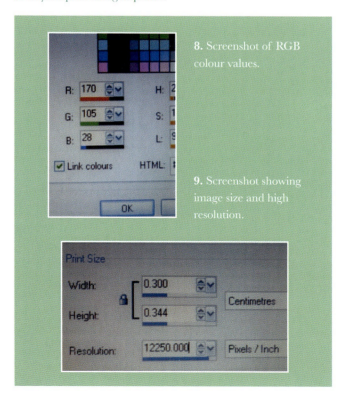

8. Screenshot of RGB colour values.

9. Screenshot showing image size and high resolution.

Steam trawler *Akranes* FD33

A TREASURE FROM THE PAST

by Neil Howard

When I was asked to write an article about building a model steam trawler I struggled; not on what to write, but more about the subject. It had to be something that was unusual, a reincarnation that stirred the soul, a leviathan the likes of which would not be seen again.

STEAM TRAWLER AKRANES FD33

My reasons for choosing this particular model to write about are twofold: it was the first steam trawler to be brought to Fleetwood by the fledgling offspring of the mighty J. Marr & Sons of Hull in 1900, which was history in itself (although Fleetwood did have steam trawlers operating successfully from the port before Marr arrived), and secondly it was an

unusual type of trawler generically known as the 'Bridge Aft Sider', which denoted that the wheelhouse was set abaft the funnel on the aft end of the engine casing, and that she fished using either fixed beam or otter door trawling methods from either or both port and starboard sides.

Being so old, the prototype is but a mere photographic memory in the pages of books, and as such little 'real' knowledge of her exists.

However, she was one of many like-built ships of the period of the late 1890s to the early 1920s and plans of similar ships do exist. Plans in books and those obtainable

Below: Finished model of J. Marr's *Akranes*, the first steam trawler to arrive in Fleetwood in the year 1900.

from other sources can be used to great advantage in order to build up a picture of what this ship would have looked like, when matching such information with the photographs available, and this is what I did.

The scale was chosen as 1:32 to give a hull length of 47in overall, and this equated to a standard hull length of 125ft overall, with a beam of 21.1ft. Countless numbers were built by shipyards up and down the country. *Akranes* was built at North Shields in 1899. Such early trawler hulls were very similar, I could utilise the hull lines of a generically similar trawler that I already possessed.

Regrettably I did not take photographs of all stages of the model and have substituted generic photos showing how certain stages of the model were built, so please excuse me for using a little artistic licence when talking of specific processes, as some photos will not fit the build.

THE HULL

I chose to build the model using GRP for the hull and main superstructure, using my own plugs.

The hull was constructed using the plank-on-frame method whereby I used 4mm birch-faced ply for the backbone and frames of the hull, and obeche planking held with picture framing pins and an aliphatic quick grab resin to glue in place.

This was then skimmed with P38 type car body filler and sanded to a smooth finish. Final treatments to the hull in order to prepare for plating consisted of cellulose sanding sealer, rubbing down with wire wool between coats.

The hull was now ready to plate with all detailing including rubbing strakes, bilge keel plates and all hawse and freeing port markings before moulding. This was done using 120 gram card (similar to old document file card) of which I have a good stock.

I started with the keel plates and worked from the stern for'ard in matching rows, with a space in between plates so that the overlapping (or joggled) plates sat on top of those already laid. The final row of plates was the bulwark set which overlap or joggle on to the next set down the hull.

These plates were glued to the hull using a 70:30 PVA-water mix. Once the hull was fully plated it was given liberal coats of sanding sealer to harden up the card.

The main superstructure was also built at this stage so as to mould all the parts at the same time. This was constructed using block obeche and then plated (again using card) and 'riveted' using small blobs of cyano gel superglue to represent the rivet points, administered using cocktail sticks dipped in a pool of glue to give uniform head sizes along the seams of the plates. Again the finished dry product was painted with liberal coats of sanding sealer.

The ship's boat was carved from a solid obeche block, split

Above: View of fore deck showing fish hatches and ponds.

Above: Aft boat deck and flying bridge/wheelhouse.

Above: Counter stern showing aft plating.

Above: Fore deck: note hand warping anchor windlass.

Above: Mid section. Note aft of the funnel is the Hanson patent cod liver oil boiler. Also the steam trawl winch and rollers on side of engine casing.

down the centre with a 2mm keel backbone added. This was then detailed with clinker planking using 6mm wide card planks, starting from the keel to the gunwale, with rubbing strakes and capping rail added at this time, repeating the same sealing process as applied to hull and superstructure.

MOULDING

I will not go into the process of moulding GRP in any great depth. Suffice it to say that I spent much time working on the plugs, since they had to have the same quality of finish (even though they are waste and disregarded after the process) as that which is required on the basic finished hull. As such, preparation is of utmost importance. The better the finish on the plug, the less work is needed on the moulding.

Each mould was made as a split mould; that is to say the mould is made in two halves around a centre flange to the plug so that it can be bolted together for the moulding process, and then after undoing the bolts, split in two to extract the moulding. The more complicated the hull of a boat, the more splits, and the photos are of a four-part mould with four splits for a classic lifeboat. This number of splits are required because of the tunnels and belting on the hull.

The plugs are waxed with a non-silicon based release wax and painted with a film of blue PVA release agent to aid non-sticking of GRP to the boat, and moulded up in layers.

MOULDING THE HULL AND ANCILLARIES

Once the moulds have been produced and allowed to cure for a few days, the plugs can be discarded and the moulds used to produce a set of mouldings from which the ship will be built.

Below: Engine room casing with oil burner and pole compass on wheelhouse.

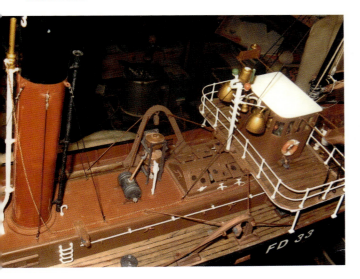

Above: Wheelhouse and ship's boat.

FITTING OUT OF HULL

At this point I made a rudder stock from polystyrene plastic (ABS type) and then pressed it into a mould of RTV (room temperature vulcanising) rubber, so that I would have the strength of a white metal rudder stock, rather than plastic, which would easily break at the boating pond.

The hole for a propeller shaft was drilled, and a suitable prop shaft bought and fitted, using cyano to hold it in place until it could be sealed from the inside permanently with polyester resin. Then the white metal rudder stock was added and pinned in place using P38 to seal it.

At this point the area for bilge keels was marked onto the moulded bedding plates. The bilge keels were to be made from modeller's 2mm ply. To fit these into the hull I employed a method I have used for years; that is, I cut a

Below: Fore deck and winch.

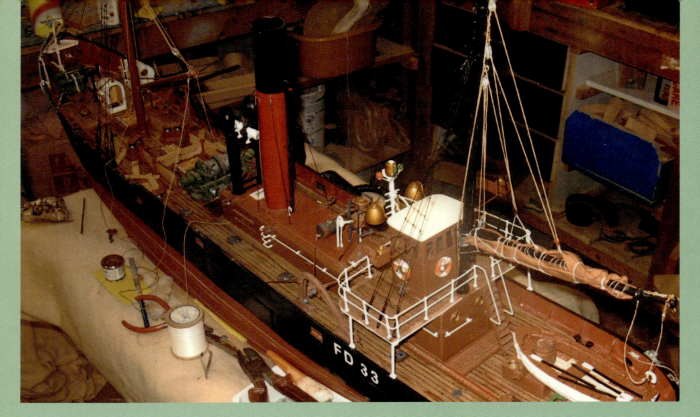

Above: Over all view of model.   **Below:** Windlass, fore companionway.

Below: Mahogany show case.

Above & below: Hull of *Akranes* decked out and scuppers cut in hull side.

Above: Bilge keels added.

centre slot the full length of the bedding plate and enlarged to the thickness of the timber, in this case a 2mm slot. Then the oversized bilge plate was placed width-ways into the long slot so that it protruded through into the hull by about 5-8mm. This was tack glued using cyano. The hull was then tilted onto its bilge and any gaps were masked with tape from the outside of the hull to stop any leaks. A small amount of polyester resin was then poured into the inside of the hull to seal in and set the bilge keel in place. The process was repeated on the other side.

These are all steps that must be undertaken whilst complete access to the hull is available and before the deck has been fitted. If the model is to be radio controlled then provisions for engine beds and battery housing beds must also be made at this point, before the decking goes on.

The final job before fitting the deck was to skim the inner bulwarks with car body filler and a final cellulose putty filler. This was done to a depth of about 50mm from the top edge of the bulwark, and sanded down to a smooth finish to

Left: Rudder frame and stock cast in white metal.

Above: Generic GRP moulds of engine room casing and funnel prior to cleaning up.

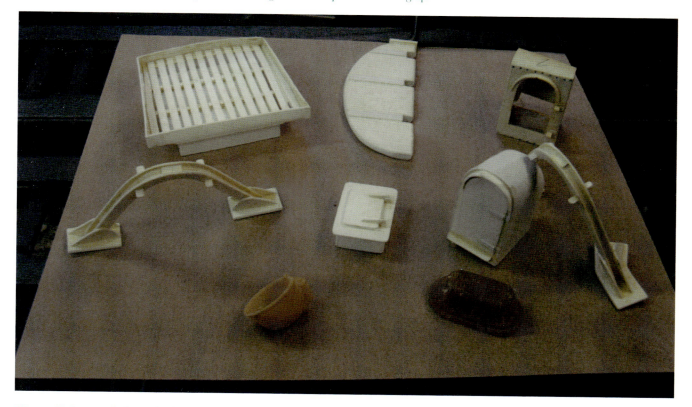

Above: Fittings made from plastic card resin.

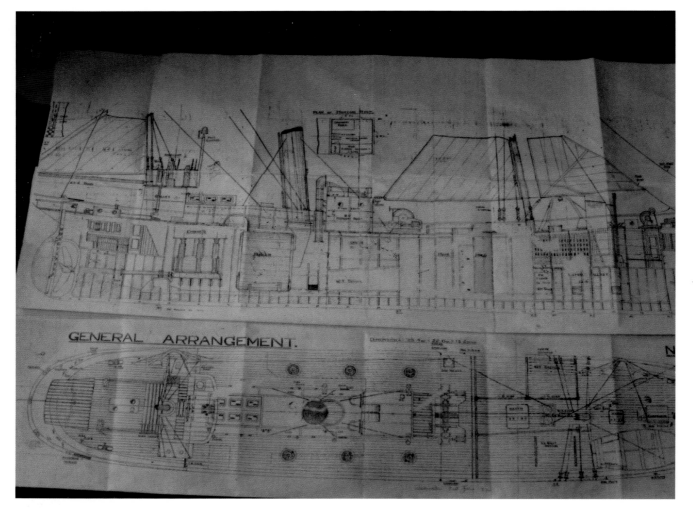

GENERAL ARRANGEMENT.

Above: Plan of similar ship to *Akranes*, used for general positioning.

remove any high points. Any low points resulting from an irregularly moulded hull were also filled.

The sanding down was done using 60 grade garnet paper and a final finishing was carried out with 280 grade wet and dry paper, used wet.

DECKING OUT

I built a 'ladder' type frame inside the hull, carefully measuring down from the top of the bulwark with a piece of 2mm ply offcut to ensure the correct depth of the deck, factoring in the thickness of the material to be used for the deck plus its cladding of planking. As this was not an even depth throughout the full length of the hull, I had to use more than one depth gauge for the purpose, especially as the measurements approached the most forward part of the deck. I also made sure that equal measurements were made on both port and starboard sides of the inside of the hull.

The longitudinal stringers, made from 6mm square obeche, were fitted first, glued into position with two part liquid epoxy, as used in the model aircraft fraternity, and held to the hull side using wooden clothes pegs. To facilitate fitting at the curve of the hull at both bow and stern, the stringers were cut partially through at 10mm spaces, which allowed the timber to bend and take the shape of the hull. Although this seems a messy and rather brutal way to do the job, it is quicker and far less time-consuming than steaming the stringers and wet fitting, which entails allowing them to dry out before then refitting with adhesive. Remember that it will never be seen when the deck is fitted.

Once glued, the cross members were fitted. The cross stringers were measured out for positioning, making sure that the cross beams and the inner longitudinal stringers gave the outline for the access hatch under the main engine casing superstructure, to allow for servicing of the motor, R/C gear and battery.

The cross beams were butt jointed to the main longitudinal stringers, but where they crossed the inner stringers, half housing joints were cut into both timbers to form a level surface on which to lay the deck.

Above: Port profile of *Akranes*.

Where the cross beams met the longitudinal stringers the butt joint was strengthened with triangular gussets made from 2mm ply, glued from the underside using two part epoxy and held with pegs.

Once the frame was in place, I further strengthened the structure by running a triangular fillet of car body filler to the underside of the long stringers that made contact with the hull side, for the full length of the boat. Not only does this strengthen the whole structure but it also acts as a watertight barrier for the deck.

THE DECK

I now made templates for the main and fore deck, there being a step between the two just forward of the main trawl winch. I used 120 gram card (cereal boxes are ideal). I cut them in sections and fitted them to the bulwarks. Once a good fit to the edge of the bulwarks is obtained they can be put together in simple jigsaw pattern. This pattern is then transferred to 2mm birch ply and cut out. The access hole to the inner area of the boat is also checked at this stage so as to align with the under frame before finally cutting out. If the boat is to be radio controlled a smaller access hole must also be cut at the after end of the deck at this stage to enable access to rudder connections.

The deck was fitted once final trimming had taken place, and glued in place using a slower setting two part liquid epoxy. Where accessible it was held with pegs around the access hole. At all other points I used old batteries and other heavy weights to ensure that the deck was held firmly to the frame until it had set.

I measured to the centre line of the deck from bow to stern and marked a pencil line. This was to be the king plank. I also marked off the small square and rectangular areas on the fore deck where the fish hatches, companionways and trawl gallows were to fit, as these areas would be framed. The edging plank line around the wash trough was also marked in pencil before any plank was laid.

The planking was made from 0.5mm (1/64in) thick birch ply cut into 6mm wide strips, measuring 180mm long. I then marked off cross lines at 60mm length on the decks, in order to simulate a three plank overlap. This would give the authentic look of a trawler deck.

These planks were glued individually, starting from the centre king plank and working outwards to the bulwarks, using quick grab aliphatic waterproof resin. I mixed a black food colourant into this glue and applied it to the edge of each plank with a small brush to simulate the black caulking used to seal a deck from ingress of water. It is easy to sand smooth and clean up once the whole deck is laid.

The waterway between deck edge and bulwarks was coated with a concrete mix on such trawlers. This was simu-

Above: View of stern section from above.

Above: View of forward section from above.

lated by painting the area with PVA glue and dusting with builder's fine sand before painting matt grey.

At this stage, before any detailing was added to the model, I cut out the wash ports and hawse holes that had been marked and moulded into the GRP mould on the master mouldings. This was achieved by masking off the outer edge with masking tape and then drilling with a 2.5mm drill bit around the inner perimeter of the hole. Small files were used to finish the edge of the masked area.

The bulwark capping rail was now added. On a trawler this part is made from steel and painted. I normally make it from layers of 120 gram card glued in place, in the first instance with cyano, building up to three layers, gluing the last two with aliphatic resin, before sealing the composite with cellulose sanding sealer and rubbing down between coats with wire wool. It is then painted a suitable colour.

Finally triangular support stays made from 1.2mm plastic card were made and glued to the bulwarks with cyano.

I had decided to fit this model for future use with radio control equipment, which meant that the main superstructure had to be removable. As such the access hole needed a coaming to be fitted round it to locate the superstructure. This was made from 2mm ply cut to width and length and glued to the stringers butting up to the access hole. The pieces were added one by one, and once set a small fillet of 3mm square stringer was glued into each inner corner to strengthen it.

The hull was sprayed using car paint aerosols; red primer to simulate the underwater part of the hull, with satin black for the area above the boot topping and waterline.

I always find it prudent at this stage to add the ship's name, number, port of registry and draught marks. This is because the hull can easily be turned on its side without the possibility of damaging delicate fittings and rigging. For this detailing I use proprietory adhesive vinyl lettering, available at good model shops in a variety of colours and sizes.

DECK FITTINGS

I have been building models of old steam trawlers for some years and have built up a collection of generic fittings that feature on such vessels. In the past these have been made from either plastic card or brass and then cast into RTV rubber moulds, for future use.

First I planned all those fittings that I could construct using plastic card, and made all of these as one long run. Items such as companionways, the toilet hut, fish hatches, escape hatches and trawl gallows were made together, rather than piecemeal, and could be painted at the same time. In this way I could make sure I had not forgotten anything. I marked out each item on the plans as I constructed it.

All other fittings appropriate to this vessel were made from either brass or plastic card and moulded into RTV rubber so that I could cast multiple fittings in white metal. These fittings included the winch, hand windlass, coaling scuttle lids, bollards and fairleads, deck lights and lifeboat fittings, etc. All were cleaned up after casting, then detailed and painted before fitting in place on the deck, where they were secured with cyano.

SUPERSTRUCTURE AND FUNNEL

I made the engine casing and wheelhouse from two separate GRP mouldings that I had made at the same time as the hull, with all surface detailing and positioning of portholes and windows moulded into them.

These two items were detailed as with the hull and decks with fittings that I had produced when planning this and other builds, and were painted prior to fitting.

The funnel is one of the focal points of this model, being a tall thin stovepipe type and a prominent feature.

I used a piece of plumber's 40mm plastic pipe for the main structure and clad this in thin card to simulate plating construction. I added rivets using small blobs of adhesive similar to the detailing in the plug for the hull. Items such as the steam whistle and steam vent pipes were made from 2mm brass rod, with a turned brass whistle and turned cup for the waste pipe. I wrapped the steam whistle pipe with a rigging thread and then painted it white to simulate asbestos insulation before attaching all these pieces to the painted funnel. The stays were attached to small eyelets made from thin brass wire and tied to the deck once the funnel had been glued in place on the superstructure. The stanchions and rails around the wings of the wheelhouse were purchased ready-made, as I find that such fittings made from white metal are vulnerable to damage, tending to bend and break very easily.

MASTS AND RIGGING

Originally I intended to fit working navigation and running lights on this vessel, and therefore needed to hide the wiring from view. As such I decided to construct the main and mizzen masts using a method I had employed in the past. This was to use hollow carbon fibre sections of fishing rod, obtainable from fishing tackle shops (I usually ask the proprietor if he has any broken rods, and invariably a generous

Above: Generic hull showing gussets added to deck beams to provide extra strength.

Above: Stern port quarter view.

quantity is given away). The masts are built to length using different diameters to represent the steps in a steel mast, and if careful when gluing the sections wiring can be passed down through the centre of the structure.

Navigation lights and running lights in this instance were from 'grain of wheat' bulbs of 12v variety, but there is now a tendency to use LED lighting as it lasts much longer and seldom needs replacing, which otherwise can be a major job. All lights were connected under the deck to micro switches operated on servo-mounted plastic cams, to give a combination of different lighting variations.

The mast booms were made from 6mm dowel. All fittings were cast in white metal, from turned brass or plastic masters.

Deadeyes, pulleys and rigging blocks, including Gilson hooks, were all from cast white metal mouldings. All rigging was of the correct size, run through a block of beeswax to seal the furry strands. However, the running rigging was first boiled in a mixture of tea and coffee and left to stand for a few hours before being allowed to dry, and then waxed. This was to give a more authentic look of well-used rope, so often found on these vessels. The standing rigging for the funnel and masts was done in black thread and secured in the correct manner. The pulley blocks and other running rigging anchor points to the upper mast sections were facilitated using six links of chain to each anchor point, and then tied off to the thread, thus allowing for movement when the running rigging was being used for hauling and other heavy work. This chain was a bought item.

SHIP'S BOAT

The ship's boat, as stated before, was constructed from a GRP moulding. It was fitted out inside using 120 gram card to simulate the interior detailing of planking and stringers from keel to gunwale. Two thwarts (cross seats) and end seats were made from 2mm ply, with all other detailing from cast white metal fittings.

FINISHING

A baseboard was made from mahogany veneered chipboard, edged with a bought moulding. The model was placed on turned brass supports. She was then housed in a solid mahogany showcase of home construction, with clear acrylic sheet 3mm thick in preference to heavier glass.

I found the construction of this unorthodox and strangely odd yet delicate looking fishing trawler both very interesting and rewarding. My only regret is that she never sailed as a model in her natural environment. The original *Akranes* was in fact sold to owners in Rangoon, Burma (now Myanmar) in 1929, and all trace of her from that moment was lost.

Shipwright Gallery

MODELS FROM THE NATIONAL MARITIME MUSEUM COLLECTION

Below: Stern gallery detail of a 50-gun two-decker *c.*1703 built in the Navy Board style. (ref. no. SLR 0218, image L2419-006)

This section presents a selection of objects from the Ship Model Collection of the National Maritime Museum, Greenwich. Curator Simon Stephens oversees the museum's world-class collection of over 3,000 models, and he was instrumental in the rehousing of objects from the Museum's old store to the new facility and gallery space at No. 1 Smithery, Chatham Dockyard (see interview, pages 8-17). During that process the majority of the collection was completely re-shot, with thousands of new photographs taken as part of the museum's ongoing digitisation programme. Simon has chosen a range of models that showcase the wealth of ship types, dates and styles that are represented in the Museum's holdings. This new imagery is presented here for the first time.

Above: Triple steering wheels from the armoured central battery of the warship HMS *Bellerophon*, 1865. (ref. no. SLR2768, image L2262-001)

Above: A contemporary full hull model of the *Victory* (1737), a 100-gun three-decker First Rate. Built in bread and butter fashion and finished in the Georgian style, the model is partially decked, fully equipped and rigged. The *Victory* itself was built in the Royal Dockyard, Portsmouth and measured 174ft along the gun deck by 50ft in the beam. In 1744, a fleet commanded by Admiral Sir John Balchen, using the *Victory* as his flagship, was sent to relieve a British squadron and convoy under Sir Charles Hardy, which had been trapped in the Tagus by a French Brest squadron. Balchen's fleet was successful in driving off the French, who retired in the face of his superior fleet without firing a shot, and Hardy's convoy was escorted safely to Gibraltar. He was returning to England when his fleet was scattered by a violent gale on 4 October. The *Victory* was lost with all hands, nearly 1200 men. It was believed that she had foundered on the Casquets, a vicious group of rocks off Alderney, in the Channel Islands. However, the wreck site was discovered in 2008, some 80km (43nm) off the Casquets in approximately 100m (330ft) of water. (ref. no. SLR0449, images L3241-004,-009,-017,-024)

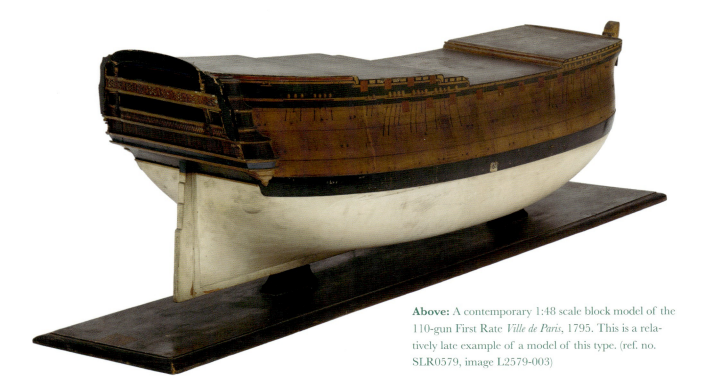

Above: A contemporary 1:48 scale block model of the 110-gun First Rate *Ville de Paris*, 1795. This is a relatively late example of a model of this type. (ref. no. SLR0579, image L2579-003)

Right: Plank-on-frame model of a Chinese junk, of unknown provenance, *c.*1860. Note the very fine upwards-sweeping stern and square-ended after superstructure. (ref. no. AAE0132, image L2691-003)

Below: Half block model of a motor yacht *c.*1930 in glazed mahogany case. The model is mounted on a mirror with angled mirrors at each end. An ivory plaque is inscribed: 'Motor Yacht. 34' 0" x 7' 7" x 5' 4" Scale ¾" = 1ft. Designed by C.L Estrange, Ewen, 45 Hope St. Glasgow'. (ref. no. SLR0351, image L2587-002).

Above: Builder's full hull model of the cargo ship SS *Cragmoor*, 1947. The model, built to 1:96 scale, is exquisitely finished. Most of the fittings are gold-plated to prevent tarnishing. (ref. no. SLR1614, image L2849-003)

Left: A 1:16 scale midship sectional model showing shipboard arrangements for the transportation of horses *c*.1760. (ref. no. SLR0508, image L2709-003)

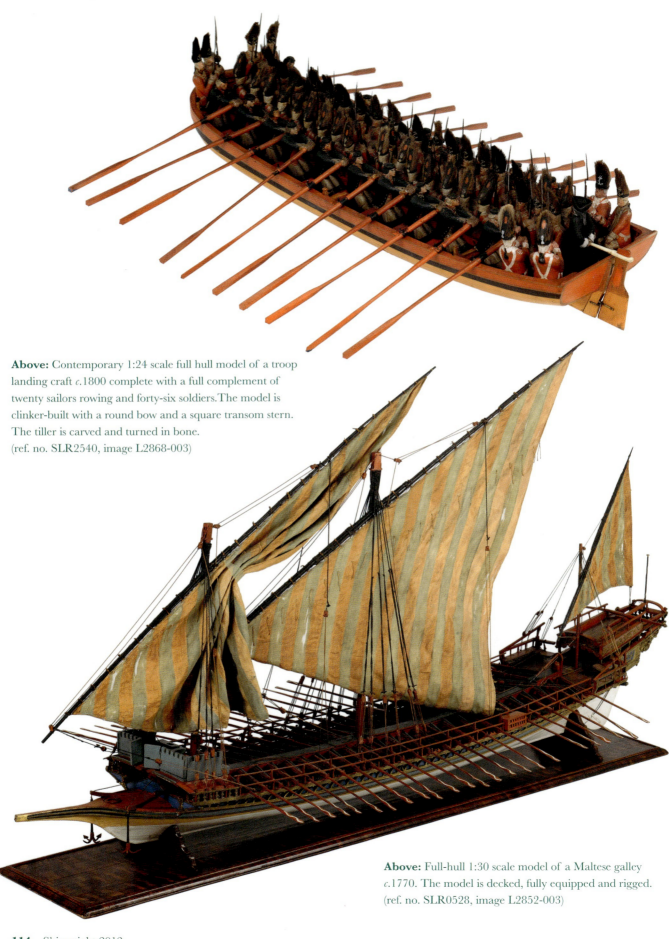

Above: Contemporary 1:24 scale full hull model of a troop landing craft *c.*1800 complete with a full complement of twenty sailors rowing and forty-six soldiers. The model is clinker-built with a round bow and a square transom stern. The tiller is carved and turned in bone. (ref. no. SLR2540, image L2868-003)

Above: Full-hull 1:30 scale model of a Maltese galley *c.*1770. The model is decked, fully equipped and rigged. (ref. no. SLR0528, image L2852-003)

Below: A full hull 1:150 scale builders' model of the LNG Carrier *Methane Heather Sally*, with the midship section cut away on the starboard side to reveal the interior construction and layout of the liquefied natural gas tanks. The gas must be refrigerated at a temperature of minus 161 degrees centigrade. The port side towards the bow shows the various colour-coded layers of the membrane containment system which comprises stainless steel, glass-fibre cloth and an aluminum foam wood sandwich. The hull is finished with red-brown antifouling paint below the waterline with upper works in black. The deck and parts of the superstructure are painted grey and white with the coamings of the top of the tanks highlighted in orange. Note various markings along the sides of the hull, which indicate tug handling points, discharge pipe arrangements, and hazards such as bow thrusters and the bulbous bow. The model was built in Korea by **KOSMO** Scientific Models Ltd and is mounted in its original wooden glazed presentation display case, complete with two plaques with principal dimensions and the model-maker's details. The model was presented to the National Maritime Museum by the BG Group in 2009. (ref. no. ZBA4653, image L0448-001,-002,-003)

Salt Water Painters

THE ROYAL SOCIETY OF MARINE ARTISTS

by David Howell PRSMA

The Royal Society of Marine Artists has the sound of a fairly grand organisation, and I suppose in many respects that's exactly what we are. Originally formed in 1939, the Society's members represent some of the finest marine painters currently working in the UK and in some cases from further afield, as the membership isn't exclusively British. Membership of the Society is achieved initially by recognition of a successful exhibiting record over a number of years at the RSMA Annual Open Exhibition in London and ultimately by election by the membership as a whole. As painters a number of members concentrate exclusively on marine subjects, but most paint pretty much anything that takes their fancy. Moreover a number are well known through their articles and books on painting in general.

Any article on painters might start by asking why those of us who do it are driven to depict what we see by applying pigment in its various forms to an appropriate surface, when there is a huge selection of digital cameras or even mobile phones that are quite capable of recording what is around us. Indeed, modern equipment can provide impressive clarity without the complexities of yesteryear, which involved the expertise needed to cope with light meters, shutter speeds, apertures, focal lengths and manual focussing.

The answer, I guess, lies in an individual painter's fascination with shapes and colours, tones and contrasts and the development over many years (or decades) of a particular way of seeing, so much so that many of us would claim that those who wander around the world with an eye glued to a viewfinder rarely see much at all. Painters who are really committed can't help themselves, and the better ones have learnt that photographic exactness isn't what is required. They have a major advantage over the photographer; namely the ability to change things to improve the picture. Composing a picture means that we can leave out the bits we don't like and other features can be moved in if appropriate. If the painter chooses they can use the basic subject as a starting point only, letting the whole composition evolve around it in terms of shape and colour.

Note that I continually refer to painters rather than artists.

1. A sketch of Pin Mill on the River Orwell in Suffolk, pencil and crayon (David Howell PRSMA).

Most good painters take the view that, apart from the occasional need to distinguish ourselves from the local painter and decorator, calling yourself an artist is somewhat presumptuous. It is only in the fullness of time that experts, dealers and the art market in general will decide whether we were just run of the mill, even if mildly skilled, or serious artists where the value of the work is destined to show significant increases over years to come. Of course this sort of modesty doesn't apply to those involved in the more bizarre end of the market that inevitably generates column inches in the media as well as TV coverage, but then most of the associated gimmicks and activities have little to do with art and everything to do with having a good PR agent.

Real painters are essentially illusionists. Unlike the model maker or sculptor their output is two-dimensional rather than three-, and therefore they have to create the impression of depth and recession by the use of perspective, colour and sheer skill. The understanding and subtle use of cool and warm colours, tones, with hard and soft edges can make all

2. The finished watercolour painting (David Howell PRSMA).

the difference in the way other individuals view the finished work, without being aware of the artifice that has created it.

The actual process of putting a painting together varies according to the painter, but many **RSMA** members work outside in all conditions. In the process they have learnt to cope with the wind, weather and tides. It isn't always possible to complete a painting on the spot but those who work in this way will have learnt to get enough information down to complete the painting in the studio. My own personal approach is always to complete at least a small sketch to 'fix' the essential details before starting the actual painting. This is because I have learnt the hard way that moving shadows, changing weather and tides all change the appearance and angle of boats – as well as possibly encouraging a timely move to higher ground! All decent marine painters will have experienced the dubious joy of the realisation that while they have been immersed in their work their painting gear has been similarly inundated and has just floated away. The walk back to dry land often means at least getting the feet wet, and in extreme circumstances can necessitate some serious wading.

The pictures illustrated in Figures 1 and 2 were produced at Pin Mill on the River Orwell in Suffolk, with rain in the air and the tide most definitely advancing across the mud. The easy way would have been to take a quick photograph and perhaps retire to the 'Butt and Oyster' for a pint. The drawing in Figure 1 probably took less than 30 minutes, by which time the water was lapping round my feet, and the process will have included the necessary adjustments to ensure that the composition worked effectively. It is this selectivity and creativity that is so much better than using a photograph. Materials used in this instance are just soft pencils and coloured crayons but the sketch provided sufficient information to produce a finished watercolour painting back on dry land– see Figure 2.

There are of course those magic days when the weather holds good, when the location you've chosen is out of the way and you can just quietly get on with it. David Curtis is one the RSMA's greatest advocates of open air painting and his watercolour of Polperro (Figure 3) is a classic example of sunlight and shade among the cottages and round the harbour. This sort of picture records a sense of time and place. The fishing boats in the harbour are very much of current times but fit in nicely with their older surroundings and make the whole scene ideal for a typical 'David Curtis' watercolour of this Cornish fishing village.

Both David Curtis and myself might be considered amongst the conventional figurative painters of the Society, but other members specialise in historical depictions that require considerable research. In some cases this might well rival that applied by the most exacting model-maker, and this background work invariably takes far more time than the eventual construction of the painting.

We have a number of specialists in this area including Past President Geoff Hunt, who is well known for his depictions of Nelson's Navy and for his jacket illustrations for the front covers of Patrick O'Brian's acclaimed historical novels featuring Jack Aubrey. Typical of Geoff's work is Figure 4, 'HMS *Sutherland*'s Last Battle'. The background research for a painting like this will undoubtedly take far longer than the painting itself and involves a considerable amount of study of the vessels' construction, the sea conditions and weather at the time of the event, and also an examination of how the ships involved were handled and deployed. Most importantly however, despite all this complexity, this information is being used to create a painting that works from an artistic point of view and is quite simply good to look at.

4. 'HMS *Sutherland*'s Last Battle', oil on canvas (Geoff Hunt PPRSMA).

Another of the RSMA's historical specialists (and indeed another Past President) is Mark Myers. Mark works from a studio on the Cornish Coast and has a considerable amount of experience of actual square rig sailing. He again spends a large amount of time on the background to a particular picture, and the illustrations opposite show how this process

3. 'Incoming tide at Polperro', watercolour (David Curtis RSMA ROI).

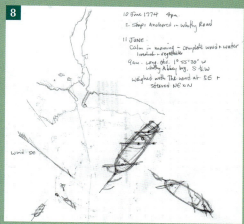

5 & 6. Preparatory pencil sketches, HM ships *Carcass* and *Racehorse* at anchor off Whitby, 1773 (Mark Myers PPRSMA F/ASMA).

7. Preparatory pencil sketch, *Carcass* and *Racehorse* getting under way on the morning of June 11th 1773 (Mark Myers PPRSMA F/ASMA).

8. Compositional sketch, showing relative positions of ships at Whitby on that morning (Mark Myers PPRSMA F/ASMA).

9. The final painting; 'The *Racehorse* and *Carcass* sailing from Whitby Roads, June 11th, 1773', watercolour (Mark Myers PPRSMA F/ASMA).

evolves. This painting was a commission; its subject a voyage by the vessels *Carcass* and *Racehorse* in 1773 when they anchored off Whitby, before proceeding northwards towards the North Pole under the command of Constantine John Phipps, the English Explorer and Naval Officer. Mark's drawings give some idea of the meticulous work that goes into the preparatory stage of a work of this type in compositional and detail terms. He has worked out precisely where the ships were moored, using information from Phipps' journal, combined with research as to the wind direction and the state of the tide when the ships weighed anchor to continue on their voyage. Apart from studying historical documentation Mark will have visited Whitby to produce drawings and photographs of the location and background where the ships were located, helped considerably by Phipps' giving a bearing on Whitby Abbey, which is still a dominant feature overlooking the harbour.

Figures 5–7 show alternative compositions. The first two feature the vessels at anchor taking on stores, and Figure 8 depicts them getting under way on the morning of 11 June 1774. It was this composition that was eventually chosen for the finished painting, and Figure 8 is an excellent illustration of Mark's background research showing the exact conditions that morning.

Figure 9 shows the final painting, entitled 'The *Racehorse* and *Carcass* sailing from Whitby Roads, June 11th, 1773'. What is perhaps most extraordinary is that this work is a

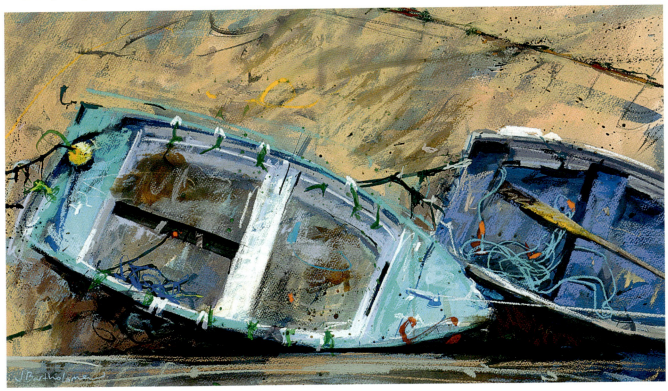

10. 'Quayside boats, St Ives', watercolour & pastel (James Bartholomew RSMA).

11. Yachts off the Isle of Wight, oil on canvas (Rowena Wright RSMA).

22in x 30in watercolour, a medium that is singularly unforgiving when it comes to making even minor adjustments. A complicated painting like this requires the painter to know exactly where he is going with it.

The painting of James Bartholomew (Figure 10) stands in complete contrast to Mark's work. This work is an example of a painter using a motif – in this case, dinghies – as a starting point, but deliberately letting the imagination and the creative process turn the painting into a dynamic composition of shape and colour. It is not so much about detail and location as about creating something with visual impact that would brighten any environment in which it was placed. The medium in this instance is pastel, which when used with this sort of freedom makes a very attractive painting. The fact that much of James's work is on a seriously large scale only adds to that.

In a short article like this it is difficult to include all the variations on the marine theme that appear in an RSMA show. The overriding consideration is that the pictures exhibited in conjunction with the RSMA must have something to do with the sea or tidal waters. That in itself is open to wide interpretation and we see still life, pictures of fish, children on beaches, tidal creeks, landscape with a glimpse of the sea in the distance and of course contemporary vessels and yachts.

Typical of the latter is Rowena Wright's work. Rowena is based in the Isle of Wight and specialises in the yachts and racing events that are right on her doorstep. The oil painting illustrated in Figure 11 is typical of her work as one of the Society's yachting specialists.

Not surprisingly in a country with a strong marine heritage, the Autumn RSMA Annual Exhibition in the Mall Galleries, London is one of the most popular events in the gallery's yearly programme. The interest shown by a new generation of painters and sculptors in submitting work for possible selection should ensure that the Society does not stand still and that we will continue to attract new generations of marine artists and enthusiasts of marine art.

Jack Aubrey's Minorca

WINNER OF THE CONWAY MARITIME SAIL PRIZE

by Matthew Jones

This year's winner of the Conway Maritime Sail Prize, awarded for a painting of outstanding merit at the RSMA Annual Exhibition, was Geoff Hunt, for his depiction of Jack Aubrey's Minorca, a superb high-angle panorama of Port Mahon *c*.1800. The theme of the painting will be familiar to all Patrick O'Brian readers, as it evokes a key episode in the series – when Jack Aubrey assumes his first command and meets his voyaging companion-to-be, Stephen Maturin, in the very first novel, *Master and Commander*. It can be taken to be the moment when Stephen, on shore, sees the brig *Sophie* sailing away, and fears that he has been abandoned; although all turns out well, as Jack returns to collect him before the evening. Along with HMS *Sophie*, other elements from both the actual location and O'Brian's imaginative setting have been represented; notably Pigtail Steps, which descend from the town to the quay, and the Crown, the fictitious inn where Jack and Stephen dine – its bay window, from which the pair flick their oyster shells, appears in the extreme right foreground. This wealth of detail captivated and charmed the judging panel, and we hope you will agree that the work is a worthy winner.

Below: 'Jack Aubrey's Minorca: Port Mahon in 1800, HMS *Sophie* leaving harbour', oil on canvas (Geoff Hunt PPRSMA).

Sindia (1887)

FOUR-MASTED BARQUE

by Ian Hunt

Sindia was built by Harland and Wolff at Queens Island, Belfast, Northern Ireland, in 1887. She was launched on 19 November of that year and delivered to her new owners, T & J Brocklebank & Co. of Liverpool, on 6 February 1888. The steel-built vessel was 3,068 tons and 329ft 4in (100.3m) long with a beam of 45ft 2in (13.7m) and a depth of 26ft 8in (8.14m). *Sindia* and her sister-ship *Holkar* were the largest sailing ships in the world at the time of their launch. Prior to her launch *Sindia* was known by her yard number, Hull 204; *Holkar* was Hull 205.

They were named for the rulers of the Mahratta nation. 'Sindia' was the equivalent of 'Rajah' or 'King'; 'Holkar' was female and meant 'Ranee' or 'Queen'. The ship was named for the greatest Sindia – Mahadji Sindia (1750–1794); the leader who captured the fortress city of Gwalior and led the Mahrattas from nomadic life to nationhood, eventually controlling central India. Gwalior became the state of Madhya Bharat in the New Republic of India in

Below: Afloat. Note the wave patterns running down her sides.

Above: Planking is of Fijian Kauri Pine. Due to its massive construction the hull is very strong.

1948 and the titles of Sindia and Holkar were abolished.

For most of her life the ship was engaged in the jute trade between India and Dundee, Scotland, but in 1900 she was sold to the British Anglo-American Oil Company of London.

Still under British registry she was long-term chartered to John D. Rockefeller's Standard Oil Company of New Jersey,

USA – now the Exxon Corporation – to carry case oil (kerosene) to Japan, returning with general cargo.

On 15 December 1901 she ran into a snowstorm with gale force winds. During the night she stranded on the beach at Ocean City, New Jersey, near the 17th Street Pier. All the crew were saved and some of the cargo taken off, but salvage proved impossible and the wreck was abandoned to sink into the sand where it remains to this day.

Holkar was sold to D. H. Watjen of Bremen, Germany, in

Above: Early days. Planking nearly completed. Note solid section at bow.

Above: The main deck is over 7ft long, with hatch and deckhouse openings.

Above: The figurehead is Mahadji Sindia (1750–1794), the great Mahratta ruler.

1901 and renamed *Adelaide*. Re-sold to Norway in 1913 her name was changed to *Odessa* and later to *Souverain*, eventually becoming the *Hiddalos* in 1923. She was broken up in Holland in 1924.

THE MODEL

Time spent on research and forward planning, particularly for a very large model such as this, is never wasted; indeed it is almost essential if work is to proceed smoothly. Like the original ship, it is necessary to build up from the keel, deciding each stage in advance and, if possible, planning the next two or three stages prior to construction.

The model was built only of wood and brass. The only two plastic items used on the model are the lenses of the port and starboard side lights which are cut from two coloured pencil sharpeners – one red, one green. The model is 10ft 6in (3.2m) long, height 5ft 10in (1.88m) with a beam of 15in (0.38m). The three lower yards are each 30in (0.77m) in length, the weight of the model without the detachable sailing keel is 91lb (40.4kg).

The detachable sailing keel is effectively a long, deep,

narrow hull 6ft 9in (2.05m) long, 14in (355mm) deep and 3.5in (89mm) wide. Empty it weighs 14lb (6.3kg).

Carried internally are eight removable cast lead ingots with a total weight of 246lb (111.8kg).

The strongly constructed keel has a frame of 3in (76.2) x ¾in (20mm) pine with a ¼in (5mm) three-ply covering.

A full-length rubber cap ⅜in (10mm) thick fits along the top to act as a soft seal between the hull and the keel.

The model is built using standard plank-on-frame con-

Right: The fore part. The forward hawse pipe was used for towing purposes only.

Above: Working replica of the gravity-activated anchor release gear.

struction, a total of thirty frames with eighteen stringers.

The two keels, upper and lower, are ¾in (20mm) square Tasmanian oak separated by seven pressure posts of the same size and stock.

The shaped stern piece is of ¾in (20mm) Pacific maple, while the stern post for rudder attachment is a length of ¾in (20mm) square teak.

The stem piece is a sandwich of two sections of ¾in

(20mm) thick rose maple separated by a slice of 2mm hoop pine plywood which does not extend right forward, leaving a 2mm slot at the front.

The hull planking is only laid from the first to the last frame. The stem and stern are filled in with solid Pacific maple blocks and hand-shaped – by eye and with card templates – to the finished size.

When this was completed the final plywood slice was fitted into the slot in the front of the stem piece and cut to the exact curve of the steel cutwater.

The upper and lower keels are pierced by four ½in (13mm) brass tubes running through the hull top to bottom carrying four ½in (13mm) threaded steel rods which also pass through the detachable sailing keel, linking the two units together.

The model is planked with ¼in (6mm) Fijian kauri. Each ½in (13mm) wide plank shaped and chamfered to fit exactly alongside its neighbour. On a large model it is not practical to plank in one continuous length like a model yacht hull, nor is it necessary as the frame is ¾in (20mm) thick. Weight was not a problem. Each frame was built up from four separate pieces of native Australian timber, both hard and soft. The timber was salvaged from a Forests Department display that was going to be discarded as scrap! All were machined planks – 4ft (1.22m) x 3½in (8.89m) x ¾in (20mm) – of brown alder,

Left: The anchor windlass under the fore deck. Note bevel gear – centre – for vertical drive to main capstan on deck above.

sassafras, brush mahogany, beech, rose gum, Pacific maple, mountain gum, alpine ash, pink wood, white beech, red cedar, teak, Monterey pine, ivory wood and Victorian ash.

Since it does not leak it is unnecessary to waterproof the interior of the hull.

All planks were fastened with a locally-made two-part epoxy gel – Megapoxy 69. This is superior to liquid epoxies as it does not seep out of the seams and any excess can be scraped off when it cures to the jelly stage.

THE HULL

Hull plating was the next stage; something I had not previously attempted. I used an overlay of 0.75mm birch three-ply from Finland, cut into 1½in (38mm) strips to accommodate the sheer off the hull.

The plate lines were marked out in pencil and using a flexible steel straightedge plus a very sharp craft knife, the surface wood fibres were lightly cut.

With the aid of the straightedge a very fine ballpoint pen was run down each of the cuts. The aim is to lightly groove the wood, not crush the edges of the cut, which results in a jagged line. The ballpoint must be dry and the ink cartridge is, of course, cut off and discarded before use.

Before the decks were laid the hull was painted and finished in the colours of T & J Brocklebank, which thankfully did not include the painted ports style.

I am fortunate to have a copy of a wonderful painting of the *Sindia* by the well-known marine artist H. Neville-Cummings, painted in 1888 at the time of her first voyage. I also have a beautiful copy of a work by an Indian artist – Lai Singh of Calcutta – painted in 1888 at the time of the ship's first arrival at that port.

The slightly different approaches to the same subject by two very talented artists at two ends of the earth is most interesting and both provide a wealth of deck and rigging detail, plus the vitally important hull colours. Only flat finish paints were used and the entire hull was hand-painted using brushes only. Airbrushes are not for me.

Below: The completed model. It is 10ft 6in long overall, 5ft 10in high.

Above: Deck framing completed.

DECKING

Sindia had steel plate decks overlaid with yellow pine planking usually 5in (130mm) wide and 3in (80mm) thick. The seven centre planks on the foredeck were double width – 10in (260mm) – to reduce the number of seams under the heavy weight of the main capstan.

An under deck of 3mm hoop pine three-ply was fitted using a large card template to ensure an exact fit.

The main deck is 7ft 8in (2337mm) long and is over-planked with individually laid Kauri planks. The planks are fastened with Araldite mixed with satin finish black paint. Any surplus can be scraped off when half cured. The planking is then lightly sanded with fine paper and rubbed down with soft steel wool, giving a slightly blurred line. Razor sharp black deck seams look fine on a millionaire's yacht, but are quite out of place on a model of a cargo-carrying square-rigger. It was necessary to plank the entire main deck first as it extends fore and aft under both the fore and poop decks. The main deck ends are unreachable once the other two decks are fitted in place.

The planking of the fore and poop is laid in the same way, but the plank ends are joggled into the curved margin planks.

Deck details – or the lack of them – are one of the yard-sticks by which a model may be judged. Nothing should be left off if scale credibility is to be achieved. The theory that many fittings are too flimsy for a working model or are likely to get in the way is, in my opinion, just not a valid excuse.

FOREDECK FITTINGS

The spike bowsprit was an I-section girder with a steel plate covering. It was flat for its entire underside length, the curves being restricted to its top and sides, giving it a slightly hump-backed look. Two metal jackstays run along the top port and starboard sides supporting wide stirrups that carry footropes for the entire length of the bowsprit.

The inner and outer bobstays are long steel rods, not the more usual chain, while the side stays are steel wire.

Right up forward at the apex of the deck are the large double sheave fairleads required for mooring ropes. Immediately behind is a heavy wood, freestanding belaying pin rack with massive turned supports. Brass belaying sheaves are fitted into the base of each leg.

The foredeck has a total of eight bollards, twenty-four ringbolts and, situated at the ladders leading down to the main deck, two further single sheave fairleads.

The main capstan, mounted in the centre of the deck, is complete with a ring of six pawls on a slotted ring base, tapered and curved whelps and a cap square slotted to accommodate the capstan bars, a double rack of which extends along the rail at the break of the deck.

Two anchors are stowed midway down on each side of the

Above: Starboard side view. The lens of the port and starboard copper lamps are the only plastic items in the model.

deck. One is bedded down into blocks with chain gripes, the other hangs over the side, held by the anchor release gear. Both anchors are hand-cut and filed to shape from brass stock.

Fitted alongside the anchors are scale, working replicas of the original anchor release gear, detailed drawings of which can be found in Harold Underhill's book *Deep-water Sail*.

Using this gear and by literally pulling the pin each anchor can be dropped overside as on the original vessel. The screw collars on the removable guardrail section are reproduced for the sake of scale accuracy. The ship's bell with white bell rope is suspended from a curved wooden arm at the break of the deck.

The foredeck deck fittings are completed with two tall ventilators positioned right at the rear of the deck just in front of the two capstan bar racks. Both extend down through the foredeck to the main deck extension below. The

Above: Break of forecastle. Note anchor windlass just visible under deck and the main ventilators passing through two decks, hand-carved from white beech and painted.

bases are located just each side of the anchor windlass.

Hand-carved from white beech, the five main ventilators were undoubtedly the most difficult parts to make on the entire model. Carving the cowls to get exactly the same shape and then hollowing them out to $^1/_{16}$in (1.5mm) thickness was a test of both a steady hand and much patience. The vertical stems are hollow up into the cowls. Three were scrapped during the making due to my taking the hollowing out process too far. All are fitted with grab handles, turned brass bases, and were painted white, with the inside of the cowls red.

THE MAIN DECK

At this point the main deck extends forward and under the foredeck and all the detail in that area had to be completed and painted before the foredeck was fitted. The fittings include entry doors to the crews' quarters, each equipped with non-working door hinges and handles, along with brass portholes and the port and starboard heads for the use of the crew. The whole area is U-shaped with an open space in the centre directly under the foredeck.

Filling this space is the anchor windlass, a massive piece of deck machinery consisting of eighty-eight separate hand-made parts including side webs, frame, chain gypsies, drums, heavy cast gear wheels, brake drums with shoes and brass control wheels and rods.

A heavy vertical shaft is mounted front centre, driving the main capstan mounted on the foredeck overhead. At the base of the shaft a two-part bevel gear transmits the drive from horizontal to vertical. The windlass took three months to construct and is entirely hand built. All the gear wheels are cut from hardwood blanks, with individual filed teeth. Each gypsy is hand-shaped with two matching and opposing faces.

Stud link anchor chain is fastened into the inboard end of

Above: Forward deckhouse with scale 24ft double-ended lifeboat. Donkey engine boiler on lower left of skylight and galley exhaust.

the hawse pipes, led over the gypsys and down into the spurling pipes on the way to the chain locker.

Mounted on the inside of the bulwarks and running port and starboard for the entire length of the main deck is the main rail or pin rail, supported every 3in (80mm) by an angled steel stanchion.

The main rail carries the bulk of the 234 belaying pins fitted to the model, with others set into the fife rails and spider bands.

A small fore hatch is placed just forward of the foremast. Like the other three hatches it has a tarpaulin-covered, removable hatch cover with side battens held in place with brass cleats. Ten ringbolts are spaced around the base.

Between the hatch and the mast sits a cargo windlass of the period complete with drums, rollers, brakes, brake control wheel and drum control levers. Out on the port side is an extension shaft mounted on a heavy A-frame to support the gypsy needed to carry the chain messenger drive forward

to the anchor windlass.

The foremast is the next major item, surrounded on three sides by three free-standing heavy wooden fife rails mounted on sturdy turned wooden supports.

Each rail carries six belaying pins. A spider band with a further eight belaying pins encircles the mast just above a lug band.

A set of bollards is situated each side of the deck just abaft the two forecastle ladders and two more are behind the fife rails. A freestanding set of bilge pumps is mounted just in front of the forward deckhouse. Built up from brass rod, tube and wire they can be hand operated or power driven by the chain messenger.

The foredeck house is the next major fitting. All three deckhouses are built in the form of a removable cap which fits closely over four internal sides and ends that extend up inside to deckhead height, making this entry point to the interior of the hull completely watertight.

The deckhouse is painted white with panelled sides and ends. Doors have non-working hinges and handles, and each door has a scribed brass kick plate on the coaming below it.

Grab rails are fitted to all four sides.

The planked roof of the house supports the galley smoke exhaust along with a standard six-window skylight with brass safety bars. At the aft end of the house the stationary steam engine boiler stands up out of the decking topped by the exhaust funnel. The boiler is built of wood overlaid with a skin of shellac-coated thin cardboard plates, each plate overlapping the next as on the original. Small details such as this are important. It is not enough to fit a big black tube to represent a boiler.

Riveted plate seams are marked out by the use of fine brass nail heads. Two wide grey-painted steel doors occupy much of the back of the house covering the entrance to the engine room and boiler house. A vertical ladder giving access to the roof is placed at the rear port side.

Below: Main deck looking forward, The double grey doors are the entrance to the boiler house and steam donkey engine main pumps can be seen at the extreme lower left.

Two scale 24ft (7.5m) double-ended lifeboats are carried port and starboard on double skids with open slat-type (sparred) decking each side of each boat.

The boats rest in hinged crutches and are secured by rope gripes lashed down to ringbolts.

Each boat was built upside down replicating the original method of clinker-planked construction, and internal construction features include stringers, frames, thwarts, hooks, knees, spreaders, bottom boards and double sheer strakes.

The sheer strake pads are drilled out and brass bushed to take the rowlock spigots.

Each boat is equipped with six oars. The blades are tapered and curved with the aid of a pressure jig, designed and built by myself, plus one slightly longer steering oar, rudder with separate tiller bar, mast, lugsail yard and bailer.

A ringbolt is fitted to the stem post. Attached to this is a 19in (48.5mm) length of 0.7mm hemp rope. The original carried a 55ft (17.5m) length of grass line.

The large main hatch occupies the deck space behind the

house, while a cargo windlass is positioned directly behind the hatch.

One of three identical units, the windlass is mounted on two side webs cut from five-ply. The filigree cast design was filed out with the aid of a rat-tail and fine triangular files. Equipped with drums, rollers, gear wheels, roller-change levers and brake drums with control wheels, they impart an air of realism to the deck fittings.

Surrounded on three sides by a heavy U-shaped fife rail the main mast is a noticeable feature.

Carried right across the fife rail just behind the mast is another set of pumps – the standard up and down cylinder and piston type with two flywheels. These could be operated by hand or chain drive.

A spider band holding eight belaying pins rings the mast along with a lug band. A further eighteen belaying pins fit on the three-sided fife rail. All of the heavy turned fife rail supports are pierced at their bases for a brass sheave used for belaying purposes.

Positioned on the deck behind the pump and inside the arc of the fife rail is the cylindrical header tank for the main freshwater tank below. A hand-operated brass pump is mounted on the rear fife rail for dispensing the daily freshwater ration from the main tank.

Standing clear on the deck and directly in front of the main deckhouse is a single tall cowl ventilator.

A major fitting, the large main deckhouse measures 11in (276mm) long and 5in (126mm) wide. It occupies the centre of the main deck and is painted white with four panelled sides and a planked roof. Grab rails run the full length of each side.

Roof fittings are sparse; only a pair of box-type double sheaves, a double bollard, six ringbolts and a large six-window skylight, the glass of which is protected by brass safety bars. On each side of the deckhouse, mounted on brass and wooden boat skids, is a pair of 22ft (6.9m) transom stern lifeboats.

The two boats are built and fitted out exactly the same as the double-enders previously described. The only difference is that these two can be lowered into the water alongside using the pair of fully working radial arm davits.

The boat chocks are hinged, as were the originals, and fold outwards, allowing the boats a neat sideways exit from the chocks.

Above: Forward view of main deckhouse. The lifeboats can be launched overside using the working davits.

A vertical ladder for roof access is fitted to the rear port side of the house. Twelve brass portholes complete the unit.

On the main house the port side carries three supporting rollers for the long length of the chain messenger drive. No safety guards were fitted.

Another cargo windlass is bolted behind the house. On the port side is an extension arm carrying a gypsy for the chain drive. The whole assembly is mounted on a sturdy A-frame.

Another tarpaulin-covered hatch comes next, followed by the mizzen mast which is flanked by two flat-top deck capstans and freestanding fife rails on three sides.

As usual the capstans are mounted on a circular slotted ring base with pawls, while the upper drumhead is square slotted to take the capstan bars, two racks of which fit across the front face of the aft deckhouse; eight bars in all.

On the inside of both capstans the deck is laid out with twin half circles of wooden cleats, one inside the other. The outer ring has twenty cleats; the inner one has twelve.

This was to provide the crew with a grip on the deck when the capstans were in use. Rubber sea boots were unknown in the nineteenth century. The crews' boots were made of leather with wood-cleat soles. They didn't give much grip on a wet wooden deck, hence the double pattern of cleats.

The fife rails and spider bands are of the usual pattern.

Next in line is the aft deckhouse of the same design and layout as the others. However, this one has three panelled doors on the aft end.

Right: Model and trailer together weigh just over 400lb.

The planked top of this house carries two mushroom ventilators, eight ringbolts and a beautiful wood-sheathed and brassbound standard compass. The compass bowl is hollowed out and fitted with a brass-ringed glass face. Clearly visible inside the bowl is a properly marked compass card.

A quadrangle sphere is mounted on each side of the bowl for magnetic compass correction, and a rope walkway leads up to the instrument from the edge of the house.

Built of brass, a replica of a three-section demountable flying bridge leads across to the poop deck from the aft end of the house. A rope guardrail is rigged on each side.

It was necessary to dismantle the bridge while in port so cargo could be worked out of the small booby hatch below.

The model is built in three sections to accurately replicate the original ship.

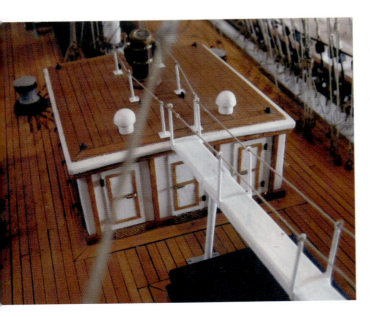

Above: The removable after deckhouse, looking forward. Remountable flying bridge to poop. Note brassbound standard compass complete with compass card in brass bowl.

Above: Recessed break of the poop. Jigger mast passes through both decks. After hatch is removable, as is flying bridge.

THE POOP DECK

This deck is entirely surrounded by white-painted brass rails, fitted with a wooden capping rail, totalling 5ft (1.52m) in length. I used the following method to assemble the rails.

First, an exact copy of the poop deck was prepared from a piece of expendable chipboard. Thin plywood templates of the curved covering boards surrounding the deck were cut to shape, marked out and drilled to accommodate the vertical rail supports. The success of this job depends on the very accurate marking out and drilling of the holes. Errors cannot be rectified later. Using the templates, the poop deck covering boards and the chipboard replica were drilled out so each was an exact copy of the other.

The brass rod rails were cut to size and soldered together in situ on the chipboard replica. Alligator clips held the rail together during the soldering process.

A small plate ¼in square (6mm) was fitted to each upright as a base with the end of the upright protruding ¼in below.

The small plates, although thin, are easy to prepare in quantity if produced in reverse. Make the holes for the uprights first, then cut the plates to shape around them. A strip of thin brass is marked with the squares and the centre punched for the drill. Once the holes are drilled, they can be cut into squares.

If cut into small squares first they will always curl or distort when drilled. As about 100 were required, a quick mass production method was needed.

Prior to fitting the wooden cap rail, the assembled unit was painted white. The cap rail was built up using the covering board template as the cap is an exact duplicate at the top of the rail as it is at deck level below. The complete unit was then lifted off the chipboard replica and dropped into place on the deck. Thanks to accurate marking out and drilling the railing fitted precisely into place. If it does not fit into place first time, the only alternative is to start again from scratch.

The poop deck is 22in (558mm) long and 14in (355mm) wide, providing plenty of space for deck fittings.

First is the jigger or fourth mast that runs right through the poop deck into the recessed area of the main deck below.

As usual, at poop deck level, the mast carries a spider band with eight belaying pins, plus a heavier mast band supporting the spanker boom gooseneck. Up against the rail, port and starboard, are two freestanding belaying pin racks, each mounted on four sturdy, turned pillars.

Immediately behind the mast is the main companionway leading down into the interior of the ship. Panelled, it has two hinged swing doors and a sliding roof.

Fitted with six windows protected by brass safety bars, a large skylight sits in front of a small, round top warping capstan. This is of standard pattern with slotted ring base, four pawls, the barrel fitted with tapered and curved whelps.

On either side of the deck are two freestanding capstan bar racks, each holding four bars.

A large square ventilation trunk is placed aft of the capstan. The roof opens up on each side and is equipped with heavy brass roof hinges.

Two more cowl ventilators stand each side of the trunk.

Next is the binnacle; like the standard compass it is brass bound with wooden sheathing. Again the glass-fronted brass bowl has a floating compass card.

The wheel box and steering wheel are the last major fit-

tings. The wheel was built up in segments with separate
spokes mounted on a central brass-faced hub.

The centre spoke, in the midship position following tradition, is of brass. The spokes are lathe-turned, the outer wheel
ring is made up from four separate pieces. Not easy to make,
but the finished article repays the effort.

The panelled wheel box is of the usual design with a
brass-hinged lid top. Placed each side are wood grating seats.
Usually curved half-violin shapes were supplied, but for
reasons unknown Harland & Wolff-built ships always had
wheel box seats in a plain right-angle triangle design, not a
curve in sight – it became a company trademark.

Two strongly built helmsman's stools fit each side of the
wheel and four white lifebelts are lashed outside the rail.

Sixteen ringbolts, nine bollards and four fair leads complete the range of fittings.

Right forward on the deck, across the break of the poop
between the main deck ladders, are two deck bucket racks.
Each holds four buckets fitted with rope handles.

Below: Scale 24ft double-ended lifeboat on forward deckhouse.
Note pads on sheerstrake, drilled and bushed to accept rowlocks.

RIGGING THE MODEL

The rigging of this model is of such complexity that attempting to describe the subject in any great detail could easily run
to a small book.

The model has a total of just over 1,600ft (48.8m) of rope
rigging, all of it made on my monorail-based 48ft (14.78m)
long ropewalk. Hemp ringing cord sourced from Italy forms
the basis of the rope. The rope is three-strand, right-hand
hawser-laid in a variety of sizes ranging from 0.75mm

Above: Main shrouds and backstays, starboard side. Note hinged washport at lower left.

Above: View of the starboard side from foremast level. Alternate single and double-hinged washports. The ship was not painted with a waterline, just a junction of two courses.

through to 3mm. Four-strand and waterlaid rope can be made if necessary. For the sake of scale accuracy it is vital that properly made rope is used, not the rigging cord sold in model shops which when used on a model looks little better than string.

Harold Underhill's classic tome *Masting and Rigging the Clipper Ship and Ocean Carrier* is more than merely an aid, it is a necessity when rigging a very complex model such as this.

Right from the start the decision was made to rig the model exactly as the original. The option of radio control was never considered, as fitting 32 sails with exact scale rigging cannot be achieved if radio control rigging is installed. It is just technically impossible and, for me, scale accuracy is paramount.

The masts and yards are made of white beech, reduced to sixteen sides and finished off with sandpaper and a model-maker's spokeshave tool.

Sindia was built with steel masts and yards. The lower masts and topmasts were in one piece, so only the topgallant masts needed doublings.

Each mast was built separately as a complete assembly, lower and topmasts in one piece, topgallants fitted into doublings and two sets of tops on each mast. The mast bands (complete with lugs and eyes), all yard cranes, trusses and parrells were fashioned from brass rod, wire and strip, and were attached to each mast prior to stepping the mast unit into the hull. Stepping each mast involved a plumb bob and a mast rake gauge that I designed, details of which appear in *Model Shipwright 105*.

A brass sheave was let into the squared heel of the topgallant mast for hoisting and lowering purposes and the mast itself fitted through hard brass caps and sat squarely on the fid. Each topgallant carries a truck, sheaved for flag halliards, at its apex.

The masts were rigged with shrouds, backstays and

Right: Topmast shrouds and back stays. Note upper left chain halliard and gin block.

futtock shrouds after they were stepped.

One advantage of building very large models is that much of the rigging, in fact almost all, can be fitted after the masts are in position. The shrouds and backstays are attached to the hull and inner bulwarks with chainplates and Harland & Wolff's own patent design rigging screws, which were only seen on ships built by them.

Compared to the simple turn-buckle, bottle-screw types, they are complicated. Each comprises seven separate parts plus three-part chainplates. As there are ninety-six of them it involves a total of 1056 hand-made parts. A jig was designed and built, and a production line set up – nine weeks later the job was done. They are quite unique and add greatly to the scale appearance. Whether they were more efficient than the more standard type is, I imagine, open to debate.

Before they are slung on the masts, the yards are completed with jackstays on the top surface, plus wire stirrups supporting the foot ropes.

Yardarm bands with lugs and eyes are placed at each yard end and a brass sheave is slotted into the yardarm for the square sail sheets. Circular fairleads are set into the underside of the yard to channel the sheets to the large triangular

Below: View forward of Poop Deck. Capstan bar racks are visible port and starboard. Also note ventilation trunk and binnacle lower left. The ventilators were hand carved from solid wood blocks. Skylight and main companion way at centre.

block at the underside centre of the yard and then down through fairleads to belaying pins at deck level.

Using the sliding parrels of the upper topsails, upper topgallant and royal yards, the three yards can be hoisted up or lowered down the mast using the halliards. The chain halliards run through sheave slots let into the masts.

The fore main and mizzen plus jigger mast stays are rigged in the conventional manner, but her lower and topmast stays are doubled, separating just above bulwark level and finally made fast to heavy metal thimbles bolted to the deck on each side of the mast.

All square sails are fully rigged with clew lines, bunt lines, sheets, down hauls, reef tackles, clew garnets on the courses, leech lines, tacks and lazy tacks, and reef points.

Bunt lines are channelled up the front face of the sail by

means of small rope thimbles, two for each bunt line, and then passed through the bunt line blocks on the jackstay.

Fore and aft sails are equipped with outhauls and downhauls which are carried through wire lizards hanked to the stays. Port and starboard stays complete the rig, while the spanker has both outhauls and downhauls plus three brails each side.

Cotton japara cloth is used for the sails which is, I believe, the closest scale version of the nineteenth century flax canvas and is off-white in colour.

The seams of the 24in (610mm) wide sail cloths are marked out in soft pencil and double sewn as are all sail seams. Single line stitching is not convincing. Reef bands and bunt line

Below: Brass spreader and top gallant doubling. Yards can be hoisted and lowered using working halliards.

Below: The 81in long detachable sailing keel is packed with eight cast lead ingots internally. The total loaded weight is 246lb (111.8kg). Note the four long holding bolts which fit up through *Sindia*'s hull up to deck level.

cloths are added and each sail was roped with bolt ropes to provide stiffening to the hems. Bolt ropes are only attached to the port side of the fore and aft sails, never the starboard side, and are only fitted on the rear side of square sails.

In all *Sindia* carries just over 1,600ft (480m) of rope rigging. This total does not include the stainless steel wire shrouds and back stays.

She is equipped with 362 single, double and triple sheave blocks in total plus 20ft (6m) of both plain and stud link chain, all hand-made.

The red ensign and Brocklebank's blue and white house flag were cut from a fine cotton handkerchief. Painted with a fine point brush and thermofixable dyes, a very realistic result can be obtained. Painted paper flags are too stiff.

Below: Two chain halliards visible on left side. The ship carries a total of 1,668ft of homemade hemp rigging of various sizes, ranging from 0.75mm to 3mm diameter.

LAUNCHING THE MODEL

This was a step-by-step team effort, involving four strong young men and myself – I am neither young nor strong!

As the model is so big and liable to damage, she has to be transported in a felt-lined carrying cradle, equipped with lifting side bars. She was driven to the lakeside in a three-ton closed truck.

A six-wheeled, 7ft (2.15m) long launching trailer was then loaded with the empty sailing keel, which was in turn weighted down with eight 30lb (13.6kg) cast lead ingots plus one 7lb (3.2kg) tube ingot.

Once filled with lead blocks it is not possible to lift the keel so, with the aid of two lifting cradles, the model was removed from the carrying cradle and lowered down onto the four vertical steel shafts which run through the keel and the ship.

Below: Model mounted on keel and six-wheeled launch trailer. Non-scale sailing rudder fitted to stern end of keel.

Above: Afloat for the first time. Down by the stern – 6lb extra ballast aft as she tends to bury her head under sail; all square rig models do. Extra stern ballast ensures that she sails upright and level.

Guided up into the four tubes leading through the hull, they were then tightened down on to the upper keel by four heavy nuts and washers, screwed down firmly with a tube spanner. The soft full-length rubber cap on top of the keel ensured a firm junction with the hull.

The whole heavy assembly – trailer, keel and model weighing over 400lb (181.8kg) – was then launched into the water. Once the water was deep enough the model just floated off the trailer, which by then was completely submerged. The procedure is reversed for recovering the model.

Experience with two previous square rig models convinces me they sail best with the wind on either quarter. They will never match a fore and aft rig model for handiness afloat.

Sindia was trimmed just down by the stern as square rig models tend to bury their head and swerve upwind if hit by a strong gust. This trim and her long keel kept her quite steady.

Sindia made her first voyage on 6 January 2010 at Wentworth Falls Lake, a fresh water lake located in the Blue Mountains 62 miles (96km) west of Sydney. My very dear granddaughter Rachel Hunt, aged 12, performed the naming ceremony with grace and charm.

The day was sunny with an 8–12mph (12–19kph) breeze perfect for sailing. She looked both imposing and beautiful as she surged along steady as a rock with only a slight heel. She was the epitome of the beauty of sail.

The long, deep keel proved its worth. She held a straight course, free sailing, no rolling or pitching. The waves ran down her sides as she cut through them like the real thing, the massive weight kept her steady, no chance of bobbing about.

Our inflatable chase boat was skippered by my son Anthony, with my son-in-law Houston Spencer filling the role of cameraman. I was present only as an interested observer! We circled *Sindia* several times and Houston captured some superb action shots.

I would estimate *Sindia* was sailing at approximately 6 knots. As the electric-driven inflatable would only do 8–9 knots, thank heavens the wind stayed light! Seeing her riding the waves convinced me that the time she took to build – 9,208 hours over 14 years – was a worthwhile investment.

I now have three large, working scale model square-riggers – a unique fleet in Australia. A fourth is already building, the Blackwall frigate *Dunbar*. A smaller model, she will only be 8ft 1in (2.4m) long, a three-mast full rigger with single topsail and top gallants.

ACKNOWLEDGEMENTS

I am deeply in debt to the late Thomas Adams of Linwood, New Jersey, USA, who with typical American generosity poured a flood of *Sindia* wreck memorabilia including original photos dating from 1901, newspaper cuttings, history and help in every way down upon me.

Thanks to the editor and former publisher of *Windling World* magazine Mark Steele of Auckland, New Zealand, for his enthusiastic support and publicity of my activities over a long, long period of years.

Unforgettable is my dear wife Ruth and my supportive family for their unflagging backup and encouragement over such a lengthy and seemingly endless project.

Thanks also to the launch team – my son Anthony, son-in-law Houston Spencer, and keen volunteers Ronnie Fortune and Wayne Pratt – who braved the cold waters of the deep lake. Without them the first voyage just would not have happened. Not forgetting a host of friends and supporters, some of who drove over 250km to be present at what did not turn out to be a fiasco.

Above: A following wind showcases the beauty of square rig. Not an everyday sight.

Below: The long keel kept her steady. No head burying here.

The Aviation Cruiser *Kïev*

BUILDING A SOVIET WARSHIP

by Dave Wooley

ORIGINS OF THE *KIEV*

The *Kïev* was not an aircraft carrier in the traditional sense but a hybrid similar in respects to the Royal Navy's *Invincible* class. Interestingly, the original definition for the *Invincible* was through-deck cruiser, a political euphemism of the time. Such a euphemism was used to enable the Kiev to transit the Bosporus, thereby avoiding the direct wording of the 1936 Montreux Treaty forbidding the passage of aircraft carriers.

Kïev was launched at Nikolaev shipyard on the Black Sea in December 1972 and entered service with the Northern

Below: *Kïev* underway.

Above: Seen for the first time, a colour picture of the forward bridge area. SS-N-12 launch tubes can be seen along with the SA-N-3 twin arm launcher in its loading position.

Above: A starboard side view of the superstructure on *Kiev*.

Above: The Soviet answer to the Harrier VTOL fighter, the Yak 38 Forger A.

Fleet in May of 1975. The class consisted of *Minsk*, *Novorossiysk* and *Gorshkov*. *Kiev* displaced over 42,000 tons and was almost 274m in length overall with a beam of 48m. Unlike the carriers of the United States Navy which formed part of an integrated battle group, *Kiev* could operate independently, and was primarily tasked with anti-submarine warfare. A diverse array of weapons gave *Kiev* the flexibility no other carrier possessed.

AIR DEFENCE

This arsenal contained both conventional and nuclear missiles. On the conventional side *Kiev* had a formidable air defence array, which consisted of the AK630, a multi-barrel Gatling type close-in weapons system using a local tracking system call Bass Tilt. She also boasted a retractable SA-N-4 intermediate Surface to Air Missile (SAM) system and the long range SA-N-3 (Goblet) SAM fired from the twin arm launchers both fore and aft of the superstructure.

The effectiveness of the Yak 38 as a viable aircraft for combat air patrol and defence was a more debatable asset. Although possessing deficiencies in range and payload the Yak 38 was capable of carrying various air defence weapons though had limited ground attack capability. Despite possessing a higher top end performance than its NATO counterpart, the Harrier, it never matched the latter, particularly in engine reliability and it was not a popular aircraft amongst Soviet pilots. The Yak 38 in all its designations was never really put to the test in air combat other than spells assisting Soviet ground forces in Afghanistan in the 1980s. Also included in this inventory of anti-air warfare (AAW) was a more conventional weapons system, the two twin 76.2mm guns mounted fore and aft of the superstructure.

ANTI-SUBMARINE WARFARE

Kiev was fitted with an array of anti-submarine warfare (ASW) weapons. At the core of this prime task was the KA 25

Above: The original GRP hull was not a good representation of *Kiev* and had to be extensively rebuilt.

Hormone B capable of deploying dipping sonar and delivering torpedoes and depth charges. Forward on the forecastle was an array of ASW weapons. First was the multi-barrel RBU 6000 launcher. Its rockets had an effective range of 4000m to a depth of 1000m. Abaft of the RBU was the twin arm launcher for the long range nuclear-tipped Fras-1 missile, which was guided to target by the use of bow mounted sonar or variable depth sonar (VDS) which could be deployed from the stern.

Unusual for any carrier in modern times *Kiev* was fitted with 2 quintuple banks of 533mm torpedo tubes housed forward behind concealed doors above the water line. It could be argued that their usefulness was limited and having seen pictures of these tubes and their location in the ship, the space was indeed wasted.

ANTI-SHIP

During the Cold War *Kiev* was more than just a carrier or ASW platform. Housed in eight launch tubes forward was one of the most formidable weapons carried by *Kiev*: the long range SS-N-12 Bazalt anti-ship missile. During the period of the Cold War when *Kiev* was deployed at sea it was a constant

source of speculation as to the exact purpose of such a weapon system that could deploy either a conventional or nuclear warhead. From what I have learned its purpose was either to take out United States Navy carriers or obliterate NATO battle groups.

Kiev, although much maligned, did pose a significant threat to NATO navies but thankfully its potential was not put to the test. As a foot note *Kiev* was sold to China in 2004 and converted to a military theme park in Tianjin. *Minsk* was sold to a China based consortium and is now a theme park in Shenzhen province. *Novorossiysk* was scrapped whilst the *Gorshkov* was sold to India, modernized in Russia and is soon to enter service as the carrier IN *Vikramaditya*.

THE 1:144 SCALE MODEL

My interest in the Soviet Navy goes back some years after seeing various copies of the magazine *Recognition*, a military publication that was circulated around RAF establishments back in the 1960s, which included pictures of Soviet warships of the day. After completing a 1:100 scale model of the cruiser *Sverdlov* in 1989 followed by the helicopter cruiser *Moskva* in 1:128 scale in 1994, I made a firm decision that at some point in the future my next project would be the aviation cruiser *Kiev*. Unfortunately, due to the lack of drawings and specific information on the vessel, my interest in building

Above: Access into the interior of the hull had to be carefully planned in order to disguise the deck joint whilst providing maximum space.

a model would remain on the back burner for a considerable length of time.

In 1999, however, I had a visit from a Russian model maker friend who had acquired a set of unfinished drawings of the carrier *Kiev*. The general arrangement drawing was relatively basic but other sheets contained the lines and body plan essential if the model was to become reality. However the essential ingredient, information and on board pictures, remained incomplete and out of reach. Thus, the prime task before construction could begin was to accumulate as much information as possible; a task which was initially far more difficult than I had expected. All of this was to change significantly (but more on that later).

In 2003, whilst visiting Europe's largest model festival, the Intermodellbau in Dortmund, an unexpected opportunity arose that was to affect the entire direction of the *Kiev* project. During one of the evening discussions following a day's trek amongst the exhibits friends mentioned that a vendor had a GRP hull of the carrier *Kiev*.

I thought, 'nothing ventured, nothing gained', and the following day I made an early beeline to check out this report. Sure enough this vendor had a single hull, which by a

quirk of fate was manufactured in Kiev in the Ukraine to a scale of 1:144. On initial inspection it appeared reasonably acceptable so a decision was made there and then to purchase this hull.

On arrival back in the UK the first job was to assess just what I had bought. Unfortunately, any resemblance to the *Kiev* was coincidental. Thus the box and the hull remained tucked away for the next 3 years. I could not make a decision as to what to do, either to break it up or think the unthinkable and try to reconstruct a GRP hull. Most of my models to date had been scratch built from the keel up so the very idea of the reconstruction of a far from accurate hull was an anathema to me. Given the circumstances and the long gestation period of this project I made the decision to make the best of what I had and reconstruct the hull.

THE HULL AND ENGINEERING

I spent the next three months identifying the inaccuracies and then how they would be corrected. First and foremost parts of the forward section of the hull had to be removed and, with the aid of patterns lifted from the drawing, reformed to the correct shape. This involved internal supports and re-building the hull with GRP and fillers.

Although the general configuration was free from any major keel line twist the entire flight deck overhang was

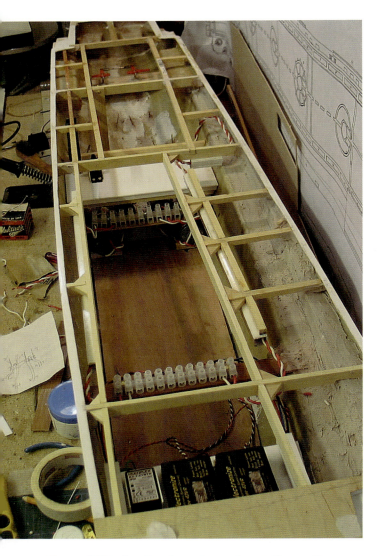

Above: All the electrics, electronic speed controllers, radio receiver, rudder servo, linkages and batteries could be easily fitted or removed.

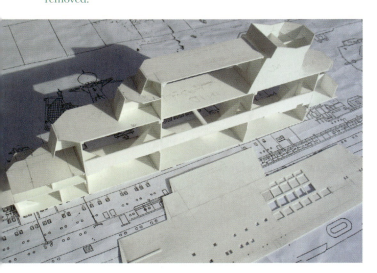

Above: The basic internal framework for the superstructure.

twisted and was far from the correct size or shape. Using a combination of the body plan and profile, plus a number of photos showing the port side overhang work, I rebuilt this, but the work was painstaking and slow. The subsequent work involved salvaging what could be salvaged, removing what was unusable but inevitably having to rebuild the entire overhang from timber and GRP.

The next step required the reshaping of the forward sponsons. These would eventually support the AK 630 close-in weapons system and associated tracking radar. (The complex shape is clearly visible in the first picture). In retrospect, a scratch built hull would have been the easier option but I considered the GRP option a challenge and ultimately worth the effort.

FLIGHT DECKS

Although the hull for *Kiev* is 1:144 and thus considered a small scale for a working model it retains a significant physical size and, as a working model, due consideration must be given for access into the hull. Here a balance needed to be struck between authenticity of appearance and necessity. It was envisaged that only a section of deck need be removed to allow access for the electrics and batteries, which would also double as ballast.

First and foremost, most of the deck beams at this initial stage of construction had to be laid with these considerations in mind. It was decided that the opening would be on the starboard side where the superstructure will fit. All of my models are essentially 'working' but I try where possible to either limit or disguise any cuts made in the deck that are essential for removing part of that deck. For *Kiev* this required some lateral thinking. The deck has a white broken double line running the length of the flight deck. Here the cut was made that would accurately coincide with this natural break in colour from the green to white. The deck was cut from 1.5mm marine ply.

ELECTRICS AND ELECTRONICS

Unlike a static model, building *Kiev* as a working model requires some thought on how to install all of the internal fittings. Firstly, these included the running gear, shafts, rudders couplings and motors. Secondly, internal linkages to rudders, servos, electronic speed controllers, radio receiver and batteries. I apply the premise that if it could go wrong, it invariably will. Thus, most of the internal fittings are disposed in such a way that all are easily accessible from the single opening.

Also, all the electronic equipment was raised to the highest point possible within the hull; this limits the possibility of any water damage. The need to keep all the cabling directed through common trunking on either side of the hull and marked for identification makes for a tidy and easy to maintain working model. While the planning for the model was underway I had no inkling whether it would sail – something that could only be assessed once completed.

Below: Both fore-and-aft bridge assemblies were constructed to be removable for ease of airbrushing and glazing.

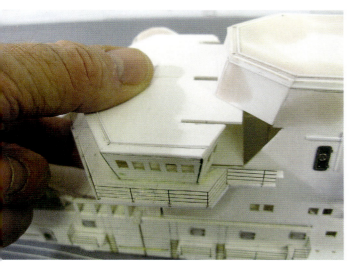

The hull was placed keel up for the installation of the running gear and rudders. The four shafts and A frames were installed with the use of a simple jig, fitted across the hull aft and marked for the height of each shaft at a given point along the hull. This ensured that the angle of the shaft and clearance of each propeller beneath the hull corresponded with the drawing. The two rudders were made from a combination of brass and filler moulded to the correct shape and fitted using a simple jig. This held the rudders in position whilst a temporary bond was made to the rudder post within the hull. When set the jig was removed and a more permanent internal arrangement made.

SUPERSTRUCTURE

For ease of construction and assembly the superstructure was divided into three parts. The foreword section houses the twin arm long range SA-N-3 SAM launcher and blast screens. The centre section comprises the majority of the structure whilst the after section includes the after SA-N-3 launcher and 76.2mm gun housing.

As the majority of the superstructure is designed with

Below: The superstructure is almost entirely constructed from styrene sheet.

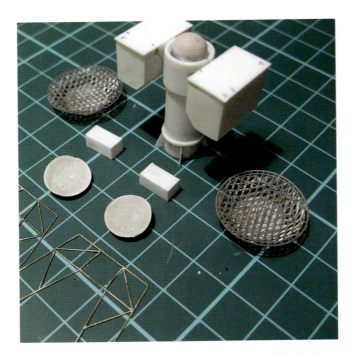

Above: Some of the component parts that make up the 'Head Light' radar.

Above: A completed 'Head Light' Radar array.

sloping sides (a method employed on *Kiev* to limit radar cross-section) it was essential to construct the shape from the inside out. Here, four basic internal vertical inward sloping shapes were lifted from the plan and transferred to a 2.5mm styrene sheet. These were then added to a 2.5mm styrene base with 90 degree triangular supports fitted to each of the vertical sections. These provided firm supports while the horizontal decks were incorporated at each level. Further longitudinal bracings were fitted on either side, adding strength whilst providing an additional surface to which each side of the superstructure could be attached.

It was decided at an early stage to glaze the fore-and-aft bridge areas even at 1:144 scale. To enable this without necessitating major constructional work both fore and after bridge areas needed to be detachable with a removable roof. As a solution each bridge would slot into the superstructure and could be removed for air brushing, replaced and later removed for glazing, thus eliminating the need for the use of an adhesive. Using this method also allowed access for glazing to other internal areas of the upper superstructure.

Essentially, the three sections of the superstructure were built up and various platforms and walkways added including hand rails. It remained essential that the structure could be dissassembled into its three main constituent parts for air brushing and be easily reassembled, this of course included each of the bridge assemblies.

To ensure that the entire superstructure was located into the same position every time location pins were inserted into the base. These also acted as final securing pins when

the time came to fit the superstructure permanently onto the deck.

'HEAD LIGHT' 'C' ILLUMINATOR RADARS

There are a plethora of radar arrays fitted to *Kiev* so unfortunately space does not allow a full and detailed appraisal of the construction of each and every one. A choice was made that best demonstrated some of the constructional details and rationale of Soviet naval radar in general and the 'Head Light' radar in particular.

'Head Light' Radar is NATO code for this type of array, which illustrates certain visual characteristics and functioned as a track and guidance radar for the SA-N-3 surface to air missile system. The basic configuration of four dishes, two large (4m) and two small (1.8m) was to facilitate vertical and horizontal scanning.

Although this is a complex structure I was fortunate to have retained all the information from the building of the ASW helicopter cruiser *Moskva*. This allowed for some fine tuning in the methods applied, improving both the building sequence and the authenticity of the completed array.

To improve both the stages of construction and convey the method of assembly, each and every fitting was reduced to easily identifiable parts, no matter how small.

An example of this approach can be seen with the construction of the 'Head Light' array showing the centre pillar and side boxes, radar dishes and support frame work.

The material of choice was styrene, using two diameters

of styrene tube to form the pillar, styrene sheet for the panniers and smaller control boxes associated with the upper radar dishes. These dishes were also formed from styrene whilst the larger dishes were formed from a combination of photo etch and zinc mesh with litho plate forming the stabilizing panels. All the supporting frame work of .31mm brass was constructed in sections, fitted to a jig and, using a temperature controlled soldering iron, soldered as a single frame.

DECK CRANES

Kiev is equipped with two large heavy lift cranes, one mounted on the starboard side forward, the other to starboard, inboard of the superstructure aft. The former is an enclosed steel frame type crane with two purchase points; one fixed, the other at the head of the jib, with a self adjustable frame and pulley. This was used primarily for reloads of the SS-N-12 anti-ship missile via a specialised loading cradle. The other crane, an open tubular frame type, was used for lifting ordnance and general stores. The construction of the latter is explained first.

The method for the construction of a framework such as

a crane jib was discussed at length by P. C. Coker in his 1972 publication *Building Model Warships*. Both references and illustrations were by the Japanese warship model-maker Kozo Izumi. The principle is both simple and effective.

GENERAL LIFTING CRANE

Whilst a crane jib at 1:144 scale can seem a daunting prospect in any material, soldering together each and every strut of brass rod would seem impossible. Not so. Using a timber former the entire assembly can be soldered together in less than 15 minutes. Preparation is the key.

As no drawing existed for either crane, it became necessary to create a working sketch for both cranes from available information. Using the scale drawing both the left and right sides of the frame were cut to size, laid out and soldered using a high temperature solder and a variable temperature soldering iron with a fine bit.

The next stage involved the construction of a timber

Below: Soldering a complex shape for a crane is made easy with a wooden former.

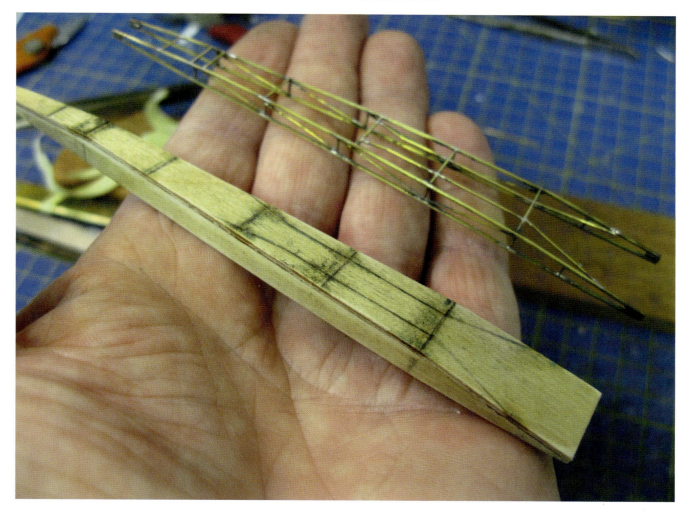

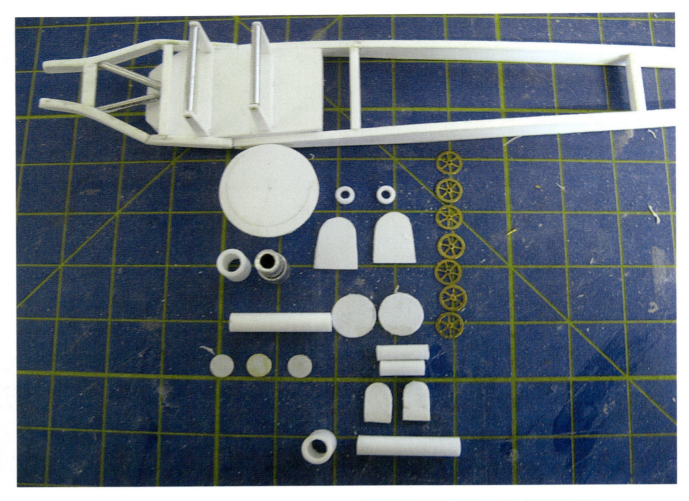

Above: Winch drums and drive motors ready to be fitted to the larger missile handling crane.

former which mirrored the internal shape of the jib. This done, the left and right sides of the jib were taped to the former and soldering each of the top and bottom struts with diagonals could be undertaken comfortably using a low temperature solder. This basic combination of solders was used throughout the assembly of the radar arrays, associated platforms, spars and masts, although paper clips helped as heat sinks. The soldering of photo etch parts was limited to the use of solder paste or cyanoacrylate.

With the entire frame of the jib soldered around the wooden former, all that was required was to withdraw the former from within the frame of the jib.

The next phase of this assembly was to identify the various mechanical parts of the crane mounted on the base, for example drum winches and drive motors. Once done, a simple sketch allowed each of these parts to be constructed and fitted to the base. The jib was added last incorporating the various pulleys along the length of the jib. With the stores crane completed, attention shifted to the larger and slightly more complex missile handling crane.

BAZALT MISSILE HANDLING CRANE

This crane, unlike the one previously discussed, was made in box sections. To replicate this type of assembly a working sketch was generated and styrene sheet and strip styrene formed much of the basic structure. Aluminium tube provided cable supports across the base and supports for the construction of the rear-lifting arm. Although an easier fitting to construct, a greater number of identifiable parts were incorporated. Help in this regard came from unexpected quarters (see acknowledgements).

Once again various diameters of styrene tube provided the winch drums and drive motor casings. To ensure that there was a degree of freedom as to how the crane jib was to be deployed, lifting or stowed, the jib fitting to the mounting was made adjustable by inserting a length of brass rod through the ends of the jib and through the base, in much the same location as the original.

BAZALT SS-N-12 MISSILE LOADING CRADLE

Kiev was fitted with an extensive narrow gauge rail system. This allowed stores and particularly ordnance to be shifted from one end of the ship forward as far as the RBU 6000 multiple ASW rocket launchers to dispersal at aft.

Installation of the track was a simple but a lengthy undertaking and to avoid the problem of repetitious work becoming tedious, a start was made on a number of complex fittings. One of these was known as the Bazalt loading cradle. For all of the period *Kiev* was in service there was speculation in western naval circles as to how the SS-N-12 anti-ship missiles were loaded into the large tubes forward. It was only on rare occasions that the loading cradle was seen aboard *Kiev* at sea, other than that it was assumed loading and unloading of the tubes was undertaken in port.

Thanks to a friend residing in China it was possible for him to get a visit arranged to go aboard the *Kiev*'s sister ship *Minsk*, now a military theme park. Here was a superb opportunity to gain what I had always thought necessary: on board pictures. These included shots of the loading cradle and a veritable gold mine of pictures relating to many other parts of the ship and its fittings. With many detailed shots I now had the information to sketch a drawing.

Unfortunately, the information as to how the Bazalt missiles were loaded into the tubes remained conjecture. Thankfully, however, pictures arrived showing how the tubes were loaded. More importantly, from a modelling point of view, there was a detailed view of the Bazalt missile during the loading process, for what was mounted on the cradle aboard *Minsk* was a very poor mock up of the Bazalt missile.

I had known for some time that the cradle was divided into three separate frames but was unaware of how they functioned. Now that this information was available I was in a position to construct an actual working cradle, having informed myself as to how the upper frame loaded the missile directly into the tube. Also there are a series of tracks running across the deck on which the cradle could move and line up with each tube. This was repeated in a sequence until all the tubes were loaded.

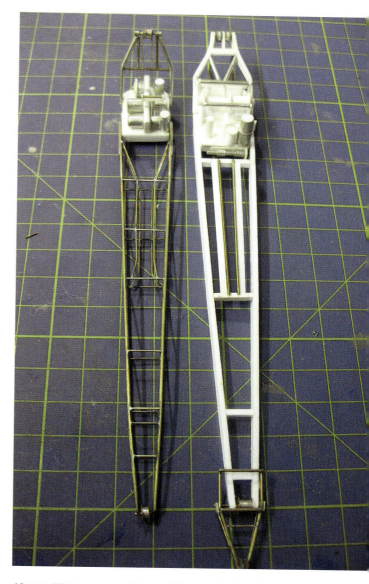

Above: The two types of heavy lift crane fitted to *Kiev*.

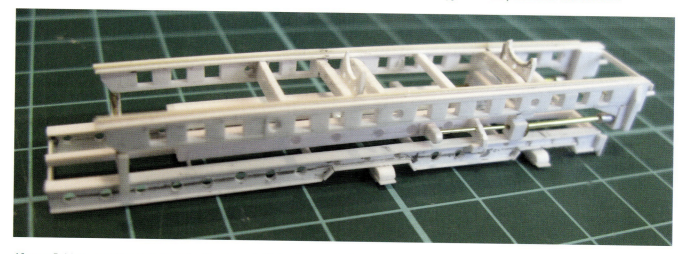

Above: Initially, no information existed for this missile loading cradle but photographs taken on board *Kiev*'s sister *Minsk* made all the difference. A cradle fabricated from styrene was constructed in three separate sections and joined together.

With some knowledge as to the mechanics of the loading operation, work could begin on generating a working drawing and the parts for the cradle.

For ease of construction each level was built separately and assembled to allow the centre frame to move along the lower frame as per the original. The framework for the cradle was constructed entirely from styrene with the drive linkages assembled from 0.41mm brass wire and 1mm OD brass tube. On the original cradle small bogies were fitted to the underside of the bottom frame. These bogies connected with the rails running athwart ships and enabled the entire frame, loaded with missile, to move across the deck to any of the launch tubes.

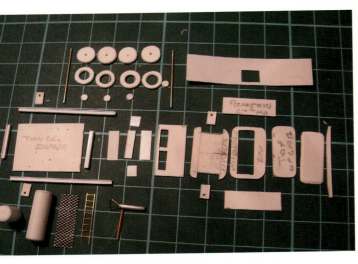

Above: The component parts for the Gazz 66 fire tender arranged ready for assembly.

Above: The completed Gazz fire tender. Compare the size with a Humbrol enamel tinlet.

GAZZ 66 FIRE TENDER

With the Bazalt missile cradle complete, attention shifted to another of the more obscure but necessary additions to the *Kiev*, the Gazz 66 fire tender. As mentioned much of the detail on *Kiev* was indeed obscure if not unknown until I embarked on the construction of this model and none more so than the fire tender. Fly by pictures of *Kiev* showed what looked like a truck parked on the flight deck but no further information existed as to what it was, let alone how it was fitted. An email to a modelling friend that served aboard the *Kiev* back in the early 1980s revealed all. It was an all-purpose utility truck, in Russia the ubiquitous Gazz 66.

This truck was turned out in the thousands and was used extensively throughout the former Soviet Union in civilian as well as military roles. Once again, using pictures of the Gazz, a working sketch was drawn, which included many of the additional parts that were incorporated for fire fighting purposes. A working drawing was made defining all the individual components. This included the body shell, flat bed, axles and wheels, foam generator and monitors.

Construction began with the basics of the body shell connected to the flat bed. This was followed by the axles and the remainder of the cab. The tyres were added and the Gazz was ready to be fitted out with its fire fighting equipment. Only the size and shape of the fire monitor was changed, apart from that the assembly went together well and a reasonable representation of *Kiev*'s foam truck was made. I followed the detail as in the photographs; however, there was a question as to the colour scheme. It was pointed out to me that the entire tender was painted red whilst other reliable sources mentioned that the cab and flat bed were painted buff, with the foam tanks painted red. It could be concluded that both observations might be accurate and represented the Gazz truck at different times in *Kiev*'s career.

AIR GROUP – YAK 38 FORGER A

As mentioned in the initial appraisal of *Kiev* the primary purpose of the Aviation Cruiser was anti-submarine warfare. For this purpose *Kiev* was equipped with the Hormone B ASW helicopter, fitted to carry depth charges and homing torpedoes.

As an extended range air defence component *Kiev* embarked twelve Yak 38 VTOL fighters. Unlike the British Harrier, the Yak 38 was not as successful, having limited lifting/payload capacity and a shorter range.

As with much of this project only basic information existed during the beginning of the build. As the scale was 1:144 it was envisaged that that I would be able to purchase the entire air group in kit form. After two years' fruitless search no such kit existed, so the options were to either scratch build using the 1:96 scale kits as a pattern or order

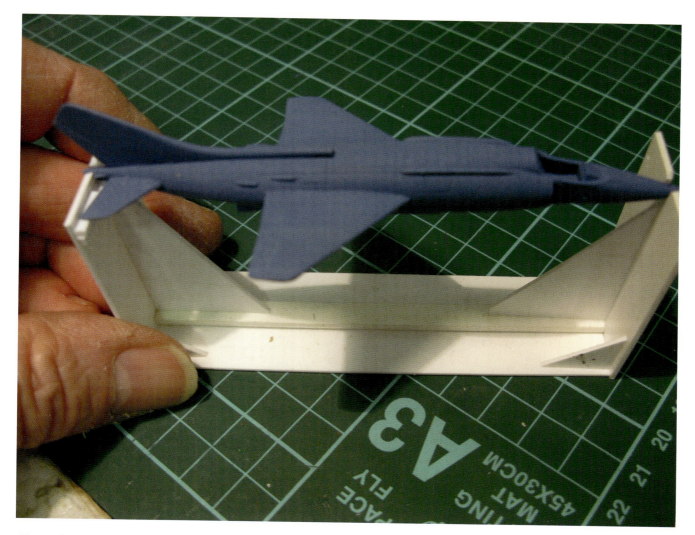

Above: One of twelve bespoke Yak 38 fighters on a custom-built spray jig.

bespoke kits of the entire twelve at considerable cost. Whilst I was deliberating I received a set of drawings of the Hormone B helicopter. This was followed by a drawing of the Yak 38 and very fortuitously a book; *Yakovlev – Yak 36, Yak 38 and Yak 41: The Soviet Jump Jets* published in the UK by Ian Allan. This was indeed a stroke of luck as the book was the definitive work on this type of aircraft. To that was added the flood of pictures I was receiving of detailed shots of the Yak 38 which show the fighter in service aboard *Kiev*.

Eventually a prototype model was produced, but this took so long that the latter avenue of ordering bespoke was decided upon. I contacted Nostalgic Plastics in the US who specialize in 1:144 aviation models. Via a manufacturer in China they undertook to supply twelve Yak 38s to my specifications. They duly arrived and I was not disappointed. The quality of the mouldings was excellent. The model came complete with ejector seats and a clear canopy, which was top of my list of essentials.

Though the parts consisted of fuselage, flying surfaces, undercarriage, cockpit detail, external stores pylons, rocket pods and canopy; building the models was relatively easy as I knew each and every part. Additional parts that needed to be made were undercarriage and lift exhaust doors and more importantly the suction relief door above the lift engine intake scoop to the rear of the canopy.

Assembly of all the parts was undertaken much like a production line and twelve basic Yak 38s were soon ready for the next phase: airbrushing.

AIRBRUSHING THE YAK 38S

Building a very small model is one hurdle but painting it is quite another. My preference throughout the build of *Kiev* has either been spray or airbrush painting with only the very small items such as tyres relying exclusively on the brush. Each assembled Yak 38 was given a matt blue undercoat, which proved to be ideal for the type and shade of blue that was to follow. As a point of interest White Ensign Models (a well established company specializing in authentic paints,

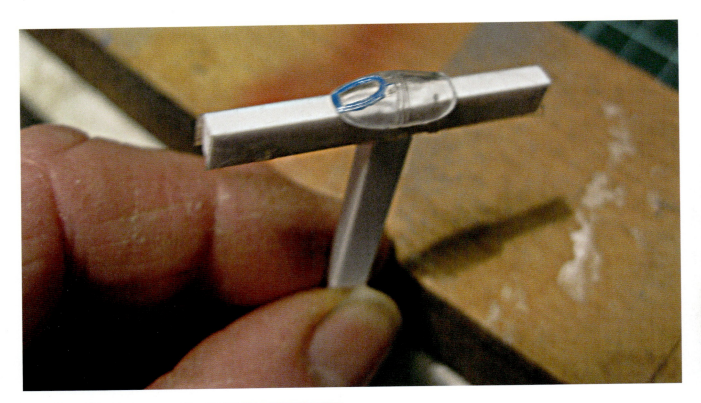

Above: A simple T bar makes a difficult job less so.

extreme end of the airframe. This method would allow the airframe to be turned through 180 degrees to allow the underside to be airbrushed using the same mounting. It proved to be a highly successful method. First the top surfaces were airbrushed in a satin royal blue and matt white mix. After all twelve were completed and allowed to dry the upper surfaces were masked off and the lower panels, including the underside of the wings and tail surface, were airbrushed matt olive green.

PAINTING THE CANOPIES

It was important that the canopy of each model was fully transparent. I have seen too many good ship models spoilt by the aircraft on board featuring one-piece fuselage and canopy mouldings, with canopies merely painted to represent glazing. All canopies have some form of frame work and although the canopy of the Yak fighter is a small item, if painted incorrectly it would spoil the effect of the completed model. The problem of painting the frame lines of the canopy was solved through the simple expedient of a styrene T-piece and a small strip of double-sided tape. The T-piece was held firmly in a mini vice whilst all of the concentration was directed at producing the fine lines of the frame around the canopy.

Right: All of the RAS equipment fitted to the starboard side of the superstructure.

Above: RAS equipment for *Kiev*. The heavy jackstay hoist, double receiver and single receiver sets.

particularly naval) supplied all the paints for the hull, decks and superstructure. These have been accurately blended to Soviet/Russian navy specification. Colours for the aviation, and particularly the Yak 38s, were achieved through my own efforts in blending Humbrol matt 25 with light blue satin.

From previous experience it was decided to provide a stable platform for airbrushing. The principle and method was simple, lengths of styrene were cut to form a base with two vertical ends while the model was supported at the

Above: Masking and preparation for airbrushing the white stripe above the black boot topping.

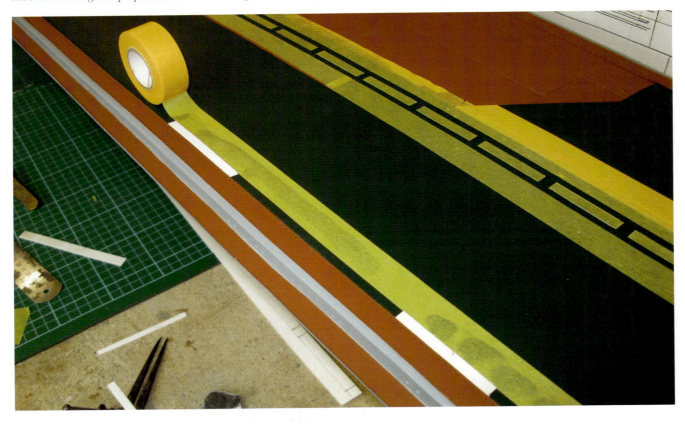

Above: Masking areas on the flight deck that will be airbrushed white.

REPLENISHMENT AT SEA EQUIPMENT

This model has a large number of fittings that were modelled for the first time. This created its own set of problems. Chief among these was obtaining access to information as to how these fittings were used, as this required detailed pictures of their appearance. Given that this article is limited in scope I have extracted only a small number of builds to convey just some of the effort inherent in both research and construction. A good example of this is the Replenishment at Sea (RAS) gear. There is little doubt that without the on board pictures of *Minsk* and those from ex-crew members I would have not been in a position to add these fittings as part of the model. *Kiev* differed slightly from *Minsk* in the type of heavy jack stay hoist used but each of the refuelling receivers were identical. *Kiev* was fitted with two single sets and one double set of receivers. Having the information was one problem solved, replicating their appearance was quite another. Like so much on *Kiev* making the RAS equipment was new modelling territory.

THE HEAVY JACKSTAY

Kiev was fitted with two heavy jackstay hoists. In its basic form the heavy jackstay was used for transporting supplies from one ship to another whilst underway. On *Kiev* this consisted of a vertical post onto which a hoist was connected. This hoist was raised or lowered by cables connected to a drive motor at the base of the post. For the model, aluminium tube was used for the post while the drive motor was made from a combination of styrene rod and tube. The hoist and top support were made from styrene sheet.

REFUELLING AT SEA RECEIVERS

Like so much on *Kiev* where only photos existed, first and foremost some form of drawing had to be generated. Again, a further example is the heavy jackstay hoist and the RAS receivers. Essentially the receiver into which the probe fits consisted of a splayed inlet and a rotating 90-degree outlet which feeds a hose line to a deck connector. Constructing these parts presented few difficulties. The receiver was made from 2 diameters of aluminium tube while the rear is formed from styrene tube. Each receiver was secured via the hose line support to a steel plate. The hose line support can swivel through 30 degrees either side, while the receiver nozzle can move up and down in a U frame fitting. This was replicated using strips of litho plate. Above each nozzle of the receiver was an L-shaped roller guide onto which the hose line could rest. This was made up from 0.31mm nickel silver wire with 0.50mm OD fine tube for the roller.

The mounting and hose line support for the double receiver was shaped differently, taking into account that it

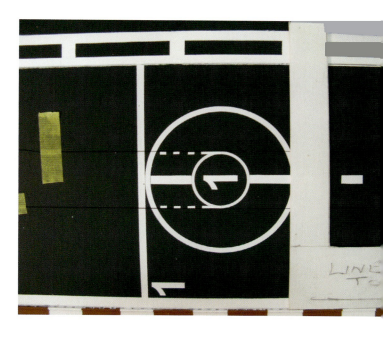

Above: Methods used for lining up the landing take off circles.

supported two receivers. Apart from that the function was the same as that of the single receiver.

With all of the RAS equipment completed and airbrushed, the next step was to fit these to the superstructure. In addition to what has been discussed, each receiver unit was fitted with access ladders and operating platforms. Detailed photos were made available to me of a RAS underway aboard *Kiev*. These gave me a much clearer understanding of how this operation was performed, and importantly other details in the pictures helped to improve the appearance of these fittings.

AIRBRUSHING AND PAINTING

This model of *Kiev* was to represent the vessel as she was in the early 1980s as part of the Northern Fleet. Unlike NATO warships the pennant number on Soviet warships was changed periodically. The colour scheme, however, remained and thankfully almost exact matches could be found through White Ensign Models.

On *Kiev*, as with other ships of the Soviet Fleet, the decks were painted in a matt brown/red shade while the flight decks of Soviet carriers also received a matt dark green. As mentioned I much prefer the use of an airbrush and use a single action type in which the outlet can be adjusted to give either a narrow pencil or wide spray angle. For general coverage the angle is opened to maximum. The angle is reduced depending on the type of job. The hull was airbrushed in White Ensign Models Northern Fleet grey, applying a single undercoat and a single finishing coat. The red anti-foul paint was represented with Humbrol 73.

Above: *Kiev*, trimmed and looking quite life-like in the dull conditions of a February day.

BOOT TOPPING

Other areas of the hull required a different treatment. For example, *Kiev* received black boot topping with a narrow white band immediately above. To aid application a simple device that many readers of *Shipwright* may well be familiar with was used: a right-angled set square with a pencil attached to correspond with the height of the boot topping from the keel as shown on the ship plan. Following the boot topping the white line was added, first by running out low tack masking tape to correspond with the top of the back boot topping. To ensure a constant width for the white band spacers of peel-off vinyl were placed on the top edge of the low tack tape and the upper band of tape added. This done, the spacers were removed and the exposed strip was ready for airbrushing.

FLIGHT DECK MARKINGS

The purpose of the carrier is to deploy aircraft. Although *Kiev* was termed a cruiser the flight deck was arranged for the management of aircraft, both fixed wing and rotary. To this end the flight deck was fitted with conspicuous signage. On *Kiev* this was a combination of circles, numbers and lines (landing/take off spots), a series of white broken lines that ran the length of the flight deck and a yellow strip aft of the

Above: Underway at last: the model's one and only cruise as she approached completion.

flight deck. Each and every line had a purpose and was highly noticeable. Thus getting the markings right was one of the more time-consuming but very rewarding aspects of the model.

The position of the lines had to be carefully marked, remembering that one edge of the full length broken white line needed to match exactly the point where the deck separates if it was to effectively disguise the joint along the deck that gave access to the internal workings. The initial measurements had to be right or the joint would be obvious. Thankfully, my concern was misplaced as the marks for the full white line were spot on. All that was required was to lay

out the low tack tape, exposing only the areas that needed to be airbrushed white. To ensure accuracy strips of styrene were used to form spacers. All other exposed areas were covered over.

Kiev has six landing/take off circles and right forward on the flight deck a circle marked with the letter 'C'. This is usually reserved for the SAR helicopter which is clearly identifiable by its orange-painted engine covers. As mentioned a yellow strip is painted over to starboard, aft of the superstructure. This separates the flight deck from the dispersal area, clearly defining that division in less than clear flying conditions.

I make it a point where possible to airbrush or paint all such lines or markings. This ensures that any lines are flush with the deck surface. However circles such as those on *Kiev* were better served using fine white peel-off vinyl. These were easily cut with a compass cutter to various sizes and widths. All other division lines across the flight deck were airbrushed. To ensure that all the circles were on the centre line I used the tried and trusted method of placing a string line fore and aft of the flight deck. For lines across the deck, I employed a simple made-for-the-job line tool. This combination of line tool and string lines ensured that there was no misalignment of any of the circles or deck markings.

GETTING UNDERWAY

From the beginning of the project I had decided that *Kiev* would be, first and foremost, a working model. As it turned out she would sail only once, as the model was donated to the Fleet Air Arm Museum at Yeovilton in February 2011. Preparations were well advanced by the end of January 2011 but it was decided that the deck dioramas would not be added until the model had completed its one and only sortie.

Unusually February was a quiet month on the weather front in the UK and the opportunity was taken to commission the model at the Boat Museum at Ellesmere Port, a venue I am well acquainted with. Successful ballast trials were conducted three years previous so all that was required was to place the batteries into the hull to make the model ready to sail. Thankfully those early trials and a methodical internal arrangement paid off. Although a little deep in the water *Kiev* performed faultlessly. Seeing the model on the water allowed me to compare some of the angles of the fly-by shots taken by NATO aircraft back in the 1980s. I have attempted to recreate these – I hope with some success.

Right: Bringing some deck activity to the model; preparing to load the Bazalt missile.

Above: Loading up the rocket pods on a Yak 38 whilst the KA25C SAR helicopter takes up its spot on the flight deck.

FINISHING

The large radar arrays that dominate the upper platform forward of the funnel were now fitted. Each array was placed using the locating pin fitted at its base. Installing these was well practised as they are inherently fragile – any mistake could cause damage.

The first to be fitted was the tall tower housing the aircraft navigation control sphere, generally referred to as Top Knot. The entire lattice work was made up from a combination of styrene sheet, rod and brass wire of various gauges. Various jigs were created to form all of the spars, with the dome being made from fillers and shaped around styrene formers.

The smaller of the two radar arrays is the Top Steer 3D radar. The basic mattress arrays are photo etched whilst the remainder of the frame work, feed horn and stabilisers were constructed from a combination of brass wire and litho plate. Producing the tapered shape of support pillars required a simple combination of styrene tube and filler, a method that worked well. The forward Top Sail 3D array on *Kiev* was the main long-range (300nm) air search early warning radar. This was constructed using a similar method to that used for the Top Steer radar.

Above: Pre-flight checks on a Yak 38. Figures depicted are 1:144 Preiser N-gauge.

ON DECK DIORAMAS

A carrier, unlike any other warship, is optimised for a considerable amount of deck activity and *Kiev* is no exception. My intention from the outset was to instil into the model that sense of activity. For example, the SS-N-12 Bazalt missile launch tubes are being made ready for loading. Pilots and ground crew are preparing a flight of Yak 38s VTOL fighters for a combat air patrol. In one scenario ground crew are

Above: *Kiev*, almost complete.

loading the under wing rocket pods. The crew of a towing vehicle have just disconnected the tow bar from one of the Yak 38s and a crew member stands close to one of the many foam monitors.

In another scenario a pilot has completed his pre-flight checks and is making ready to climb the ladder into the aircraft. On the flight deck aft aircraft are being brought to the flight line whilst others are being prepared in dispersal. Looking very closely there are other members of the crew going about their routine duties or manning the fire tender and fire monitors, one crew member is even having a casual breather on the close-in weapons sponsons right aft.

Finishing involved much more than is outlined here. There are four types of ships' rails fitted to *Kiev*. All of these had to be drawn and prepared in photo etch, along with numerous Soviet Navy style watertight doors. *Kiev* was fitted with many hundreds of life raft containers strapped in place along the sides of the walkways. All of these were cast and mounting frames made.

Added to that are the internal arrangements for the recessed boat galleries, including the davits and the ship's motor boats. These were designed from the outset to be fitted out externally and slotted into place on completion. The detail right forward included the unusual Trap Door targeting radar. The mechanics of operation were only revealed during the construction of this model and have been an enigma for many years. Fifty or more Preiser 1:144 N-Gauge figures were each individually painted. *Kiev* was now completed and just one journey remained.

A DISPLAY OF SOVIET NAVAL AIR POWER AT THE FAA MUSEUM

As the era of the Cold War fades into history, various museums have begun displaying artefacts and establishing exhibitions that mark events of this period. In the UK the RAF Museum at Cosford has created an entire pavilion highlighting various aspects of the Cold War from 1948 to 1992, displaying aircraft and other military artefacts of both NATO and the Warsaw Pact. Other UK museums are considering marking this period – amongst these is the Fleet Air Arm Museum at Yeovilton.

In the FAA museum various episodes of the Cold War are well covered, such as Korea, where Royal Naval Aviation was represented as part of the UN mission. But the museum authorities and particularly curator David Hill were keen to present a model that illustrated the development and deployment of Soviet naval aviation during the Cold War period.

The model of *Kiev* was therefore donated to the Fleet Air Arm Museum. I believe it is the only detailed large scale model of this Soviet carrier outside Russia.

CONCLUSION

For me, researching and building the *Kiev* has been an ambitious but rewarding project. I embarked on the building of the model knowing I had insufficient information, yet as the build progressed information became available from the most unexpected sources and it is to these sources that I am eternally grateful. I hope that in this model I have perhaps, in some small way, added to our knowledge of the function and form of a carrier that represented cutting edge technology of its day – but a technology that thankfully was never put to the test.

Below: *Kiev* is now on permanent exhibition at the Fleet Air Arm Museum Yeovilton.

REFERENCES AND ACKNOWLEDGEMENTS

Soviet Warships by John Jordan

Conway's All the World's Fighting Ships 1947-1995

Guide to the Soviet Navy Fourth Edition by Norman Polmar

Aircraft Carriers of the World 1914 to the present: An Illustrated Encyclopaedia by Roger Chesneau

Kiev and Kuznetsov: Russian Aircraft Carriers by Barry Dean

Yakovlev Yak 36, Yak 38 and Yak 41: The Soviet Jump Jets by Yefim Gordon

My thanks to former members of the crew of *Kiev* for their kind assistance during the course of this project. My thanks to Steve Cuplan for his contribution of detailed pictures taken aboard the carrier *Minsk*.

Preussen (1902)

GERMAN FIVE-MASTED SHIP

by Robert A. Wilson FRSA

The *Preussen* was unique in that she was the only commercial cargo-carrying five-masted full-rigged sailing ship ever built.

She was built in 1902 by J. C. Tecklenborg, Geestmunde, Germany, for the famous Flying P Line owned by F. Laeisz of Hamburg. She was an enormous vessel of 5,081 gross tons with a length of 407ft, a beam of 53ft 7in, and a depth of 27ft 1in. She was built specifically for the nitrate trade, sailing from Hamburg and rounding Cape Horn to the nitrate ports situated on the west coast of South America.

The standing rigging amounted to about 6.7 miles of steel wire rope. There were a further 8.2 miles of wire rope running rigging, 10.7 miles of hemp running rigging, and about 2,500ft of chain rigging, giving a total of about 26 miles. There were over 1,200 blocks and her standing rigging was set up on 248 rigging screws. The mainmast stood about 223ft from keel to truck. The main yard was slightly over 100ft long, while the main royal yard was 52.5ft long. Thirty square sails could be set with a further seventeen fore-and-aft sails, including the spanker. This gave a total area of about 50,000 square feet of canvas.

The ship could carry about 8,000 tons of cargo. Although she was mainly employed on the nitrate run, she did visit other ports such as New York and Yokohama. Her final voyage, number thirteen, ended at Hamburg on 20 August 1910.

Below: Completed model on display base.

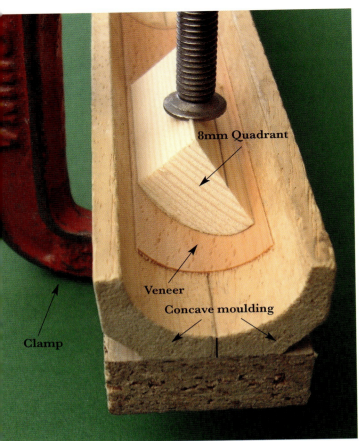

Left: Veneering a quadrant using a concave jig.

8mm Quadrant

Veneer

Concave moulding

Clamp

She was lost in 1910 when, following a collision with the British cross-Channel vessel *Brighton*, she went ashore beneath the White Cliffs of Dover, becoming a total loss.

The first model I constructed of the *Preussen* was completed in early 2007. It depicted the ship fully loaded and under full sail in a fairly calm sea.

Recently I was asked to build another model of the ship, showing her at anchor in a calm sea, not quite fully loaded and with all the sails furled on the yards and stays. When I built the first model, plans were something of a problem. I eventually obtained deck, lines and sail plans from separate sources, namely from the books *The Great Age of Sail* (Lines); the rigging plan, showing all rigging and braces, from *Sailing Ships Rigs & Rigging* (Underhill); and a deck and basic sail plan from the German technical journal *Jahrbuch Der Schiffbautechnischen Gesellschaft* of 1907.

Since then, the plan situation has improved. By entering '*Preussen* plan' in a Google internet search, a plans service advertising a complete set of lines, sail and deck plan may be located. A small scale set is included in the advert and they appear accurate, agreeing with my other plans of the ship.

I also obtained a copy of the book *Konigin der See Funfmast-*

Below: The base quadrant assembled.

Removable sea tray

Paper masking tape

Above: The sea tray, ready for the Plasticine sea to be fitted.

Vollschiff 'Preussen' by Horst Hamecher. This volume, written in German, is profusely illustrated with large photographs and also has a 1:250 scale folded plan in the back, with the lines on one side and the sail and deck plans on the other. The deck plan is very detailed, but the sail plan does not show the braces and running rigging, so I used the Underhill sail plan for rigging purposes.

The fact that the second model is shown at anchor with furled sails did not mean that it took less time to complete than the one under sail. Both models took the same amount of time within a couple of hours. I always time the work on a stopwatch and keep an accurate building log of the progress.

With a complicated ship like this, I prefer to break the work up into sections and do not proceed with a straightfor-

ward hull, masts, rigging, sea, display case sequence, but tend to work on different parts at different times, moving from one to the other as and when I feel like a change.

THE DISPLAY BASE

The chosen scale was the same as the previous model, 1in = 25ft (1:300), which gave the model a length of 16in on the waterline.

As soon as I had cut the rough hull shape, I assessed the required size of the display case base. With all my display cases, I cut and assemble the quadrant moulding first, making allowance for the bevelled wood edging that will go around the sea base inside the display case. The quadrant I

Below: The broad and narrow sea rollers.

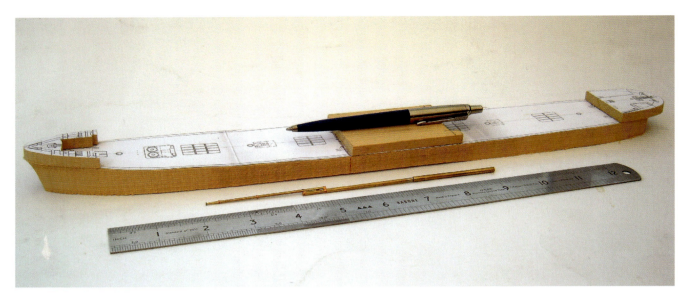

Above: Initial hull shaping.

prefer is 18mm. Cheap pine is perfectly adequate for this because I always veneer it on its curved surface with 'steamed beech' veneer. This is the name of the finish rather than a process – I do not steam it. Veneering surfaced 18mm quadrant may seem a difficult task, but in fact it is a fairly simple operation. I wet the veneer and this makes it take on a natural curve. The strip of veneer is placed in a concave support made from two strips of concave moulding glued to a long strip of chipboard. The inside surface of the veneer is

painted with Evo-Stik wood glue. After the mitres are cut in the quadrant, it is also painted with the same type of glue and pressed into the support and clamped firmly. After about half an hour, I remove it. It is better not to wait longer than half an hour as the whole strip of veneered quadrant can end up glued firmly in the support if left for too long.

The illustration on the previous spread demonstrates the principle with a short piece of moulding.

After the four quadrant sides are dry, the excess veneer is

Below: The bowsprit socket in position in the raised forecastle.

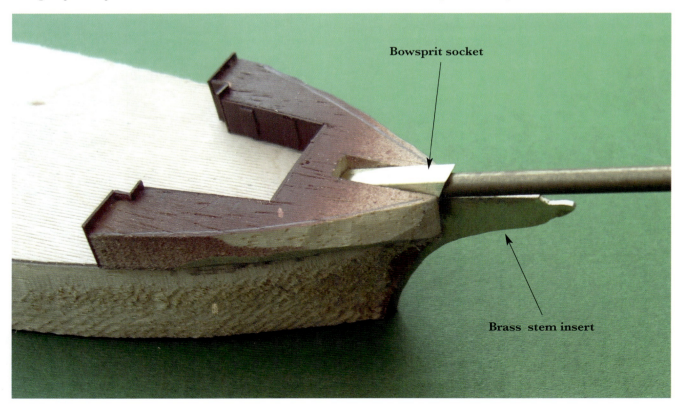

Bowsprit socket

Brass stem insert

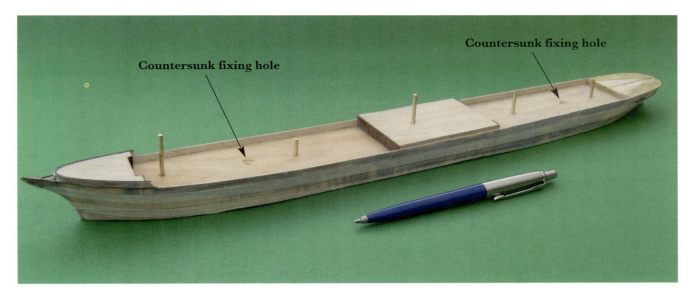

Countersunk fixing hole

Countersunk fixing hole

Above: The plated hull ready for painting.

removed with a scalpel. They are then glued and clamped together using corner clamps.

Because the model is shown at anchor, not a lot of sea was required and I settled on a display case measuring 23.7in by 5.2in and 10.5in high. That allowed about 4in (10cm) of sea between the bow and the end of the case, about 3in (7.5cm) between the stern and the end of the case and about 1.5in (3.8cm) on each side between hull and case. The height allowed for about 1.5in over the mastheads. I find a slightly wider gap between the bow and case end than the gap between case and stern looks much better than equal spacing at each end.

The four display case sides were made from 3mm acrylic cut to fit within the veneered quadrant. The two front and back pieces were fitted first, securing each with three small woodscrews. Thin strips of the inner protective backing were

removed from each end of the two pieces, to enable the ends to be glued to them. The two ends were cut and fitted, securing them with contact adhesive to the exposed vertical strips at each end of the front and back panels. These ends were also screwed to the insides of the quadrant with small wood-screws. The top was left open for the moment. Note that the four acrylic sides are only glued to each other and not to the quadrant! The inner base was then cut to be a perfect fit inside the case and edged with bevelled moulding, fixed with contact adhesive. I find it much easier to work through the open top to cut and edge the inner base to a perfect fit. Once that has been done, the top of the case may be cut to size and glued on. I always remove the under side protective backing before doing this. If it is left on, it is virtually impossible to get off again when the case is complete.

A shallow tray was then made to fit snugly inside the inner

Below: Thick white plasticard forms the top of the poop.

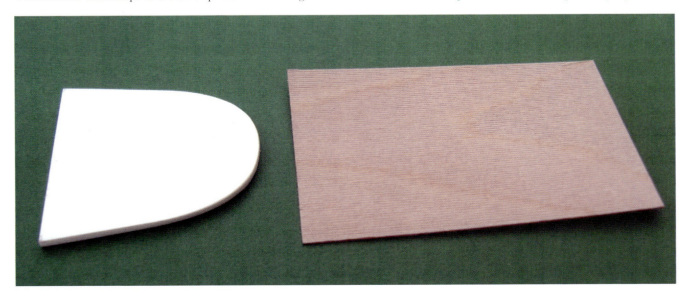

Above: Scored deck and side plating fitted.

base. This is to take the Plasticine sea. The fact that the tray can be removed allows the sea to be painted without any fear of getting paint on the bevelled quadrant around the base.

I always fit the sea with the sea tray in position. This is because pressing the Plasticine into it applies pressure to the sides that sometimes makes them bulge out slightly, making it difficult to put the sea tray back in the base when it is com-

plete. Because Plasticine itself can mark the woodwork, I mask off the bevelled moulding when fitting the sea. I also prepare the sea whilst the hull is in the early stages in order to avoid making a mess of the paintwork, which would certainly happen if I waited until the hull was plated and painted. The model shown ready for the sea is not the *Preussen*, but the *Loch Torridon*. However ,the same method is used for all my models.

The formation of the calm anchorage sea for the *Preussen* was extremely simple to make and no particular skill was required. The Plasticine was pushed into the tray around the hull and then shaped by two sea rollers, made specially for the purpose. After removing the hull, the larger one was used first, rolling it up and down until the larger undulations were formed in the surface and then the smaller one was used to finish off the sea with the smaller ripples. Because the Plasticine is pliable, it is possible to roll away randomly until it looks correct.

The construction of the sea rollers is self-explanatory. The top one is completely homemade using a plastic bead,

Below: Drilling portholes, using the edge of a steel ruler as a guide.

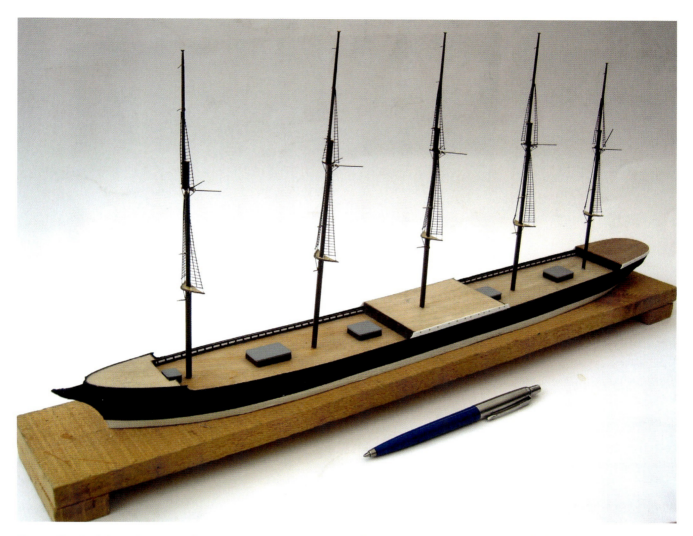

Above: The basic hull with hatches fitted.

nut and bolt, two strips of steel and a wooden handle. The narrower one was made from a device that I obtained at a car boot sale. I replaced the original milled wheel with a fairly thin steel washer with a rounded edge. The sea tray may then be removed for painting. To facilitate the easy removal of the sea tray, the base had a hole drilled in at either end before the tray was made. To remove the tray, I just pushed a thin screwdriver alternately in the holes at each end of the base. In this way, I was able to ease it out without damaging the Plasticine.

The surface of the Plasticine was primed for painting by spraying with grey matt aerosol primer. My wife painted the sea itself and the whole process only took half an hour. First a light blue coating of blue gloss was applied, and whilst it was still wet, it was streaked with a much darker blue. The two colours ran together to form quite a 'wet' looking sea.

The case was finished by veneering the edges with steamed beech veneer to match the quadrant. I cut narrow strips of the protective backing off the edges so that the veneer bonded straight on to the acrylic and not the backing.

Because the quadrant is not glued to the bottom of the display case, I removed it from the case after the screws had been removed and smoothed and finished it separately. That made it far easier as I did not have to worry about making a mess of the case. I finished the woodwork by sealing it with Evo-Stik white wood glue diluted 50-50 with water. After it was dry, I rubbed it down with fine wet and dry paper and then sprayed it with clear lacquer. I prefer a lacquer spray to varnish because it dries within minutes.

Greater care had to be taken when finishing the case edgings as it is glued direct to the acrylic. Although this is still protected by the plastic coating, it is easy to damage it.

HULL AND FITTINGS

The hull was no particular problem and the fact that the *Preussen* had a raised midship island made it easier to fit the bulwarks than the more common arrangement of just a raised forecastle and poop, with a long maindeck.

Following my normal procedure of using extra plan copies as templates, I first cut out the profile below the level

Above: The capstans and stubs.

Above: Using the lathe as a jig when soldering the stubs in place.

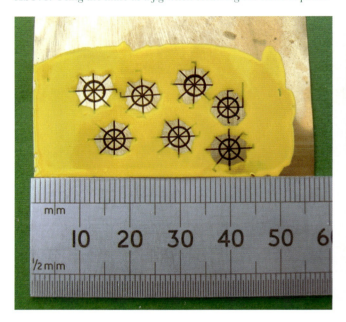

Above: Wheels applied to brass and masking added.

of the three raised decks and then pasted a plan of the full length of the hull on top of it and cut that out as shown. Between the hull and the ruler is the first of the five masts. Because of the complexity of the rig, I began making the masts and spars very early in the construction. This is not really necessary, but it is a very good feeling when, on completion of the hull, the five masts can be fitted and rigging can commence immediately. The three raised decks are just placed in position at this stage.

Two sheets of $^1/_{32}$in marine plywood, scored to represent deck planking, were then glued on top. The junction between the two pieces lay under the raised midship deck. It is more accurate to score in relatively short lengths, so the midship deckhouse worked in my favour in this respect.

I made the width of the three raised decks slightly less than the full hull width on each side. This allowed me to glue the bulwarks along the hull in two complete strips, the ends and centre, fitting directly to the sides of the decks and filling it out to the full hull width. The bulwarks were made from $^1/_{32}$in marine plywood.

The raised poop and counter stern was a piece of wood of the correct thickness, sandwiched between two thin pieces of 0.005in brass shim. The upper piece was the shape of the top of the poop deck, and the lower one, the shape of the counter at the level of the knuckle. Using these two pieces of brass as a template, the counter was carved into shape with a scalpel.

The midship island was a piece of wood of the correct thickness, less the thickness of the bulwarks on each side. The forecastle had a fairly large section cut out at the forward end to take the bowsprit socket. In previous models, the socket was round. When it came time to make the socket for the *Preussen*, I found that I had no round tube into which the bowsprit would fit snugly, so I used square tube. I was pleased to find that fitting a square socket was much easier and served the same purpose. Future models will all have square sockets. It was seated in chemical metal, sometimes known as

plastic padding and used for filling dents in car bodies.

Note that the forward end of the socket is slightly higher that the top of the forecastle. Although this was not intended, I found that the upward tilt of the top of the forecastle deck was slightly more pronounced than the level of the top of the forecastle block. The raised socket corrected this perfectly when the scored deck was glued on top. The gaps at the side were filled with chemical metal.

Preussen did not have a figurehead, but a simple shaped prow. The stem insert was cut from brass and glued into a vertical slot before the bowsprit socket was fitted. A similar insert was fitted into a vertical slot cut in the stern. The two pieces of brass shim in the counter were so thin that they did not damage or impede the saw blade. Any fairing of the ends of the hull into the stem and stern inserts was achieved using chemical metal. After smoothing, the hull shell plating was represented by strips of paper masking tape. I drilled two fixing holes in the hull beneath where two of the cargo hatches were to be fitted. These vertical holes went through the model and base, coming out underneath in two counter-sunk holes. Two long 6BA bolts were fitted to the model and initially were used to hold the unfinished model to the rough building board. On completion, the model was inserted into the sea and screwed in by adding two washers and nuts underneath and gently tightening them up with a 6BA box spanner.

Before the forecastle was fitted, the bulkheads and recess were faced with plasticard and spray painted brown. In the first model, I had the raised deck bulkheads white, but the

Preussen book obtained later showed that they were dark and I assumed that the most likely colour was brown.

The scored forecastle and midship decking was glued on before painting. The poop, above the level of the bulwarks was left off at this stage because it is white.

Rather than paint the poop sides, I used thick white plasticard cut to shape. The scored decking was then glued to the top. This method was used because the side plating on the poop above the rails is vertical all the way round and the after end does not slope to meet the counter below it. After the scored top was fitted, the side plating, drilled with portholes was glued around the sides leaving the forward ends protruding slightly and cut in curves as shown on the plan.

The completed poop was then set aside until after the hull was painted.

To drill the portholes I mark the spacing of the ports on a sheet of thin white plasticard, lay an old steel ruler along it to act as a guide, and drill the holes with a small hand-held 12-Volt battery drill. I use an old rule for this, because the drill does damage the edge of it in time.

After they were drilled, I cut the strip and glued it to the edge of the poop deck.

A note on safety may be apposite at this stage with reference to the deep groove down the side of my left forefinger.

When drilling the fixing holes through the hull, I placed a 4in-long drill in the drill press chuck. Although it looked vertical, it was not clamped between the three jaws, but offset to one side and clamped between only two of them. Holding the hull in position with left forefinger about an inch away from the drill, I switched it on. Centrifugal force threw the point of the drill sideways where it carved a deep groove across the top of the poop deck and proceeded to carve a similar groove down the side of my finger. This was not a

Below: Clipped to a small piece of glass ready for etching.

Below: Etching in an old pencil case.

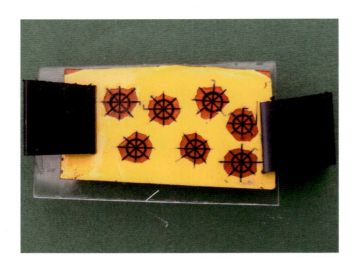

serious injury and no medical treatment was required, but it remained extremely painful for about four days before it settled down and healed. Fortunately, as I said earlier, the planked top section of the poop was not fitted at the time, so the damage was covered up when it was fitted. Fortunately, the blood flew clear of the model.

The hull was then painted. First of all the top part was masked off and the underwater paint sprayed white. I now marked the top of the white by placing a sharp pencil on top of a thin slice of wood and running it around the hull. The

black section was hand-painted using artist's matt black watercolour. After it had dried, I stuck a thin black strip of masking tape around the junction between white and black to sharpen up the line.

The white plasticard side plating above the midship bridge deck was drilled in the same manner as the poop deck and glued on after the black had been painted. This ensured a clean, sharp junction between black and white.

Throughout the hull construction, I was assembling the masts and fitting the topmast and topgallant shrouds and backstays, so that when the hull was complete, I could fit the masts and begin the rigging. I also shaped and painted all the thirty yards, derricks, spanker gaff and boom and kept them safe in a separate box with a section for each mast. With so many yards, it would be very confusing to keep them all together before they were required.

The bulwarks were made using the 'boxes, lines and squares' fonts on the Microsoft Word software. This font seems to be common to all word processing software.

A lot of the deck detail on the *Preussen* consisted of the deck machinery, comprising of ten halliard winches, five brace winches and four cargo winches. These were made during the early stages of hull construction. They were turned from brass rod using needle files, a fine jeweller's saw and a junior hacksaw to shape them rather than the more

Below: Two sets of completed ships' wheels.

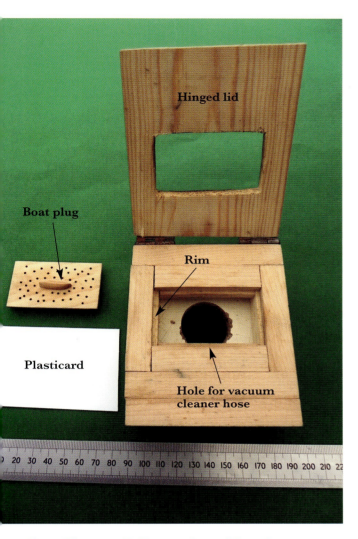

Boat plug

Hinged lid

Rim

Plasticard

Hole for vacuum cleaner hose

Above: The custom-built vacuum box and boat plug.

Above: The boat plug in position in the vacuum box.

Above: Plasticard in position and lid closed and clamped.

conventional lathe tools. The eight capstans were turned in two parts, the capstan itself and a short stub that was soldered to the base of the capstan and used for gluing them into holes drilled in the deck.

I used the lathe as a jig for soldering these small pieces together. First, I tinned the bottom of the capstan and one end of the short stub. With a drill chuck on both the left and right hand ends of the lathe, I inserted the capstan in the left side (bottom outwards) and the stub in the tailstock with the tinned ends facing each other. I then advanced the tailstock until both parts were touching. A quick blast from a small blowtorch melted the solder and joined the two pieces together very accurately.

The various components of the halliard winches, brace winches and cargo winches were made using the same principle.

A number of small square hatches were fitted on the midship deck. These were cut from square brass tube into which fixing stubs had been soldered. The tops were filled in

with chemical metal. After spray painting and fitting to the model, the white tops, each with four ports, was printed on thin card using the computer, cut out and stuck on.

SHIP'S WHEEL

The *Preussen* had a large double wheel midships just forward of the chartroom on the midship deck. I etched these from 0.002in brass shim. No special equipment was needed and the whole process was quite simple.

First, I cleaned a piece of shim and applied the pattern for a number of wheels to it. I usually make a few at a time to cover future models. To apply the design, I use rub-on circles and lines obtained from an art shop. I rub the spokes on first and then the circles on top. It is easier to centre them this way. The yellow paint serves two purposes. First, it reduces the area that the etching fluid has to eat away, thus speeding up the process. Secondly, it ensures that after the etching is complete, the wheels will remain in the brass shim, held only

Above: Boats in various stages of construction.

by the end of the spokes. This makes for easier storing. The back of the shim was then painted red in order to prevent the etching fluid eating the metal away from the back. Because of this extensive masking, only the spaces between the spokes and a small area around the wheel rims will be exposed to the

Above: The completed anchor.

etching fluid. The sheet was then clipped to a small piece of glass using two slices cut from the end of a plastic slide binder obtained from a stationery store. The glass is necessary to ensure that the brass remains below the surface of the etching fluid. My preferred etching agent is Sodium Persulphate crystals that I obtain from Maplin Electronics (UK). The more common Ferric Chloride works just as well, but it is dark brown and the etching process cannot be viewed as easily as the former substance, which has the appearance and clarity of water. I put two or three teaspoons in a small quantity of water and it takes about two hours to complete the etching. Goggles and rubber gloves should be worn when using either of these chemicals as they are mildly corrosive.

The reason I masked the back of the brass with red paint is that it shows up clearly when the exposed brass is etched away. After washing the completed etching, the paint may be removed by soaking it in white spirit. Two of the wheels were then cut from the sheet using the point of a scalpel. I blackened them with a broad-tipped permanent black marker pen. The separation between the two wheels was obtained by cutting a thin slice of $1/16$in brass rod using the lathe. This slice was glued to the centre of the first wheel and then the second wheel was glued on top. The double wheel was then glued to the front of the wheel box. Because of their extremely small size, etched wheels look very good on miniatures, even though they are completely flat and do not have shaped spokes.

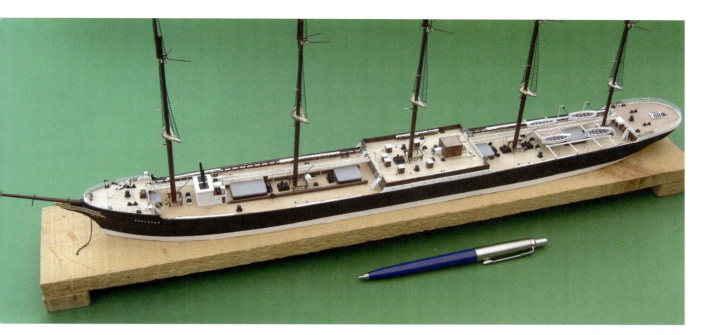

Above: The finished hull ready for rigging.

BOATS

The *Preussen* had four boats; three identical double-ended lifeboats and a fourth transom-ended gig. All four were made from 0.015in thick plasticard sheet, using a small homemade vacuum box. The top of the box measures 95mm across and 112mm on the side, with the box placed as in the photograph on p173. The suction hole in the bottom is cut so that a standard household vacuum cleaner hose plugs into it, making a tight fit. The box is divided into upper and lower chambers, separated by a rim fitted around the inside with about 15mm below it and 6mm above it. A hinged lid with a rectangular hole the same size as the one in the box is fitted.

The box works by sucking a hot sheet of thin plasticard (styrene) sheet down over a carved boat (bottom up). A boat 'plug', as it is called, must therefore be made. This is a solid boat made slightly deeper than required. It is glued bottom up in the middle of a thin sheet of plywood that is a snug fit in the vacuum box, resting on the rim. A number of small holes were drilled around the boat. This is to allow the air to be sucked out during the process. The number of holes is not critical; I simply drilled a good number in an approximate pattern, as can be seen in the images on p173.

Before placing the plug in the box, I smoothed Vaseline over the boat and perforated sheet to prevent the boat from sticking to the plasticard after forming. I find the ideal thickness of plasticard is 0.015in. After placing the plug in the box and covering the hole with a piece of plasticard, the box was closed and clamped shut with a large bulldog clip – the lid of the box, opposite the hinges, extends slightly over a lip glued to the end of the box. This is to accommodate the bulldog clip to clamp it shut. The hose of the vacuum cleaner was

then inserted into the hole on the back of the box, keeping the switch handy for turning it on when ready. The exposed area of plasticard was heated using a small heat gun – these can be obtained from hobby craft shops. I recommend giving it 30 seconds with the gun almost touching the plasticard. I am often asked whether a hairdryer is suitable for supplying heat, but it is not – a hairdryer does not produce anywhere near enough heat.

Then I switched on the vacuum cleaner. The soft card was instantaneously sucked down over the boat plug and the vacuum cleaner switched off. The boat was then cut from the

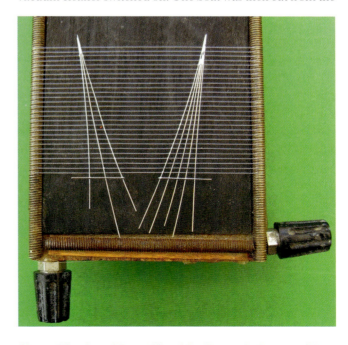

Above: The shroud frame. The old radio terminals are used for securing the wire ratlines.

Above: Standing rigging and furled fore and aft sails fitted.

sheet and trimmed up, initially with nail scissors. Then the excess height was removed with fine wet and dry paper until the boat was a good shape. A right angle was bent in a piece of straight fine wire and this was glued along the boat to form the keel, the right angle representing the stern of the boat. This initially left a gap between wire and boat in the way of the angle. This was filled in with a spot of Evo-Stik white wood glue. When dry, it shrinks slightly and gives the end of the boat a better shape. The wire was bent round the front and also glued to the plastic hull. The boat was then sprayed with white matt primer, holding it by the wire keel in a pair of surgeon's clamping forceps.

I printed the layout of the interior of the boat on self-adhesive Safmat film and stuck it on a piece of thin plasticard. I cut out the shape and glued it in the boat shell. This is very effective technique for miniature models, but I doubt whether it would look as good in larger scales. Finally, I added a black stripe round each boat at the level of the top of the gunwale. Rather than attempting to paint it on, I cut a narrow strip of black paper and glued it in position.

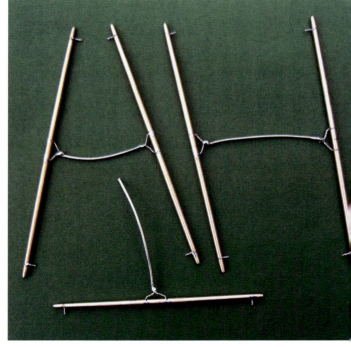

Above: The five lower yards ready for painting.

ANCHOR

As the ship is shown at anchor, only one had to be made and stowed on the forecastle, the other being at the bottom of the sea. This was made from copper wire. I took a length of wire and stretched it slightly to make it straight. A piece was cut off and bent round a metal rod to form the base, and another straight piece was cut to form the shank. These were beaten flat on a piece of smooth steel using a smooth-faced hammer. The shank was soldered to the base and the excess wire was cut away from both base and shank. The flukes were formed by pinching the ends of the base with a small pair of mole grips. The resulting flats were filed to form the pointed flukes. The same applied for the top end of the shank. A piece of thin wire was soldered to the top of the shank. This was to attach to the anchor cable leading into the hawse pipe. The anchor cable was purchased from a model shop.

The fore-and-aft gangways were made using white plasti-card channel into which I glued strips of $1/64$in marine plywood, scored to represent the planking. After the bridges were fitted, the support stanchions were added. These were made from thin copper wire that had been stretched to make it straight and then spray painted.

Above: Starboard quarter view of finished model.

MASTS AND RIGGING

The lower masts were hollow tubes and were fitted to the hull by gluing them over five short brass stubs that had been glued in earlier and bent to the correct rake for each mast.

In many ways, the deck detail was not as complicated as clippers of earlier eras, as there was no fancy panelling or decoration – everything was strictly utility. The bow and stern decoration was made from tightly twisted gold/silver wire, purchased from a craft shop. The names were printed in white lettering on a black background using the computer, shrunk to the required size, cut out and fixed in place.

The rigging sequence is quite important with a complicated vessel such as this. I began with fitting the masts and bowsprit. Next, I rigged all the fore and aft stays and their associated furled jibs and staysails. These were made from folded up airmail paper that had been painted with white Evo-Stik wood glue. This made them 'squashy' and I was able to squeeze them into the required furled shape.

I then fitted all the lines from under the tops down to the fife rails and brace winches. The rigging was all made from

Above: Completed model in display case.

thin black enamelled wire that had been stretched slightly to make it straight. Each piece was cut to length and glued on using contact adhesive. No knots were used anywhere in the model.

The five sets of lower shrouds and ratlines were made and fitted. These were made using my usual method of winding the ratlines on a small wood frame using threaded rod glued around the edge as spacers. The shrouds were soldered across them. Tinned copper wire, rather than enamelled wire, should be used for this. After they had been cut from the frame, they were spray undercoated with Red Oxide primer and finally sprayed Satin Black.

Once all the shrouds and ratlines were in place, it was just a matter of settling down to rigging all the many backstays. Although this was a tedious job, it was rendered much easier by the fact that there were no knots to deal with. Using wire to rig a model greatly simplifies the whole process.

By the time I had reached this stage, all thirty yards had been made and painted. I began this tedious task shortly after starting the model. These were all made either from brass or copper rod.

Two slots were turned in each yard close to the centre and two more just short of the ends. Twisted wire was fitted into these, forming the landings for the braces at the ends of the yards and the trusses at the centre. Short pieces of tinned

copper wire temporarily joined up two pairs of yards, whilst the odd one had its own piece. These wires were simply to hold the yards in surgeon's clamping forceps whilst spray painting. As soon as they were dry, the wires were melted off again with a small soldering iron.

The furled sails were pieces of white airmail paper, rolled and bound with fine tinned copper wire and glued to the top of the yards. The clews (corners) of the sails were glued on separately.

The fitting and rigging of the thirty yards was not very difficult, but it was extremely tedious. I began with the five lower yards, working from fore to aft and completing all the rigging before moving upwards. I found that I could manage five per day. This was very time-consuming until I got above the upper topsails. The remainder had much simpler brace rigging, so it became easier as I moved upwards.

On completion, I lowered the model into the sea and secured it by adding washers and nuts to the two securing bolts, tightening them up gently with a small box spanner. The junction between sea and hull was filled in using clear liquid acrylic, applied with a fine brush. The final task was to glue the end of the anchor cable into a small hole in the sea and fill it with liquid acrylic.

As the display base had been completed some time earlier, it was only the work of a few minutes to place the case over it and secure it with six woodscrews driven upwards through the edges of the base, thus completing the model.

Modeller's Draught

M/Y *GRIFFIOEN*

by J. Pottinger

The subject of this article is a type of motor yacht that has always carried considerable appeal. It is generally known as the 'trawler yacht' type, a description applied solely for the reason that they have some resemblance to the seaworthy fishing boats, in contrast to the other more extreme types of luxury yacht that are often labelled 'gin palaces'. Study of the waterlines on Sheet 2 will show an almost double-ended shape, giving a balanced motion in a seaway.

Griffioen is such a vessel. She was designed by Dutch naval architects De Vries Lentsch Design, and built of aluminium by Bloemsma & Van Breemen of Maakum in northern Holland, the Netherlands.

The owners' brief included a stipulation that the vessel height was not to exceed 6m so as to enable navigation of canals and inland waterways. As such *Griffioen*'s two light-weight masts can be lowered by means of hydraulically operated mechanisms. In addition, however, her qualities of seaworthiness enable her to make extended ocean voyages.

This type follows a number of similar designs common to some yacht designers and builders in Holland, in contrast to many of the more extreme motor and sailing yachts.

The legendary reliability of the British-built Kelvin engines is attested to by the fact that the yacht is propelled by a single TBSC8 535 BHP engine of this type. The engine provides an economical cruising speed of 11 knots to give a range of 4,800 nautical miles. The exhaust exits by an opening in the hull on the port side amidships, instead of being carried up through a casing and trunk through the wheelhouse.

Below: *Griffioen* at sea, showing her purposeful lines and general seaworthiness. (Courtesy of Bloemsma van Breemen shipyard)

Above: Foredeck capstans and bollards. Note the complex arrangement of the laid decks. (Courtesy of Bloemsma van Breemen shipyard)

Above: The seating arrangement at the aft end of the wheelhouse. (Courtesy of Bloemsma van Breemen shipyard)

Two tenders are carried on the fore deck, the larger being a custom-built fast robust craft able to land in exposed and difficult shores, the other being a popular RIB type, both being handled by a retractable hydraulically powered davit. There is a glazed skylight positioned between the two craft.

The usual areas for relaxation on deck are provided; a semi-enclosed seating casing is arranged at the aft end of the forecastle. Note grab rails along the top at the sides which are a continuation of the access ladders port and starboard. Similar seating arrangements with a table are provided on the main deck at the aft end of the deckhouse (note that this should be at the starboard side, not as shown) and an open air dining area is located aft of the wheelhouse, sheltered by overhead and side extensions to the wheelhouse at the port side. Additional seating with deck lockers underneath is arranged around the curve of the after bulwark with triangular-shaped tables handy nearby. Seats are also fitted in front of the wheelhouse. Liferafts in canisters are carried on both port and starboard on this deck.

The high standards of the deckhouse and other fittings are evident in the teak capping rails that are fitted on top of the bulwarks on the main deck and bridge deck, continued around the enclosing guardrail. A grating platform is arranged right forward inside the curve of the bow. The two anchors are handled by twin vertical cable lifters with prominent wheel-operated cable clamps, with gypsy barrels to take the forward mooring ropes. The mooring bollards are sited directly inside the openings in the bulwarks, as shown in the scrap detail on Sheet 1. Small capstans are incorporated between the bollards aft to handle the mooring ropes.

Main particulars
LOA: 90ft
LWL: 75ft
Beam: 24ft
Draft: 8ft
Displacement: 140 tons
Engine Kelvin: TBSC8
Max. Speed: 12 knots
Builder/year: Bloemsma Van Breemen Shipyard 2006

Colour Scheme
Dark Blue: upper hull, upper section of runabout motor boat
Red: hull underbodies
White: deckhouses, white line above waterline on yacht and small boat, rubbing strake line at deck edge, mast and boat davit, inside of bulwarks
Natural wood colour: planked decks
Varnished wood: deckhouse and wheelhouse access doors

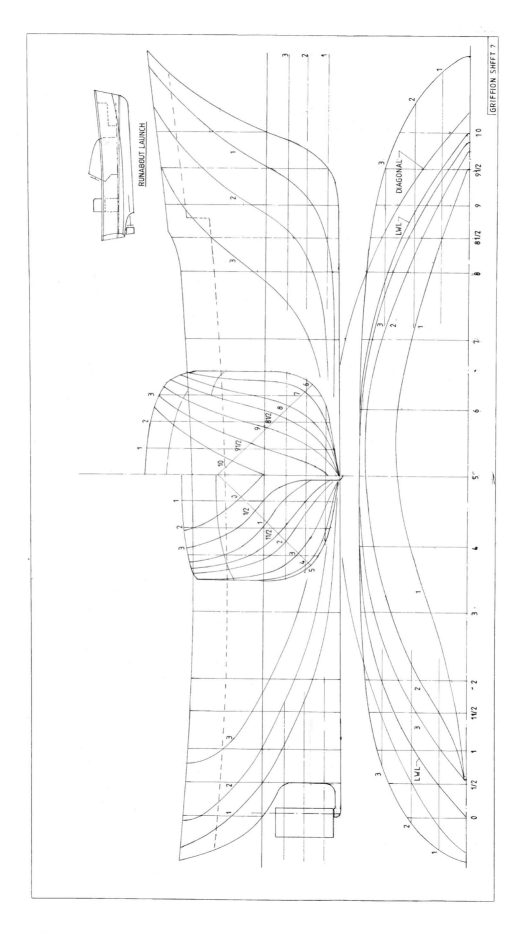

RUNABOUT LAUNCH

GRIFFION SHEET 2

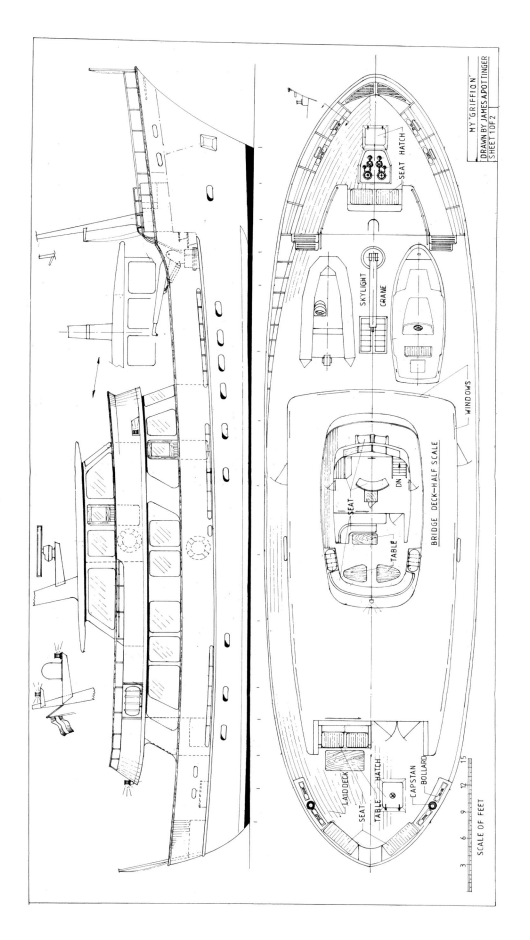

MY 'GRIFFION'
DRAWN BY JAMES A. POTTINGER
SHEET 1 OF 2

SEAT HATCH

SKYLIGHT

CRANE

WINDOWS

SEAT

DN

TABLE

BRIDGE DECK—HALF SCALE

LAID DECK

SEAT

TABLE

HATCH

CAPSTAN

BOLLARD

SCALE OF FEET

3 6 9 12 15

STS *Tenacious*

A MODERN SQUARE-RIGGER

by David Mills

The Jubilee Sailing Trust (www.jst.org.uk) is a registered charity that was set up in 1978. It was inspired by the idea of Christopher Rudd that the integration of able-bodied and physically handicapped persons crewing a full-rigged sailing vessel would be a worthwhile benefit to all concerned. Their first ship, the *Lord Nelson*, designed by Colin Mudie, had her maiden voyage in 1986, and was such a success that in 1993 it was decided to build a new ship, this time designed by Tony Castro. Very imaginatively it was to be made of wood so that

the unskilled labour of the able-bodied and physically handicapped could be used in its construction. Therefore it was built under cover, upside down, turned upright, put on to trolleys, and rolled out on to a barge, which was towed out and sunk, leaving the *Tenacious* to float off; the first wooden square-rigger to be built in a British yard for a hundred years.

I previously made a model of the *Lord Nelson* (MS 119) to

Below: The completed model of *Tenacious.*

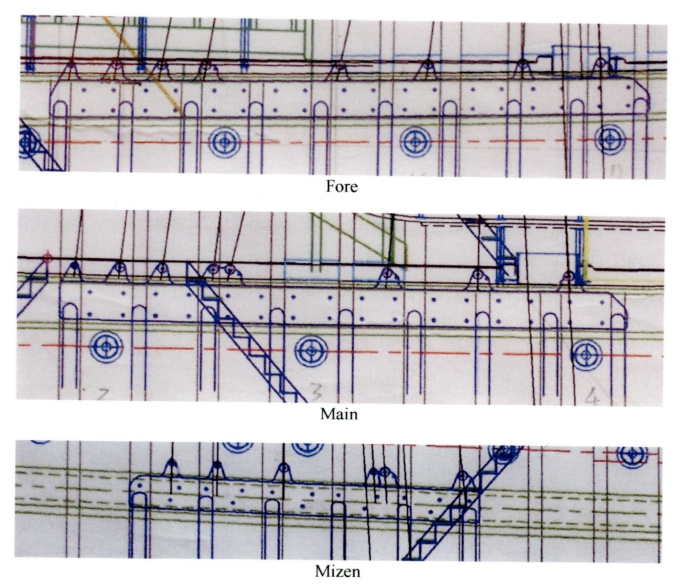

Fore

Main

Mizen

a scale of $^3/_{16}$in = lft (1:64) and so to show their relative sizes I made *Tenacious* to the same scale, though my work space was barely large enough to accommodate the model during construction. I was able to obtain copies of some of the working drawings from the Trust, though I discovered the hull lines were from a discarded draught. I had to make corrections which, it turned out, were not quite right. The drawings were augmented by several photo-visits made whenever the ship was at Southampton.

HULL AND BASE

The keel, stem and stern posts were made of strip ramin. Three holes were drilled vertically through the keel to take the long screws that would go through the supporting pillars and baseboard. *Tenacious* had sixty-nine frames, but as can be seen I reduced this to forty, made from 6mm plywood and slotted into the keel assembly. This whole skeleton was then mounted upside-down on a temporary base and covered with strips of $^1/_{64}$in ply up to the level of the main deck. In one pair of planks grilles were cut for the bow-thrusters and in another hawse holes were cut. Small gaps and imperfections were made good with filler and then rubbed down. This was followed by the fitting of propeller shafts and propellers, which were carved from boxwood, as was the rudder, which had a short stock that fitted into a hole drilled in the counter against the stern post. With the hull in this position I applied the anti-fouling paint up to the waterline.

Although the case would not be required for some time I built its plinth with bull-nosed moulding (which now seems to be called 'large rounded skirting architrave'). I fitted an internal shelf of 120mm x 6mm softwood to take the baseboard using screws from the outside, covering up the holes with filler before veneering. It is important the shelf is at such a

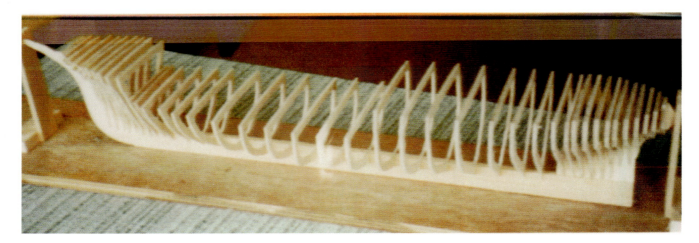

Above: The framed hull ready for planking.

Above: Rubbing strake and shroud and backstay straps. Also shown are the emergency chute and the top platform for the accommodation ladder.

depth that the baseboard assembly is proud of the edge of the plinth, otherwise difficulty will be had when lowering the upper assembly into position, as the acrylic is liable to bend. The end panels of the acrylic were cut about 25mm longer than the sides so that they slotted into the gaps at each end (see Figure 1, p191). The assembly could then be screwed to the plinth through a hole drilled in the bottom edge of the acrylic end panels.

The baseboard was cut from 6mm MDF to fit the inside of the plinth, allowing for the edging strip and the thickness of the acrylic. It was then veneered with sycamore leaves matching along the centreline, and three holes were drilled to take the screws of the supporting pillars. On the underside I glued 120mm x 6mm softwood strips along the edges, and finally sycamore edging strips all round, covering the edge of the baseboard and the softwood. The top was varnished, pol-

ished, and covered with soft paper and two pieces of MDF. These incorporated three semi-circular cut-outs on one edge, to accommodate the brass pillars, which were butted along the centreline. The MDF was held in position along the sides and ends with duct tape. The hull was mounted on these brass pillars on the baseboard – the MDF covering made a useful working surface. Next the forecastle and poop were covered with $^1/_{16}$in ply. In the latter, rectangular ports were cut and backed with exposed developed film, whilst the frames, etched from brass shim (not as successfully as I had hoped) were glued around the edges. The portholes around the poop and indeed everywhere else in the hull had slightly projecting rims, so I made them exactly as I did on my model of the paddle steamer *Glen Gower* (see *Model Shipwright 117*). The rubbing strakes around the main deck and poop were made up from strips of thin ply incorporating the chain plates; this is shown in the photograph immediately above. The latter were cut from 0.015in brass with holes drilled in the lugs to take studs of brass rod, to secure straps to the rigging screws. These straps, which were of different lengths depending on the mast and whether they were for shrouds or backstays, were cut to length from 0.010in brass.

DECKING AND DECKHOUSES

A sub-deck of $^1/_{64}$in plywood was fitted overall and the two deckhouses were built up from the same ply, with square softwood corner strips. The plywood sides were cut with two or three lugs, depending on the length, to fit into narrow slots in the sub-deck. The poop deckhouse was centred round a block of softwood to take the mizzen mast. Windows were cut out, edged with etched brass frames and glazed with clear or roughened plastic as appropriate; similarly reduced openings were cut out for doorways, which were covered with doors cut from 0.75mm plasticard, with clear plastic insets. The doors were fitted with handles and grab rails; hand rails ran around both houses, which also had deckheads made from the thin plywood and edged with a strip of thin plasticard. I laid a cover plate of 0.75mm plasticard around the edges of the main and poop decks with extensions for bollards and pin rails. This was slightly thicker than the planking, which was cut from 0.7mm plain sycamore veneer. With the deckhouses temporarily in place the planking was laid yacht-style using individual strips. Margin and king planks were cut about double width. Before laying the forecastle deck I located the hawse holes and spurling pipes and fitted the trays which contained the stoppers for the windlass and fairleads. These were made from thin plasticard and painted with a metallic paint. The guiding strips to assist blind and partially sighted persons were cut in the same way as the planks but with the blade set as close as possible.

HANDRAILS AND STANCHIONS

The stanchions were made of 1.2mm brass rod, except those around the poop supporting pin rails, which were 1.5mm diameter. Two holes 0.4mm diameter were drilled in each using $^1/_{16}$in brass angle as a jig pre-drilled with guide holes (from the inside for centring) and firmly clamped as shown in Figure 3. This was rather tedious and costly in terms of drill bits. Stretched 28 SWG copper wire was threaded through the holes and soldered at the appropriate positions. When fitted in holes drilled around the deck wooden top rails 2.3mm wide were cut from 1mm thick apple wood, which I rounded on the edges and colour-varnished. Templates were made of the curves of the forecastle and poop to which the handrails were cut and then glued in place with a dab of

Above: Plank cutter.

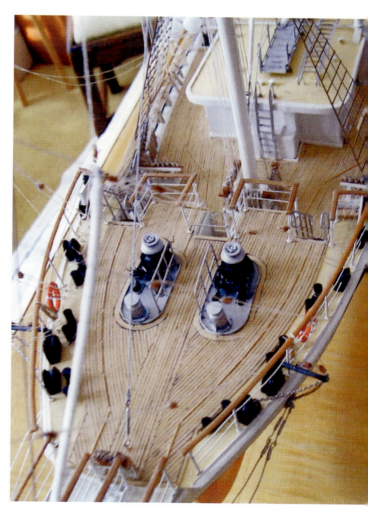

Right: Forecastle, showing windlasses, fairleads and raised strips on deck to guide the visually impaired. Note the coils of rope hanging from the pins, wooden ratlines, and gangway stowed on top of the deckhouse.

Left: Fore lower platform and forward truss.

Bostik non-solvent adhesive on each stanchion. The canvas wind breaks consisted of cigarette paper painted matt white.

LADDERS

The sides were made from thin strips of brass, to which hand rails made of 22 SWG stretched copper wire shaped around a former were soldered. Treads were cut from sycamore veneer and slotted into a jig, as shown in Figure 2. With the aid of a straight piece of wood they were made flush with one side of the slotted rack. The opposite side was then glued in position. When the glue had set the assembly was moved across and the other side glued. Here again I used Bostik non-solvent glue. When set it was somewhat rubbery and so offered a little give, which was useful when removing from the jig.

FAIRLEADS AND BOLLARDS

One half of a fairlead was carved from boxwood and glued flat on to a piece of wood, to which a small upright piece of wood was glued along one side. In turn three strips of thin wood were attached to this with elastic bands, to form a box. Into this box molten vinyl plastic was poured. When set the 'box' was removed and the mould released. A second mould was cast and the two halves were held face to face using two thin pieces of wood and elastic bands. Resin with blackening paste was poured into the mould through a small hole cut into the base and allowed to set. When released the fairlead was trimmed with a small file. As seventeen of these were needed the mould could easily be renewed if necessary. The bollards were straightforward, being made of plasticard and plastic rod painted black.

MASTS AND PLATFORMS

The lower masts were made of 7.9mm diameter polystyrene tube with a 6.4mm tube inserted to give extra stiffness, whilst the topgallant and royal masts were turned, tapering from one piece of straight-grained Parana pine. These slotted into the lower masts. They were fitted with trucks and jackstaffs. Royals were also fitted with caps, into which two small holes were drilled to take a flag halliard. The mast platforms were made using a jig. A small section of polystyrene tube the same diameter as the masts was inserted as a guide; $1/16$in x $1/64$in brass strip was bent around the former and soldered to the crosstrees and tresstrees made of $3/64$in square brass strip

Left: Windlass. Note one of the guide strips fitted on the deck to assist blind and visually impaired persons.

Above: Large blocks, centre of windlass, plug for half a fairlead mould, and small blocks.

held in slots as shown. I used Carr's paste solder, using the higher temperature on the rim and the lower on the centre joints, though so long as the rim was held tight it survived any loosening of the solder when the other centre joints were hot. After drilling holes, fitting the stanchions and painting they were slid down the masts to rest on a thin ring cut from a larger sized polystyrene tube, and supported by stays, made of the same square section brass. To fit these into the masts I soldered a small piece of brass shim at one end, which slotted into a cut in the relevant mast. When cut to length these were glued to the underside of the tresstrees.

Finally each section of the handrail was cut to length and secured to the stanchions with a dab of glue. At this stage I fitted small eyes of bent wire for stays, lifts, halliards etc., but later I was glad that I had invested in a flexible drive to my Minicraft drill, which enabled me to drill holes that I had forgotten until after the masts had been stepped. The slides for the upper two yard trusses were made from pieces of small plastic channel covered with a metallic paint.

SPARS

As the upper topsails, topgallants and royals were roller-reefed these were shaped from a square sandwich of veneer and two pieces of straight-grained pine as shown in Figure 4, so that when carved a slot was left for the roller-reefing. The lower yards, spanker boom and gaffs were carved from single pieces of pine. The lower yard trusses were made from two pieces of $^1/_{16}$in square brass soldered together in the form of

Above: Platform jig.

a 'V', the end of which was glued into a small piece of brass channel. A short length of rod had been soldered into the base of this; the other ends were then soldered to two strips of brass shim wrapped around a former the same diameter as the appropriate yard. They were then painted a metallic colour and slipped on to the yard, fixed with a dab of glue and pegged with a small brass stud pushed through a hole in one of the rings on the under-side. Other bands around the spars were made from strips of metallic-painted cigarette paper with holes drilled through them to take necessary eyes when the glue had set. The upper three yards and the lower two had a single jackyard along the top; these were made by sliding a piece of thin piano wire through a series of small eyes made from thin copper wire glued into holes drilled into

Above: Showing boats, davits, winch, kedge anchor, starboard lift in upper position and port lift in lower position.

the yard. Sails on the lower yards were made of strips of the finest lawn I could get, and cut so that when rolled up some of the clews were left to hang down a little to take the clew-lines and sheets. They were then fastened with cotton gaskets around the forward jack yards. Dabs of glue helped them to sit fairly snugly on the yards. The stirrups for the footropes were made from blackened copper wire with an eye to go round the jackyard and an eye at the other end through which the foot-ropes were threaded.

They were then bent round the curve of the spar and held with a spot of glue. Eyes for the lifts and brace pennants were fitted at each end.

BOATS

The semi-rigid boats were made from U-shapes carved from a fruit wood, with a deck cut from plasticard and glued to the underside. The outboard motors were carved from boxwood.

DAVITS AND DECK FITTINGS

The davits were made from boxwood. The lip along the top and bottom of the jib was formed by gluing on slightly over-sized pieces of thin brass shim. The lever system was cut from plasticard, the drums from plastic rod, and the switchgear boxes were small pieces of boxwood.

The windlasses were turned from boxwood with webs of plasticard glued vertically around the lower pedestal. The same method was used for the mooring winches in the stern and main deck, and also the fairleads to the windlasses.

Lifebelts were made from rings of polystyrene tube with the edges slightly rounded. The mounting for the repeater dial in the pelorus, of which there was one each side of the bridge, was shaped using a fine saw and file from a ring of $3/16$in diameter thin-walled brass tube about $3/16$in wide fitted tightly on the end of a wooden rod (see Figure 5). On removal a small length of brass rod was soldered on to the lower part to sit into the pedestal. The bowl was turned on

Left: Pelorus on board ship.

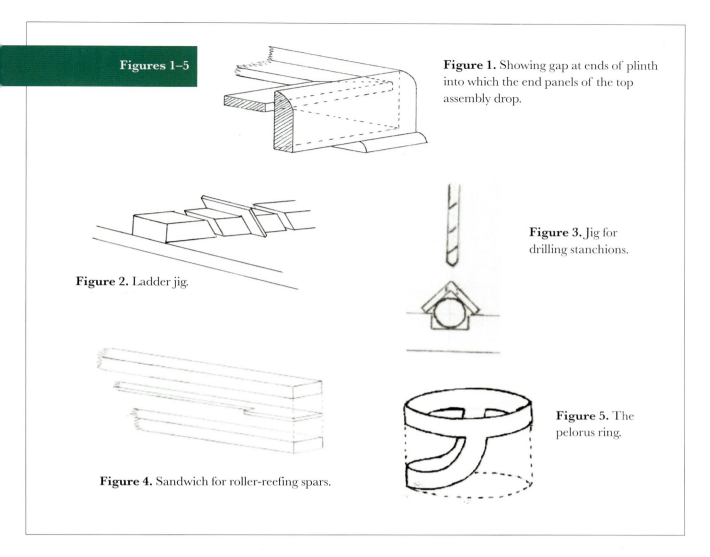

Figure 1. Showing gap at ends of plinth into which the end panels of the top assembly drop.

Figure 2. Ladder jig.

Figure 3. Jig for drilling stanchions.

Figure 4. Sandwich for roller-reefing spars.

Figure 5. The pelorus ring.

the end of a piece of boxwood, cut off to size and fitted into the ring, and the whole mounted on a pedestal.

The ship was equipped with three vertical lifts for wheelchair crew. These were made by soldering a framework of $^3/_{64}$in square brass with thin pieces of plasticard for the sides. The gangways were made from thin brass. Treads were made from $^1/_{32}$in angle and glued on. The 'bathing' ladder was also made up from thin brass strips as treads, with angle for the sides. The stowed inflatable life rafts were made from polystyrene tubes plugged with plaster domes at each end.

RIGGING AND BLOCKS

The standing rigging was set up using Amati black rigging thread of various thicknesses, but I used their natural coloured 0.8mm diameter dyed grey for the running rigging.

The blocks were made as described in my previous article *Restoring a Model of an Unnamed Brig*, featured in *Shipwright 2010*. Rigging screws were made by sliding a length of sleeving off a strand of telephone wire and cutting off pieces to represent the body of the screws, threading through another piece of wire, the ends of which had protruding eyes. As I have never been satisfied with the hang of my cotton rope coils from belaying pins, I made the coils from wire.

DISPLAY CASE

It would have been less hazardous to have made the cover when I made the plinth, but I had no convenient place to store such a large structure whilst the building proceeded.

The cover for the case was made from acrylic sheets, which are considerably lighter than glass. They were cut to size with the end panels measured about 30mm longer, with holes drilled in each so that they could be screwed firmly to the inside ends to the plinth. Then the side and top panels were glued into place using contact adhesive. The frames were made of angled softwood strips veneered with sycamore to match the plinth. These were then glued along the edges with 'No Nails' adhesive and held in position with masking tape until set.

Intermodellbau Dortmund

MARINE EXHIBITS AT EUROPE'S LARGEST MODEL SHOW

by Dave Wooley

I have been attending Intermodellbau Dortmund, Europe's largest model show, for over a decade. The sheer volume and variety of models and model-making disciplines dispersed amongst the eight large halls never ceases to amaze me.

Intermodellbau attracts over 100,000 visitors and the variety of model interest is almost endless. My own personal interest is focused on all things marine but the models and activities associated with the various disciplines varies enormously, from magnificent model railway displays in two halls through to model trucks, tanks and any other form of mechanical vehicle. Then there are the aircraft, airships, card models, miniature models, engineering and fairground models. The latter category in particular is a real eye opener, with its complex array of models incorporating audio and light displays. Intermodellbau is not just a giant exhibition, it is an experience in itself.

Below: A general view of just one part of Hall 5 – the boat hall.

Above: A good example of imaginative displays and exhibits.

Intermodellbau is held at the Messe Westfalenhallen, Dortmund, and this venue is very easy to reach via the underground rail network either from the airport or the rail station. Transport in Germany is quick, frequent and inexpensive, making a journey from any of the major airports relatively straightforward. For those wishing to return less than empty handed, however, travelling by car or as part of an organised coach trip is recommended. A number of travel companies now run coaches to cater for foreign visitors.

Below: Results of a live figure carving demonstration on the Historischer Schiffbau stand.

Above: The German equivalent of the Model Shipwrights.

THE BOAT HALL

Although Hall 5 is the dedicated boat hall, having a large pool where R/C ships are more prevalent, there is a strong static input from various clubs, societies and groups. Germany, like the UK, has a strong maritime identity and this is very much reflected in the displays. Some have nautical themes, constructing stands to represent the bridge of a ship (complete with funnel), for example. Others show complex models with many working features, which are a

Below: Other stands also displayed traditionally built models such as this Lustyacht, *Kirsten*, complete with cradle.

great attraction in Germany. There are also dedicated stands; 'Die Seenotretter', the German equivalent of the RNLI, for instance. Others like 'Meine Kleine Schiffswerft' display steel ship building in model form, again generating a constant flow of interest from modellers and public alike.

Although many of the models on display are working, there is the German model shipwrights association, the Arbeitskreis Historischer Schiffbau eV. This association have been demonstrating their traditional woodworking and model ship building skills for many years, and they bring to the Intermodellbau some of the most outstanding models of the show. They also had entries in the Naviga C class World

Above: The *Zirfaea*, a research and survey vessel, at 1:75 scale by Naviga C Class Champion Werner Toller.

Championship, which was held at Dortmund Intermodellbau in 2010. Although clearly focusing on period ships and the age of sail, their maritime interest also embraces warships of the German Navy from the ships of the Hanseatic period through to the Imperial and post-Imperial navies.

Below: Jurgen Scharfenberg's all-brass cargo vessels employ the same method of construction to that of the full size ship, including riveting.

Above: Models of river vessels are very popular, particularly those operating on the Rhine.

There is a huge interest in vessels associated with the oil supply industry, oceanographic research and, of course, river craft of all types. A good example of this are the number of models of steamers or commercial vessels from the Elbe, Rhine and Danube. Many were seen sailing elegantly around the indoor pool. Others were seen on stands such as the IG Binnenschiffe Duisburg, demonstrating feathering paddles on the Rhine steamer *Köln* with the simple expedient of a mirror.

Many of the top German ship model makers come to Dortmund. Werner Toller presented several of his Naviga models including the Dutch Research and Survey vessel *Zirfaea* in 1:75 scale. Equally the standard of the club models is impressive, to say the least, and there is always an eye for detail. Often models feature stunning paint finishes that are far from reality when compared with the original ships. Nonetheless, they are all a credit to their builders.

MARITIME SCENES IN OTHER HALLS

Naturally the ship models in the boat hall (Hall 5) are the centre of attention. Yet not all ship models are confined to this space. Often superbly built and authentically displayed models are used as part of a much larger display, especially by railway modellers. Here they form parts of dioramas depicting ports or coastal towns and are cleverly integrated into the scenes, some even generating their own steam as if

Right: Just some of the deck detail worked into one of the Rhine river ships.

preparing to depart the dock or quayside. Other examples include container port facilities, where alongside busy rail activity there are often large and complex ship models.

CARD MODELLING

Marine card modelling is a major model-making discipline in Germany. As such it is represented with a wide range of content, from full hull miniature models to huge dioramas of harbours, docks and ports; the themes are seemingly endless. There is also a strong manufacturing base for such models, which in turn generates further enthusiasm.

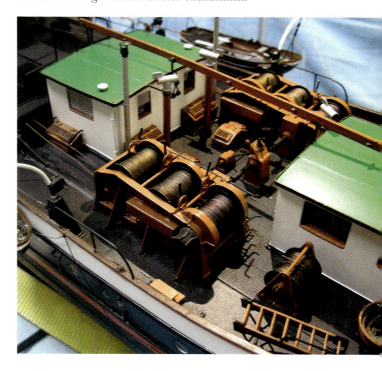

Above: All the models on the Meine Kleine Schiffswerft stand are built in brass by Jurgen Scharfenberg.

Above: Demonstrating hull construction on this model of German *Vorpostenboote* or port protection boats.

Above: Just some of the detailed work on the *Zirfaea*.

Above: An interesting way to display the feathering paddles on the Rhine steamer *Köln*.

Above: Models such as this coaster were found in the railway hall.

Above: A roll-on-roll-off train ferry, made almost entirely from card.

Above: The stern wheeler *Mississippi Queen* attracted considerable attention.

VENDORS

The model trade is an integral part of Intermodellbau and all the major manufacturers attend, including big names such as Revell, Graupner, Krick, and many more specialist suppliers. It is here that there is a crossover of interest as tools, electronic equipment and materials are all available under one roof on a vast scale. Often what is available in the aircraft hall will do just the job for a boat modeller and the same can apply throughout all the halls. For the first time this year I witnessed a really strong rise in model engineering. Surprisingly, Intermodellbau has been slow on the uptake in this sphere of modelling but not any more. There is also a growing interest in computer controlled cutting, whether to a lathe, milling machine or more sophisticated forms of pattern making. Here industrial technology is now being made available to the model maker at affordable prices. This is indeed a sea change.

Below: The bomb vessel *Salamandre* on the Historical Ships stand.

Above: The Austro-Hungarian coastal defence ship *Monarch*.

CONCLUSION

If you have not had the opportunity to visit Intermodellbau then try to make at least one trip – it is more than just a model show; it is an experience not to be missed. Be prepared to spend some time exploring the halls, as one day is simply not enough. The boat hall alone will absorb a whole day. I like to start when the doors open at 9am and to be one of the last out at 6pm. In 2011 I spent two whole days and yet managed to see only half the event. In 2010 I did not leave the boat hall for two days. Entrance for each day is €11.00, with cheaper rates for children. Dortmund is very accessible and taxis are widely available. Transport from accommodation to the exhibition is fast and inexpensive, particularly if four or more share a cab. One final thought – be prepared to walk! There are many refreshment outlets within each of the halls but it can be a long trek from Hall 2 to Hall 8, to say nothing of the time spent totally absorbed in the many thousands of models on display.

Above: Card modelling in all its forms is very popular at the Intermodellbau.

Book News

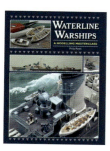

Waterline Warships – An Illustrated Masterclass
Philip Reed
Seaforth Publishing, 2010
Hardback, 128 pages
ISBN 978-1-84832-076-5
£25.00

If there is an afterlife and Norman Ough's spirit made it through the Pearly Gates he is surely delighted that so many still admire his superb warship models, particularly HMS *Queen Elizabeth* with attendant destroyer and his model of HMS *Hood*, and continue to use his drawings, especially warship fittings, as well as his written description of such.

Philip Reed and this reviewer have long been admirers of Norman's skills and Philip follows his example in building a miniature waterline warship using minimal engineering techniques and maximum use of simple materials such as wood and paper.

The author has a deserved reputation as a builder of sailing-ship models and his previous books include *Building a Miniature Navy Board Model* and *Period Ship Modelmaking*. However over the years he has built sixteen, mainly World War II, warship models; starting with plastic kits but quickly progressing to scratch-built. Many of these are described and illustrated at the end of this new book.

The book is not an encyclopedia of the many methods of building waterline warships but primarily a detailed and beautifully photographed description of Philip's 16ft to 1in model of HMS *Caesar*, sister to HMS *Cavalier* at Chatham, the actual ship being laid-down in 1943. She was one of the 'Ca' Class destroyers with the classic and elegant single-funnel ships that stretched from the 'Js' to the 'Battles'. The author details her history before embarking on descriptions of his workshop, tools, and materials used. The model has a wood-block hull, plywood superstructure and bridge-decks,

with extensive use of paper for plating and detailing. Philip does allow himself some limited use of plastic and etched brass, but in the main he follows Norman Ough's proven methods and materials to produce a first class ship model.

His photographs are a great help to beginners and the more experienced warship modeller, especially of such fittings as the Hazemayer-Bofors which on drawings is not easy to interpret.

His ship's boats are delightful, the photos show just what can be achieved, the clinker-built whaler being only about one-and-a-half-inches long. The sea-setting is a marvel, basically constructed from carved wood realistically painted; by no means the easiest technique.

A significant departure from Norman Ough's methods is Philip's extensive use of superglue. He and I have repaired models for museums; in my case the museum's conservators regarded superglue as strictly 'verboten', favouring the tried and tested 'natural' adhesives favoured by Norman – who knows the long term effects of superglue?

This is a book well worth buying for anyone interested in making model ships using relatively simple methods – from age six to eighty!

David Brown

17th and 18th Century Ship Models from the Kreigstein Collection
Arnold and Henry Kriegstein
Seawatch Books, 2010
Hardback, 256 pages, numerous colour plate illustrations
ISBN 978-0-98205-797-1
$85.00

This is the second, revised and expanded publication of a book which originally appeared in 2007, albeit briefly, before being removed from circulation. The publishers' claim that their new, large format edition does justice to this stunning private collection of ship models is well founded. The choice of a landscape format certainly enhances the subject matter, allowing the exquisite detail on the models themselves to be photographed in close proximity.

The Kreigstein Collection comprises a large number of 17th and 18th Century Navy Board ship models. Successive chapters are individually devoted to some sixteen First to Sixth Rate model warships, together with three bomb vessels, some admirals' barges, a troop transport, a ship's boat and, by way of contrast, a Dutch state yacht. The final part of this book will be of particular interest, dealing as it does with the all-important matter of sourcing sufficient information to allow the modeller or model collector to achieve a truly accurate representation of the original vessel. This issue has been of particular importance to the Kreigstein brothers in the past as some of their collection has been through several ownerships and previous restoration has been carried out imperfectly or wrongly in several instances.

Each of the chapters relating to the individual ship models is divided into several sub-sections entitled: Acquisition, Provenance, Description, Literature and Historical Perspective. Thus the reader is provided with an extremely detailed account not only of the model itself and how it was acquired but also of the warship within its historical context. The endnotes for each chapter add an informative guide to further research.

Two important distinctions are drawn at the start of this book which set the Navy Board ship models apart from others of their kind. Firstly, these were working objects, designed to reveal the construction of the full size ship. Thus, sections of planking are deliberately omitted on some, which allow one a glimpse below deck; the beautifully scaled fixtures and fittings provide an accurate insight into the eighteenth-century 'wooden world'. In the case of the 'bomb' *Carcass*, for example, the model comprises the midship section only; the utilitarian, cutaway style of this model is thought to have been adopted in order to demonstrate the structural modifications required to support the weight and absorb the recoil of the 13in mortars carried by this vessel.

The second distinction concerns the use to which the models were put following construction. Unlike their continental equivalents, the Navy Board Models passed into private hands almost immediately, thus establishing a tradition of use as desirable, interior decorations or as collectors' items in some of the richest homes in the country. Samuel Pepys records how the shipwrights were permitted to distribute these models to favoured and presumably influential recipients as a means of advertising their work and attracting future custom. In many cases the Kreigsteins have been able to trace the ownership of the models through the centuries before acquiring them for their own collection. Thus, the 'Acquisition' sections of the chapters make for fascinating reading. For example, finding the *Royal James*, a splendid, fully-rigged model of the Restoration-era First Rate, took the brothers over twenty years after which they were required to endure a further period of waiting before the necessary export license was granted.

This is a beautifully produced book and, while it is expensive to purchase, it nevertheless does full justice to the superb craftsmanship of the models themselves. The colour plate illustrations, the majority of which were taken by the brothers themselves, allow us to view the ships from all angles while the close-ups reveal the extent of the workmanship involved. The text is both informative and highly readable. Moreover, the sheer enthusiasm of the Kreigsteins for their subject is quite infectious.

There will be those reading this review who will deeply regret the fact that these objects of historic, national importance are now residing overseas. It is implicit in the text that the Kreigstein brothers are fully aware of this; they are anxious to stress the fact that the Navy Board models have always been in private ownership and that they are merely custodians of these items. Indeed, there can be little doubt that the care and financial investment they have lavished on their collection over the years by way of careful and accurate professional restoration has been the equal of any museum. While the brothers have been privileged to be able to acquire this unrivalled collection through the 'generous and enthusiastic' assistance of their father and their own life-time endeavours, one doubts whether these models, which have been mostly been purchased through private auctions, would have fared any better had they been dispersed among individual collections. Nevertheless, from a wider perspective, it is a sobering indication of the value that has been placed on the historical narrative of the official British shipbuilders' model that the National Maritime Museum's unsurpassed collection has been languishing for years in store and has only latterly been made accessible to the wider public in a new display area at Chatham Historic Dockyard.

Jon Wise

Legacy of a Ship Model: Examining HMS 'Princess Royal' 1773

Rob Napier
SeaWatch Books, 2010
Hardback, 210 pages plus DVD, lavishly illustrated, supported by nine Appendixes and reference data
ISBN 978-0-98205-796-4
$58, exclusively from the publishers

The challenge faced by any publication describing the construction, or in this case renovation, of a specific model is to avoid limiting its appeal by becoming purely a Builder's Manual or focusing solely on an individual vessel – and here the author has, on balance, succeeded.

The model of HMS *Princess Royal* 'examined' in this book is a Navy Board model, built to 1:48 scale contemporaneously in the same Royal dockyard as the original vessel; it is described as representing the 'Georgian Style' having a fully-planked hull with deck-planks omitted to reveal internal features, and depicts no armament, masts, or rigging.

It became privately owned and resided on the Isle of Wight for over a century before being acquired by Henry Huddleston Rogers in the USA, who eventually bequeathed it, amongst fifty others, to its current custodians at the United States Naval Academy Museum in Maryland: the book describes this model in great depth and, by association, similar models and vessels of the era – but it also does more.

Rob Napier is a professional model-maker and a master-craftsman who conveys his enthusiasm, knowledge (of materials in particular), and meticulous approach to this project in a very clear and readable manner. This is his second book and it is written from the heart as a conversation with likeminded enthusiasts yet with the clarity of an informed and well presented lecture.

The numerous high quality colour photographs are captioned informatively and well annotated with helpful graphics; the ubiquitous but subtle arrow indicating 'Forwards' soon becomes a friendly guiding-hand to orientate the reader!

What broadens the appeal of this book's specific subject is the insight that it provides to the world of professional ship-modelling, both now and back in the days when things were done very differently. Topics such as referencing the many disassembled components, returning the hull to its original shape, cleaning techniques, and the dilemma of repairing earlier repairs which themselves have become part of the model's history are relatively unusual and make interesting reading.

The standard of model-making conveyed by this book is of such a high standard that frankly it transcends merely inspirational; those of us who enjoy tinkering in the workshop can only be mesmerised by the amount of (paid) time, resources, and technology brought to bear on a project at this level; and then be humbled by the craftsmanship and dedication of the earlier 'modelwrights' (author's term) with their relatively primitive facilities and somewhat inferior lighting.

The model's external workmanship is obvious and stunning, but more so is the extent and quality of the non-viewable internal detailing that was revealed by means of fibre-optic endoscopy, X-raying, and eventually by dissection for this major overhaul.

Shipwright's readers will warm to the discovery of an original camber-template left (deliberately or otherwise) inside the hull and its use again during this renovation; the pencilled reference marks still evident beneath fittings; and, reassuringly, evidence of a few corrected measurements and overzealous timber removal to suggest some human fallibility in earlier ship-modellers!

The publication is presented as a high-quality package but notwithstanding the quality of the subject, writing, and illustrations it is somewhat let-down by 'hardware' issues.

Immediately apparent, and a distraction throughout, is the book's 'landscape' orientation (A4 with the spine on its shorter-edge): very practical for a reference book in use on a crowded desk or workbench but hardly conducive to relaxed armchair browsing; and unsightly when stowed in the average domestic book-case.

The DVD provides an overview of the model and its seventeen-month reassembly by means of some clever time-lapse photography that suggests a 'Laurel and Hardy' escapade; it offers an interesting insight to both the project and a professional's workshop and, whilst fashionable, this combination of media will not be to every reader's taste.

However DVDs lead independent lives and the book has to be able to stand-alone, which results in a very strange, and increasingly frustrating, omission – there is not one photograph that conveys the magnitude and grandeur of the actual model, 'Before' or 'After', anywhere in the text or on the outer-pages of this book: two were found eventually at the end of Appendix Nine, requiring the reader to persevere in order 'to see the wood for the trees'!

Legacy of a Ship Model provides the definitive reference to an historic artefact and a catalogue of its restoration at this stage of its life; this is a delightfully written book presenting a unique insight to the construction of eighteenth-century Navy Board Models that will appeal to ship-modellers and maritime enthusiasts specialising in this period.

Whilst not being a book about 'model-making' it should also be of interest to the less specialised maritime modeller who can relate to, if not emulate, the craftsmanship and standards achieved by professional ship modellers – both now and in the past.

Graham Castle

Histoire des cuirassés d'escadre IENA & SUFFREN
Philippe Caresse
Lela Presse, 2009
Hardback, 192 pages, 260+ B&W photos and plans, colour artworks, maps and data tables
ISBN 978-2-91401-754-1
€45.00

Philippe Caresse has previously produced English-language articles on these two turn-of-the-century pre-dreadnought battleships for *Shipwright*'s sister publication *Warship* (see 2007 and 2010 editions). In this new book from Lela Presse, which benefits from 192 large-format pages, he has been able to include much more material in terms of both text and illustration.

The text follows the general format of the articles: an account of the design process of each ship followed by a detailed analysis of technical characteristics, and finally a service history. The technical data is extremely comprehensive, and is accompanied by full sets of official plans. In contrast to the plans published in other recent French monographs these are beautifully reproduced with sharp and clearly-defined lines (although because they have been reduced from large-scale plans many of the annotations can still be read only with a magnifying glass). The photographic coverage is not only comprehensive but of exceptional quality, with many views from contemporary periodicals and photo agencies to complement those from the French naval archives. There are also sections of colour artwork for each ship, showing external appearance and livery at the various key points in their careers. These are reproduced across a single page, and are less detailed than the official plans, but nevertheless provide a useful complement for the latter and would be invaluable to any prospective model-maker.

Much of the above is accessible to the English-speaking reader with only a smattering of French. Those whose linguistic skills go beyond this will enjoy a much more comprehensive account of the design process and the ships' careers. *Iéna* was lost to a magazine explosion in 1907, only five years after her completion, while *Suffren* played an active part in the Dardanelles campaign, where she flew the flag of Admiral Guépratte, nicknamed 'Fire Eater' by the British.

John Jordan

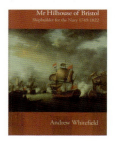

Mr Hilhouse of Bristol – Shipbuilder for the Navy, 1749-1822

Andrew Whitefield
Redcliffe Press Ltd, 2010
Paperback, 150 pages, illustrated with prints, portraits and line-drawings, supported by copious end-notes and references
ISBN 978-1-90659-368-1
£15.99

The majority of *Shipwright*'s readers will have some knowledge and an image of the City and Port of Bristol; possibly as a scene of nineteenth-century maritime activity and Brunel's involvement as an engineer and creator of the SS *Great Britain* that now lies there. Alternatively it may be viewed as an important but declining port throughout the twentieth-century, as evolving trading and shipping practices combined with the River Avon's navigational limitations to take their toll on the city that spawned the phrase 'Shipshape and Bristol fashion'.

Fewer readers will be familiar with the city's Golden Age of entrepreneurship and buccaneering that made Bristol the country's 'second port' during the early eighteenth-century and the subsequent development of a sophisticated and well respected merchant and naval shipbuilding industry – and here I have to declare an interest, and my own ignorance, of this aspect of an area that I knew intimately as a 'boat-daft' youngster captivated by its seafaring tradition.

James Hilhouse was arguably the most influential of these pioneering shipbuilders in that '… almost single-handedly, he created the city's most successful and long-lived shipbuilding company' – a legacy that endured until recent times in the guise of one of his protégés Charles Hills and Sons; significantly it was he who attracted Naval contracts to the city at a time when Their Lordships were justifiably sceptical about having warships built anywhere other than the Royal Dockyards.

He was clearly a talented, far sighted, and industrious all-rounder who in addition to running three busy shipyards and building some of the associated Navy Board-style models was also an accomplished draughtsman and celebrated marine-artist, raised and provided for a large family, and served in various high profile Civic Offices.

This very readable and well presented book gives 'Mr Hilhouse' the recognition that he properly deserves: despite a slightly off-putting but appropriate plod through the family's ancestry the author's engaging style gripped this reviewer with a fascinating glimpse into a 'can do' era, the practical aspects of building Britain's 'wooden walls', the local impact of historical international events, and the real-life saga of his extended family and Bristolian society in a period of opportunity and high adventure.

Whilst being an authoritative and well researched tribute the plot is equally enjoyable as an 'Onedin Line' setting of 'Howard's Way' and I hope the author turns his attention to further comparable projects.

For the model-maker this book offers insightful background reading, particularly so for the 'period' ship-modeller; numerous lesser-known vessels are mentioned, there are some photographs of half-models and a few very small line-drawings that may stimulate further research, aided by the comprehensive Notes and References sections.

Many years ago I cycled daily through the focal point of this narrative, but notwithstanding this fact I would have appreciated a more modern map indicating the results of the author's research into the sites of the original yards in order to 'bring them to life' – more so for readers who may only have driven through today's redeveloped area.

Mr Hilhouse of Bristol is both a laudable contribution to maritime research and a cracking-good read: thoroughly recommend for nautical-buffs who enjoy a bit of genuine swash-buckling.

Graham Castle

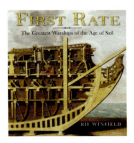

First Rate: The Greatest Warships of the Age of Sail
Rif Winfield
Seaforth Publishing, 2010
Hardback, 168 pages, 31 colour and 46 black-and-white illustrations, 60 plans and 55 photographs
ISBN 978-1-84832-071-0
£45.00

A slightly misleading title, as the First Rates of navies other than the Royal Navy are only mentioned where they have been captured or destroyed in combat, but that said the author has provided a feast of illustrations of the Royal Navy's ships, many in the glowing colours of the original paintings.

The emphasis on providing good illustrations has resulted in a large format book measuring 30 x 32 cms – not the easiest to read on your lap! However the detail in some of the illustrations and model photographs really has to be absorbed carefully and in fairness this is best done on a desk top with a good light.

The book is divided into eleven chapters, the first eight of which cover specific periods of history in the development of the Navy, the final three cover fixtures and fittings, ship structure and finally the few captured First Rates to see service with the Royal Navy. The book is topped and tailed by the author's introduction and acknowledgements, and a single page index.

Each chapter is lavishly illustrated with well chosen paintings, etchings and photographs, mainly of the Admiralty models of the ships of that period. The design and career of each individual ship is briefly described, with any particular highlight covered in more detail. Each chapter also has one or more two page spreads on an independent but related topic. This is one area where the generally high production standards seem to have faltered; sometimes these spreads have the effect of breaking the flow of the main text in rather awkward places.

The reproduction of the illustrations themselves is, without exception, superb. The early illustrations make you realise that we owe an enormous debt to the van de Veldes, elder and younger. Without their detailed sketches and paintings our knowledge of the ships of their time would be much the poorer. From the point of view of the enthusiast, many of the illustrations will be familiar, but seldom have they been so well reproduced. It only takes a visit to something like the Canaletto or van Gogh exhibitions to see that the true colours of their paintings are seldom caught by the printing process, so clearly a lot of effort here has gone into getting the colour reproduction as close to the original as possible.

Equally, the draughts prepared by the Admiralty, or their dockyards, of Royal Navy ships have provided a further essential element to the book. Wherever possible a draught has been provided of an important ship or some development in design. The pièce de résistance is a four page fold out of the draught of the *Victoria* of 1863; a full coloured drawing, replete with detail. As the later draughts, such as that of the *Victoria*, also include a wealth of internal detail, the draughtsman has had to resort to coloured inks to help differentiate internal from external detail.

This has resulted in another slight problem for the reader in that some of these coloured draughts are reproduced in black and white, but the captions refer to "red lines"; not always easy to discern in black and white! There is also a minor problem with duplicated captions on pages 19 and 20, but both refer to the same vessel and probably the same artist so there may not be much lost here.

These slight niggles aside, this is a book to be recommended to anyone with an interest in these ships, ships that clearly constituted man's greatest technological achievements during the 300 years or so they reigned supreme. In fact this book should appeal to the widest audience, from those whose interest lies in marine painting to those who build detailed ship models.

W. B. Davies

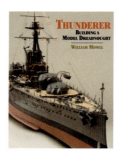

Thunderer: Building a Model Dreadnought
William Mowll
Seaforth Publishing, 2010
Hardback
£25.00

Imagine being on the south bank of the River Thames, where London's Millennium Dome now stands, but on the 29th December 1860. You are there to watch the launch of the hull of _Warrior_ from its birthplace at the Thames Iron Works at Bow Creek on the opposite side of the Thames. Imagine yourself fifty-one years later, at the same spot, watching the launch of the hull of Britain's latest dreadnought, a scene caught on film, the hull surrounded by paddle-tugs belching smoke. Fitted out and commissioned this became the _Orion_ class _Thunderer_: 22,000 tons, 581 feet long, powered by turbines with ten 13.5in guns in five turrets arranged on the centre line, for the first time in a British battleship. Models of both ships were commissioned by West Ham United Football Club, which owes its origins to the Iron Works team. The modeller was the author of this book.

As well as over 20 black and white photographs, mainly of _Thunderer_ herself and parts of the Iron Works, there are over 300 colour photographs mainly of the model and its parts under construction, but concluding with the USS _Texas_, a preserved dreadnought not dissimilar to _Thunderer_. Mowall makes clear throughout the book his admiration for those who designed and built such ships. His work to replicate the results is very much as a 'blacksmith in miniature'. He covers some of the history of the Iron Works, the construction and arming of the actual ship, naval seamanship and practice, the adoption of director firing and the Dreyer fire control table, and finally his visit to the USS _Texas_, which included parts not normally accessible to the public.

The _Orions_' main design fault echoed that of _Dreadnought_ herself, with a single tripod mast almost straddling the fore-funnel and the attendant problems of heat and gases affecting control positions. The four ships of the class were in action at Jutland but _Thunderer_ herself suffered no damage, the main action involving largely the battlecruisers, destroyers and super-dreadnoughts. The USS _Texas_, however, served with Britain's Grand Fleet in 1918 undertaking patrols in the North Sea and the Atlantic. She was rebuilt in the 1920s with one less funnel, oil-fired boilers, tripod masts, torpedo bulges and an aircraft catapult. From 1936 to 1941 she was the Training Ship, _Atlantic_. She covered the Casablanca landings in 1942 and D-Day in 1944, when her targets were the guns believed to be at Pointe-de-Hoc, later bombarding Cherbourg. In November 1944 the ship moved to the Pacific, where she was involved in the Iwo Jima and Okinawa landings. In 1948 she was transferred to the State of Texas as a permanent memorial at St. Jacinto Park, where she remains.

The book and the model are impressive, the text very readable. The author goes to considerable lengths to explain the materials, techniques and tools used to build his model. The hull of the 6ft long, 1:96 scale model is plank-on-frame using mahogony strip and ply, the interior glass-fibred to strengthen and stabilise it, the exterior copper-plated with simulated riveting, and the decks planked with obechi. The production of barbettes, guns, fittings etc. involved silicone rubber moulding as well as metal casting in static moulds and centrifuge, plus silver and soft soldering. Mowll has even managed to obtain and use a section of _Thunderer_'s teak planking, latterly part of a garden seat! The model is equipped with radio-controlled barbettes and lighting above the upper deck, but no propulsive power. Mowll details his own miniature ropewalk, construction of the ship's boats, and an unusual approach to aircraft modelling using copper sheet for the wings, worked to represent fabric shrunk over the ribs.

The author's reliance on powered machinery and various casting methods all taking place in what appears to be a large, well-lit and well-equipped workshop could perhaps be discouraging to those less fortunate, or who choose to rely mainly on simpler tools and materials, following Norman Ough's methods. However, the book should inspire many of us to greater things!

There are, however, some features which diminish the quality of the model and the book. Mowll used only 25 frames to produce a relatively light model. In this reviewer's experience more would have produced a stronger and more accurate model, especially at the stern where pre-drilled frames would obviate the need to bore out the propellor shafts later on and to use glass-fibre internally. The use of mahogany is unnecessary and wasteful: birch ply is perfectly adequate, being fine-grained, much easier to sand and to draw on, and with less vicious splinters. Mowll states that he never glazes scuttles, preferring to be able to see through the model; something not likely in many places on a real ship. Losing the reflective capacity of glazing gives the model something of a 'hollow-eyed' look, and may allow 'guests' such as spiders to take up residence. He has also not joggled the deck planking, copying a model in the Science Museum: hardly likely in real practice, and omitted some of the rigging to allow access to the limited R/C equipment.

Close-up photographs need to be selected very carefully as they can emphasise unfortunate features not so readily visible to the naked eye. For example here there is one of the cutter, which shows coarse grained highly varnished seats and obviously woven fabric for the gratings. The rigols appear far too wide and the White Ensign looks like thick canvas. The figures on the draught markings are much too close together, and the hull supports and propellers are gold plated. The influence of WAGs?

Despite these criticisms Mowll's meticulous workmanship is to be admired, and he has only to quote Frank Sinatra to explain his individualistic modelling comments and overall approach: 'I did it my way'.

David Brown

The Battle of Jutland 1916
George Bonney
The History Press, 2010
Paperback, 244 pages
Includes maps, illustrations, bibliography & index
ISBN 978-0-75245-641-6
£14.99

This is not, I suspect, a book that has been written for anyone who already has any knowledge of the Battle of Jutland. After all, in his introduction Bonney writes that:

'Evidently, this book is not primarily intended for the professional historian, rather it is intended for the reader interested in the recent past…'

However, it gives a reasonably good overview of the development of the navies of Britain and Imperial Germany in the years preceding the Great War and of the main events of the naval war up to, and including, the meeting of the two great battlefleets, on 31 May 1916. The Germans were hoping for 'Der Tag', the British for a 'new Trafalgar' or at least, a second 'Glorious First of June'. They got neither; the Germans were quicker to release details of the battle, and claimed a victory, whilst the British, more circumspect (and probably just not as good at public relations) were slower off the mark, but had won something like a strategic victory. German battlefleets did sail again to challenge the British, but there was more than a degree of truth in the American newspaper claims (the *New York Times*, I think), that the German fleet had assaulted its gaoler, but was still in gaol.

So what does the reader actually get for his £14.99? I believe that Bonney hoped to open a previously closed door of knowledge to those who are discovering the Royal Navy's part in the Great War for the first time. The fact the book carries the logo of the National Museum of the Royal Navy suggests to me that it may well be popular with visitors to Portsmouth, picking this book up after a day looking around the dockyard and museum. It is obvious that Bonney has a love of the Royal Navy and wanted to write this book to inform a wider audience about a key moment in the service's history, which sometimes only gets superficial coverage in larger histories of the Great War.

It is written with passion, and is extremely well illustrated with black and white photographs as well as maps. Essentially, though, it is a reprint of a book published in 2002 and again in 2006, the latter the first paperback edition, and as such, does not contain references to more recent research, for example the works of John Brooks, Jon Sumida and Nicholas Lambert. Bonney's book thus treads a well trodden path. However, Bonney does highlight the defects in Beatty's battlecruisers' signalling, and the continued poor performance of Seymour, Admiral Beatty's Flag Lieutenant, implying that his retention in this post after the Battle of Dogger Bank was a mistake on Beatty's part. He also throws in the odd interesting snippet of information, such as the fact that Hipper was a boyhood fan of Captain Marryatt's novels – the sort of interesting, if not very relevant piece of detail that I like!

Bonney states that his book is not intended to be simply a technical description of the battle. But, like a previous reviewer (referred to in the Introduction to the first paperback edition) I felt uneasy with the frequent asides and discussions, which I felt were never fully developed, often trying to draw parallels with more modern history, and which left me wondering why exactly they were there. I felt that they weren't necessary, and didn't add much to the narrative. I also felt that Bonney sometimes left points rather hanging in the air. On p138, for example, he mentions that the German pre-dreadnoughts were known as the 'five-minute ships' but doesn't explain why. Despite these caveats, however, I found that the book seemed to pick up once starting to discuss the battle itself, almost as if the previous chapters had been setting the scene.

Is this a book that *Shipwright* readers should buy? Certainly, if this is your first venture into the naval side of the Great War, or if you want to gain a general overview of naval developments from the launch of *Dreadnought* to the Great War and especially to the Battle of Jutland. If you already have books and knowledge about this period, I don't think that you'll learn anything new. But you may still want to buy the book to add to your library and you may even (like me), enjoy 'tut-tutting' and 'harrumphing' at the bits you don't like. In short, Bonney's book doesn't add anything new to the works on Jutland, although in these days of 'sea blindness', his enthusiasm for the Royal Navy and his desire to tell the story to others is both laudable and to my mind, necessary.

Andy Field

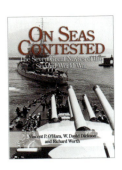

On Seas Contested
The Seven Great Navies of the Second World War
Vincent P. O'Hara, W. David Dickson, Richard Worth (eds.)
Naval Institute Press, 2010
Hardback, 333 pages, illustrated with maps, tables and photographs
ISBN 978-1-59114-646-9
$39.95 / £25.00

It is sometimes quite easy to forget that ships do not exist in isolation: they are always part of a wider scene, whether this is transporting people and goods on behalf of a commercial concern, or (as in the case of the subject of this book) the exercising of power on behalf of governments. In what can only be described as an ambitious concept, a collection of authors and editors attempt to cover all the main aspects of the navies of the seven major combatants of the Second World War in one reasonably sized volume. In this aim *On Seas Contested* by and large succeeds, and often most impressively.

There are seven sections, one devoted to each navy, and each of these follows a broadly similar structure, though there are some differences in emphasis, presumably as a result of the specialisations of the individual writers (for example there is a lot of really rather arcane material about gunnery directors in the United States Navy section). The coverage of the Royal Navy seems perhaps the weakest, but this may simply be the result of the subject being that with which this reviewer is most familiar. On the other hand the section on the Italian Navy is excellent: apart from a slight tendency to talk up the force's rather few successes, and similarly excuse away its somewhat more numerous failures, it is an absolute model in putting together a thorough, clear and informed summary and doing so in a most readable fashion. That on Japan is similarly lucid, explaining how the navy's (and hence the country's) defeat was in effect inevitable right from the start, and not just because it had chosen to take on a far bigger foe in the form of the United States, but just as much because of various inbuilt factors which, while enabling it to achieve some startling victories in the short term, meant that it never had a hope beyond that.

However analysis is only part of the story, and just as important here is the quantity and quality of the basic information. The text and accompanying tables include extensive material on not just ships but also other areas such as aircraft, weapons, administration, organisation, infrastructure, doctrine, personnel, training, strategy and tactics. The main body of the book is complemented by some useful appendices such as one giving comparative ranks, and extensive notes on sources.

Several of the individual authors will be familiar to readers of *Shipwright*'s sister annual from Conway, *Warship*, notably John Jordan, Stephen McLaughlin, Enrico Cernuschi, and Vincent P. O'Hara himself.

It must be said that the illustrations are a bit of a let down. The few photographs don't seem to have been particularly carefully selected, are reproduced at small size and rather grey, on poor quality paper, and generally add little to the book. The maps are in themselves neat and clear (though as a man of Kent, this reviewer was less than happy to see Chatham positioned in, of all places, Essex…), but they suffer badly from being constrained by the book's relatively small format, with the result that they are frequently not large enough to be as useful as they should be.

Although *On Seas Contested* is basically a reference book, it is also a very good read. For anyone studying the conflict as a whole at say undergraduate level, or even A-level, or with an informed but non-specialist interest (i.e. many readers of *Shipwright*) it is absolutely ideal. At a sensible size and a reasonable price, this 'one-stop' basic reference on the major navies of the Second World War is, at least in the near future, unlikely to be bettered.

Stephen Dent